The Dog Lover's Reader

THE
DOG LOVER'S
READER

Edited by Timothy T. Clarke

Hart Publishing Company, Inc.   New York City

COPYRIGHT © 1974

HART PUBLISHING COMPANY, INC., NEW YORK, N.Y. 10012
ISBN NO. 08055-1129-6
LIBRARY OF CONGRESS CATALOG CARD NO. 74-79928

MANUFACTURED IN THE UNITED STATES OF AMERICA

Contents

5

The Dog Lover's Reader

The Popularity of Dog Breeds

James Meyers

WHICH BREED of dog is most favored by Americans? Beagle? Collie? German Shepherd? Surprisingly, it's the Poodle. With close to 200,000 registered dogs, there are more than two times as many Poodles as there are German Shepherds, the second most popular dog. In fact, almost one in every five dogs registered in the United States is a Poodle!

The dog breeds listed below may offer a few other surprises. The large number of registered Dachshunds, Labrador Retrievers, and St. Bernards would startle those people who consider specimens of those breeds to be mere curiosity pieces. On the other hand, such supposedly populous breeds as the Bulldog and Bloodhound rank astonishingly low in actual registration.

Anyone who patronizes the dog tracks will be surprised to learn that there are only 200 greyhounds registered in the entire United States. And if you are the proud owner of a Belgian Malinois, you own almost ten per cent of all the Malinois in America.

The most interesting figure on this list, however, may well be the total. With 1,099,850 dogs registered in the country, there is now one pedigreed dog for every 200 Americans. And of course, the number of mongrels extant is anybody's guess, though one seemingly knowledgeable individual estimates the total number of dogs in the United States to be close to 40 million.

DOGS REGISTERED IN 1973 WITH THE AMERICAN KENNEL CLUB

1.	Poodle	193,400
2.	German Shepherd	90,907
3.	Irish Setter	54,211
4.	Beagle	54,125
5.	Dachshund	51,000
6.	Miniature Schnauzer	41,745
7.	St. Bernard	35,397
8.	Doberman Pinscher	34,169
9.	Labrador Retriever	33,575
10.	Cocker Spaniel	31,158
11.	Collie	28,573
12.	Pekingese	24,926
13.	Chihuahua	22,253
14.	Shetland Sheepdog	21,845
15.	Great Dane	19,314
16.	Brittany Spaniel	18,503
17.	Yorkshire Terrier	18,073
18.	Basset Hound	17,843
19.	Golden Retriever	17,635
20.	Pomeranian	16,708
21.	Siberian Husky	16,127
22.	Lhasa Apso	15,071
23.	German Shorthaired Pointer	14,814
24.	Old English Sheepdog	14,751
25.	English Springer Spaniel	12,421
26.	Boxer	12,319
27.	Boston Terrier	11,589
28.	Afghan Hound	10,549
29.	Samoyed	9,912
30.	Scottish Terrier	9,502
31.	Norwegian Elkhound	8,826
32.	Dalmatian	8,549

33.	Pug	8,420
34.	Alaskan Malamute	7,969
35.	Cairn Terrier	7,497
36.	Shih Tzu	7,473
37.	Fox Terrier	7,273
38.	Weimaraner	7,208
39.	Airedale Terrier	6,687
40.	Bulldog	6,559
41.	West Highland White Terrier	6,433
42.	Maltese	5,416
43.	Keeshond	4,671
44.	Silky Terrier	3,307
45.	Chow Chow	3,163
46.	Basenji	2,400
47.	Welsh Corgi (Pembroke)	2,290
48.	Vizsla	2,233
49.	Chesapeake Bay Retriever	2,214
50.	Newfoundland	2,010
51.	Akita	1,859
52.	Borzoi	1,703
53.	English Setter	1,603
54.	Bichon Frise	1,578
55.	Great Pyrenees	1,489
56.	Schipperke	1,366
57.	Irish Wolfhound	1,309
58.	Bloodhound	1,252
59.	Australian Terrier	1,191
60.	Welsh Terrier	1,167
61.	Miniature Pinscher	1,079
62.	Gordon Setter	1,071
63.	Whippet	1,036
64.	Kerry Blue Terrier	914
65.	German Wirehaired Pointer	888
66.	Standard Schnauzer	851
67.	Rottweiler	840

103.	Komondorok	121
104.	Kuvaszok	120
105.	Irish Water Spaniel	101
106.	Scottish Deerhound	97
107.	Flat-Coated Retriever	90
108.	Border Terrier	74
109.	Affenpinscher	73
110.	Foxhound (American)	72
111.	Otter Hound	55
112.	Welsh Springer Spaniel	52
113.	Curly-Coated Retriver	40
114.	English Toy Spaniel	38
115.	Clumber Spaniel	31
116.	Harrier	20
117.	Foxhound (English)	18
118.	Sussex Spaniel	14
119.	Field Spaniel	12
120.	Belgian Malinois	11

1,099,850

LITTERS REGISTERED BY GROUPS

SPORTING BREEDS	50,000
HOUND BREEDS	59,150
WORKING BREEDS	90,099
TERRIER BREEDS	34,350
TOY BREEDS	64,400
NON-SPORTING BREEDS	122,750

420,749

Cape Hunting Dog

How It May Have Started

Konrad Lorenz

THROUGH THE tall grass of the plain a little group of people makes its way, an unclothed, uncivilized band. They are certainly human beings like ourselves, their build no different from that of present-day man. In their hands they carry bone-tipped spears, some even have bows and arrows, but in their behaviour there is something which would be foreign even to present-day savages of the lowest cultural type, and which would strike a modern observer as being an animal trait. These men are no lords of creation that look fearlessly out into the world; instead, their dark eyes move to and fro restlessly as they turn their heads, glancing from time to time fearfully over their shoulders. They remind one of deer, hunted animals that must always be watchful. They give wide berth to bushes and the taller vegetation of the steppes which may easily shelter a large beast of prey, and, as on one occasion a big antelope breaks cover with a loud rustling, they start nervously, hastily adjusting their spears for action. The next moment recognizing the harmlessness of the animal, their fear gives place to relieved but excited chatter and finally to hilarious laughter. But this cheerful mood soon subsides: the band is downcast and with good reason. In the course of the last month, they have been forced by stronger, more populous tribes, to relinquish their original hunting grounds for the plains of the West, a country

From *Man Meets Dog* by Konrad Lorenz. Reprinted by permission of Houghton Mifflin Co.

17

which they do not know and where large beasts of prey are much more prevalent than in the abandoned territory. The knowing old hunter who was their leader lost his life a few weeks ago; he was wounded by a sabre-toothed tiger which tried one night to steal a young girl from the band. In a fever of excitement, all the men set their spears at the tiger, the leader at their head, but unluckily it was he that received the brunt of its attack. The girl was already dead and the leader died of his wounds the next day. The fact that the tiger also died a week later of peritonitis caused by a spear wound in his abdomen was of small direct advantage to the little band of people. This now consisted of but five grown men, the rest being women and children, and five men are not enough to beat off the attacks of a large beast of prey. Nor is the man who has assumed the leadership so endowed with experience and muscle-power as was the former leader. But his eyes are brighter and his forehead higher and more arched than that of the other. The depleted group suffers most from lack of sleep. In their own territory they used to sleep round the fire and, moreover, they possessed a guard of which, till now, they were unaware. The jackals that followed in the tracks of the human hordes, scavenging the refuse from slaughtered animals, surrounded their camp at night in a close circle. No feelings of friendship united the humans with their troublesome followers. Missiles greeted every jackal that dared approach too near the fire, and occasionally an arrow was aimed at them, though it was seldom that one was wasted on such unappetising creatures.

Even to-day, in the eyes of many peoples, the dog is still marked out as an unclean animal in consequence of his disreputable ancestors. Nevertheless, the jackals were a definite help to the human beings whose footsteps they followed: to some extent, they saved them the trouble of setting a watch, since the clamour they set up on the approach of a beast of prey announced from afar the appearance of the marauder.

How It May Have Started

These primitive human beings, careless and unthinking, were unaware of this usefulness of their four-legged retinue; but now that it was missing, the uncanny stillness around the camp was so sinister that even those who were not entrusted with the watch hardly dared to close an eye; and this proved most exhausting, since their vigilance was already overtaxed owing to the small number of able-bodied men that their band included. And so the little company, tired and nervous and thoroughly disconsolate, pursued its way, jumping at every sound and seizing its weapons, and now very seldom bursting into guffaws when the alarm proved to be a false one. At the approach of evening, the dread of the coming night began to weigh heavy on every mind; they were obsessed by fear of the unknown which, engraved in bygone eras into the convolutions of our brain, renders even to-day the darkness of night a source of terror to the child and, to the adult, the symbol of things evil. This is an age-old memory of the time when the powers of darkness, in the form of flesh-eating beasts of prey, sprang out of the night upon human beings. For our forefathers the night must indeed have held unlimited terrors.

The silent group of people presses closer together and begins searching for a place far from any bushy cover, where they will be safe from the attack of predatory beasts. Here, by a slow and tiresome procedure, they will light their camp fire and roast and divide the meagre spoils of the day. The repast consists to-day of the already 'high' remains of a wild boar, the leavings from the meal of the sabre-toothed tiger, from which the men had driven off after a struggle, a pack of hyena dogs. Such a mutilated carcase would hardly seem appetising to us but the members of the band cast hungry looks at their leader who is carrying the half-eaten skeleton himself in order to save any less responsible person from temptation. Suddenly the footsteps of the band halt as if at an order. All heads are turned in the direction whence they have come and, like a heard of startled deer, they all focus their senses in that one direction. They have heard a sound, the call of an animal which, strangely enough, brings no threat with it as most animal calls do: for only the hunting animal gives tongue—the hunted have long ago learned to be silent. But this sound seems to the wanderers like a message from home, a reminder of happier and less dangerous times, for it is the howl of a jackal. It almost seems as though the band, in its child-like, almost ape-like impulsiveness, will hurry back in the direction whence the howling proceeds. Strangely moved, they stand in anticipation. Then suddenly the young leader with the high forehead does something remarkable and, to the others, inexplicable: he throws the carcase to the ground and begins to rip off a large piece of skin to which some flesh still adheres. Some young members of the band, thinking that a meal is about to be distributed, come close, but with furrowed brow, the leader repulses them with a deep grunt of anger. Leaving the detached pieces of meat on the ground, he picks up the rest of the carcase and gives the signal for marching. They have hardly advanced a few steps when the man who stands nearest the leader in rank, and who is physically stronger though mentally less active, challenges him, indicating with his eyes and with head movements—not, as we would do it, with the hands—the abandoned piece of meat. The leader reproaches him and presses onward. After another ten yards, the second man falls back and moves towards the meat. The leader, throwing his booty into the grass, pursues him and, as the other raises the reeking flesh to his mouth, he rams his shoulder against him causing him to totter sideways. For a few seconds the two face each other threateningly, their foreheads puckered, their faces distorted with rage; then the second man drops his eyes and, muttering, follows the group, which is now once more in motion.

Not a man is conscious that he has just witnessed an epoch-making episode, a stroke of genius whose meaning in world history is greater than that of the fall of Troy or the discovery of gunpowder. Even the high-browed leader himself does not know it. He acted on impulse, hardly realizing that the motive for his action was the wish to have the jackals near him. He had instinctively and rightly calculated that since the wind was blowing against them it was bound to waft the scent of the meat into the nostrils of the howling jackals. The band moves on, but still no open space is to be found which could offer them a safe camping place. After a few hundred yards, the leader repeats his strange action whereupon a loud protest is raised by the other men. The third time he repeats it something like a revolt breaks out, and it is only by recourse to an outburst of primitive fury that the leader is able to enforce his will. But shortly afterwards the bushes clear and a large expanse of open plain affords them some measure of safety. The men gather round the remains of the wild boar and begin, amidst continual grumbling and mutual threats, to carve the aromatic delicacy in pieces, while the women and children gather a pile of fuel sufficient for the whole night.

The wind has dropped and in the stillness the sensitive ear of the wild man can detect sounds a long distance away. Then suddenly the leader utters that quiet sound, fraught with meaning, that commands the absolute silence and attention of the others. All turn to statues, for in the distance the cry of an animal is again audible and this time louder than before: the jackals have found the first piece of meat and, with unmistakable sounds, two of them are fighting for the plunder. The leader smiles and gives the signal for his companions to continue. A little later, the same growling and snapping of the jaws can be heard, this time still nearer. Again the humans listen attentively. Suddenly the second man jerks round his head and, with a peculiar, tense expression, stares into the face of the leader who, with a satisfied grin, is listening to the fight of the jackals. Now at last, the second man has begun to grasp the leader's intentions. Seizing a few detached ribs, nearly bare of meat, he approaches him, grinning. Then he nudges him and, imitating the barking sound of the jackals, he carries off the bones in the direction from which the band has come. In its tracks, not far from the camp, he stoops to lay them down, then, rising, he looks questioningly at the leader who has been following his actions with interest. They grin at each other and suddenly burst into loud laughter, that same unrestrained mirth that little boys might indulge in to-day when they have succeeded in some particular piece of mischief.

It is already dark and the camp fire is burning as the leader of the band again gives the signal for silence. A gnawing of bones can be heard and, in the light of the fire, the party suddenly see a jackal revelling in the pieces of meat. Once he raises his head, glancing apprehensively towards them, but as nobody attempts to move, he returns again to the feast, and they continue to watch him quietly. In the truest sense, an epoch-making happening: the first time a useful animal has been fed by man! And as at last they lie down to sleep they do so with a feeling of safety which they have not had for a long time.

Many years have passed, many generations. The jackals have become tamer and bolder, and now surround the camps of man in larger packs. Men have now added wild horses and stags to their prey and the jackals too have altered their habits: whereas formerly they remained concealed by day and only ventured abroad by night, now the strongest and cleverest amongst them have become diurnal and follow men on their hunting expeditions. And so some such episode as the following may well have taken place when hunters were following the trail of a pregnant wild mare that has been lamed by a spear wound: they are highly elated, their rations having been meagre for some time now, and the jackals are following them more eagerly than usual since they too have received little or no share of the spoils for an equal period. The mare, weakened by her condition and by loss of blood, resorts to an age-old strategy of her species and lays a false trail, that is, she doubles back in her tracks, runs on for some distance and finally turns off into a clump of bushes at right angles to her path. This strategy has often saved a hunted animal, and on this occasion too the hunters stand baffled at the point where the tracks apparently end.

The jackals follow at a safe distance, still fearing to approach too close to the clamorous hunters. They follow the trail of the humans and not of the wild mare, since, as can be readily understood, they have no desire to overtake on their own an animal which is far too large a prey for them. But these jackals have often been given scraps of large animals whose scents have thus acquired for them a special meaning, and at the same time they have conceived an association of thought between a trail of blood and the near prospect of a feed. To-day the jackals, being particularly hungry, are strongly stimulated by the fresh blood, and now something happens which inaugurates a new form of relationship between man and his band of retainers: the old, grey-muzzled bitch, the potential leader of the pack, notices something which the human hunters have overlooked, namely, the deflection of the trail of blood. The jackals turn off at this point and follow the trail independently, and the hunters, realizing that false trail has been laid, turn back too. On their arrival at the junction of the paths they hear the jackals howling from one side, and, following the sound, they see the tracks where the many jackals have trodden down the grass of the plain. And here, for the first time, the order is laid down in which man and dog shall pursue their quarry from this day forth: first the dog and then the man. The jackals are swifter than the hunters in overtaking the mare and bringing it to bay.

When a large wild animal is brought to bay by dogs,

a particular psychological mechanism plays an essential role: the hunted stag, bear or wild boar which flees from man but does not hesitate to defend itself against dogs, forgets its more dangerous enemy in its anger at its impertinent smaller aggressors. The weary mare, which sees in the jackals only a set of cowardly yappers, takes up a defensive attitude and lashes out wildly with one fore-foot at a jackal which has ventured too close. Now, breathing heavily, the mare circles but does not resume its flight. In the meanwhile, the hunters, hearing the sound of the jackals now concentrated in one spot, soon reach the scene of action and, at a given signal, distribute themselves silently around their prey. At this, the jackals move as though to disperse but, seeing that nobody interferes with them, decide to remain. The leader of the pack, now devoid of all fear, barks furiously at the mare, and when it sinks down, impaled by a spear, buries her teeth ravenously in its throat and only retreats when the leader of the hunters approaches the carcase. This man, perhaps the great, great, great grandson of the one who first threw a piece of meat to the jackals, slits open the belly of the still twitching mare and tears out a portion of gut. Without looking directly at the jackals—an act of intuitive tact—he throws it, not at, but to the side of the animals—another instance of the same tact. The grey pack-leader shrinks back a little, then, seeing that the man makes no threatening gesture, but only utters a friendly sound, such as the jackals have often heard from the side of the camp fire, she falls upon the piece of entrail. As she withdraws, holding the booty between her fangs and hurriedly chewing it, she glances back furtively at the man and at the same time her tail begins to move in little short strokes from side to side. For the first time a jackal has wagged its tail at a man and thus we get a step nearer to friendship between mankind and the dog. Even such intelligent animals as canine beasts of prey do not acquire an entirely new type of behaviour reaction through a sudden experience, but rather by an association of ideas which is only built up after many recurrences of the same situation. Months probably elapsed before this jackal bitch again ran before the hunter after a big game animal which had laid a false trail, and perhaps it was an even later descendant which regularly and consciously led human beings and brought the game to bay.

At the beginning of the later stone age, man seems to have made his first settlements. The first houses which we know of were situated on pillars and built by the lake dwellers, for reasons of safety, in the shallows of lakes, rivers, and even of the Baltic Sea. We know that at this time the dog had already become domesticated, for the skulls of the little Spitz-like Turf-dogs, which were first found among the remains of the pillar dwellings on the Baltic Sea, though showing plain evidence of their descent from the jackal, also show unmistakable signs of domestication.

The important point is however that, although jackals were at that time more widely distributed than they are to-day, there were no indigenous ones left on the Baltic coasts. In all probability, it was man, in his advance further north-wards and westwards, who brought with him the dogs or half-tame jackals that followed his camps. When man began to erect his habitations on pillars in the water and invented the canoe, two innovations which certainly meant cultural progress, a basic change in his relations with his four-footed followers must inevitably have followed. Owing to the water these could no longer surround his camps, nor could they guard the homes of their masters against attacks from human enemies on the water side. It is reasonable to suppose that when man first exchanged his camps for pillar dwellings he brought with him some few tamer specimens of the still half-wild jackals which had particularly distinguished themselves in the chase, and thus made them into house-dogs in the true sense of the word. Even to-day different peoples keep dogs

25

in different ways, the most primitive of these being when a large number of dogs surrounds a settlement but only has a very loose connection with man. We find another type of dog-keeping in every European country village, where a few dogs belong to a certain house and are dependent on one particular master. This last type of relationship very likely evolved with the development of the pillar dwellings. The smaller number of dogs which could be accommodated in the pillar dwellings naturally led to in-breeding which favoured the hereditary transmission of the characters of true domestication. Two facts strengthen these assumptions: first, that the turf-dog, with its shorter muzzle and somewhat more domed skull, is certainly a domesticated form of the jackal, and secondly that the bones of this form have been found almost exclusively amongst the remains of the settlements of the lake dwellers.

The dogs of the lake dwellers must have been tame enough either to enter a canoe or to swim the intermediate stretch of water and clamber up the landing-stage. A half-tame pariah dog would not do this at any price, and even a young dog of my own stud requires very patient coaxing before it can be induced to enter my canoe for the first time or to climb into a tram or railway carriage.

The taming of the dog had possibly already been achieved when men began to build their pillar dwellings, or, alternatively, it took place contemporaneously with it. It is quite conceivable that at this time a woman or a little girl 'playing dolls' brought up an orphaned puppy in their family circle. Perhaps the pup was the sole survivor of a litter carried off by a sabre-toothed tiger. The little creature may have cried but probably nobody bothered, for in those days man was insensitive.

But while the men were out hunting and the women fishing, we can well imagine how a little lake-dweller's daughter followed the direction of the whimpering and found at last in some cavity the tiny puppy which wobbled fearlessly towards her and began to lick and suck at her outstretched hands. The soft, round, woolly bundle no doubt elicited in that small daughter of the early stone age the desire to cuddle it and carry it round interminably, just like the little daughters of our own times; for the maternal instincts which give rise to such behaviour are age-old. And so the little stone-age girl, in playful imitation of the actions of the women, gave the puppy food, and her joy at the greed with which it devoured it was no less than that of our women of to-day when a carefully prepared meal gives obvious pleasure to guests. The home-coming parents find with astonishment but little enthusiasm a sleepy little jackal, fat with food. The father, of course, wants to drown it straight away, but his little daughter, weeping, clasps her father's knee so that he stumbles and drops the pup, and when he stoops to pick it up it is already in the arms of the child who is standing in the farthest corner of the room, dissolved in tears. Not even a stone-age father could be so stony-hearted, so the pup is allowed to stay. Thanks to abundant food, he is soon a particularly big, strong animal whose ardent affection for the child now undergoes a change: although the father, the head of the colony, takes little notice of the dog, it gradually transfers its allegiance from the child to the parent; in fact the time has arrived when the animal, in its wild state, would be breaking away from its mother. Hitherto the daughter has played the role of mother in the life of the puppy, but now the father represents the leader to whom belongs the unswerving pack loyalty of the wild dog. To begin with, the man finds this attachment tiresome, but he soon realizes that this tame dog is much more useful for hunting than the half-wild jackals that hang around the shores of the settlement and, still fearful of man, often make off at the moment when they should be holding a game animal at bay. In its attitude towards the game, the tame dog is also much more courageous than his wild confederates, for his sheltered life in the pillar dwelling has been free from painful experiences with large beasts of prey. So the dog soon becomes the close companion of the man, much to the chagrin of the little daughter, who now only sees her former charge when her father is at home—and stone-age fathers were often absent for long periods. However, in the spring, when jackals bear their young, the father comes home one evening with a skin bag in which there is much heaving and squeaking; and when he opens it—the little daughter jumps for joy—out roll four balls of fur. Only the mother makes an earnest grimace: after all, two would have been enough . . .

Did it really happen like this? Well, none of us was there, but considering all we know, it is quite conceivable that it may have done. At the same time, we must not conceal the fact that we do not know for certain that it was exclusively the golden jackal (*Canis aureaus*) that attached itself to man in the way described. It is indeed very probable that in different parts of the earth various larger and wolf-like species of jackal became domesticated and later interbred, just as many other forms of domestic animals originate from more than one wild progenitor. A very strong argument in favour of this theory is that pariah dogs do not at all tend to mingle and to re-cross with wild Canis aureus. Mr. Shebbeare has very kindly drawn my attention to the fact that there are lots of localities in the near East where Pie dogs and golden jackals abound, yet never intermingle. However, it is quite certain that the northern wolf is not the ancestor of most of our domestic dogs as was formerly believed. There are just a few breeds of dog which are mainly though not entirely descended from wolves, and these, by their very peculiarities, supply us with the best proof that they are the exception to the rule. These breeds, whose resemblance to the wolf is not merely physical—Eskimo dogs, Samoyeds,

How It May Have Started

Russian Lajkas, Chow-chows, and a few others—all originate from the extreme north. None of them is purely wolf-blooded; it can be assumed with a degree of certainty that man, in his advance further and further north, brought with him some already domesticated, jackal-blooded dogs, from which, after repeated crossings with wolf-blooded animals, these breeds arose. . . .

Greenland Dog

Gulliver the Great

Walter A. Dyer

It was a mild evening in early spring, and the magnolias were in bloom. We motored around the park, turned up a side street, and finally came to a throbbing standstill before the Churchwarden Club.

There was nothing about its exterior to indicate that it was a clubhouse at all, but within there was an indefinable atmosphere of early Victorian comfort. There was something about it that suggested Mr. Pickwick. Old prints of horses and ships and battles hung upon the walls, and the oak was dark and old. There seemed to be no decorative scheme or keynote, and yet the atmosphere was utterly distinctive. It was my first visit to the Churchwarden Club, of which my quaint, old-fashioned Uncle Ford had long been a member, and I was charmed.

We dined in the rathskeller, the walls of which were completely covered with long churchwarden pipes, arranged in the most intricate and marvelous patterns; and after our mutton-chop and ale and plum pudding, we filled with the choicest of tobaccos the pipes which the old major-domo brought us.

Then came Jacob R. Enderby to smoke with us.

Tall and spare he was, with long, straight, black hair, large, aquiline nose, and piercing eyes. I disgraced myself by staring at him. I didn't know such a man existed in New

From *Gulliver the Great and Other Dog Stories*, by Walter A. Dyer.

York, and yet I couldn't decide whether his habitat should be Arizona or Cape Cod.

Enderby and Uncle Ford were deep in a discussion of the statesmanship of James G. Blaine, when a waiter summoned my uncle to the telephone.

I neglected to state that my uncle, in his prosaic hours, is a physician; and this was a call. I knew it the moment I saw the waiter approaching. I was disappointed and disgusted.

Uncle Ford saw this and laughed.

"Cheer up!" said he. "You needn't come with me to visit the sick. I'll be back in an hour, and meanwhile Mr. Enderby will take care of you; won't you, Jake?"

For answer Enderby arose, and refilling his pipe took me by the arm, while my uncle got into his overcoat. As he passed us on the way out he whispered in my ear:

"Talk about dogs."

I heard and nodded.

Enderby led me to the lounge or loafing-room, an oak-paneled apartment in the rear of the floor above, with huge leather chairs and a seat in the bay window. Save for a gray-haired old chap dozing over a copy of *Simplicissimus,* the room was deserted.

But no sooner had Enderby seated himself on the window-seat than there was a rush and a commotion, and a short, glad bark, and Nubbins, the steward's bull-terrier, bounded in and landed at Enderby's side with canine expressions of great joy.

I reached forward to pat him, but he paid absolutely no attention to me.

At last his wrigglings subsided, and he settled down with his head on Enderby's knee, the picture of content. Then I recalled my Uncle's parting injunction.

"Friend of yours?" I suggested.

Enderby smiled. "Yes," he said, "we're friends, I guess. And the funny part of it is that he doesn't pay any attention to any one else except his master. They all act that way with me, dogs do." And he pulled Nubbins's stubby ears.

"Natural attraction, I suppose," said I.

"Yes, it is," he answered, with the modest frankness of a big man. "It's a thing hard to explain, though there's a sort of reason for it in my case."

I pushed toward him a little tobacco-laden teak-wood stand hopefully. He refilled and lighted.

"It's an extraordinary thing, even so," he said, puffing. "Every dog nowadays seems to look upon me as his long-lost master, but it wasn't always so. I hated dogs and they hated me."

Not wishing to say "Really" or "Indeed" to this big, out-door man, I simply grunted my surprise.

"Yes, we were born enemies. More than that, I was afraid of dogs. A little fuzzy toy dog, ambling up to me in a room full of company, with his tail wagging, gave me the shudders. I couldn't touch the beast. And as for big dogs out-doors, I feared them like the plague. I would go blocks out of my way to avoid one.

"I don't remember being particularly cowardly about other things, but I just couldn't help this. It was in my blood, for some reason or other. It was the bane of my existence. I couldn't see what the brutes were put in the world for, or how any one could have anything to do with them.

"All the dogs reciprocated. They disliked and distrusted me. The most docile old Brunos would growl and show their teeth when I came near."

"Did the change come suddenly?" I asked.

"Quite. It was in 1901. I accepted a commission from an importing and trading company to go to the Philippines to do a little quiet exploring, and spent four months in the sickly place. Then I got the fever, and when I recovered I couldn't get out of there too soon.

"I reached Manila just in time to see the mail steamer disappearing around the point, and I was mad. There would be another in six days, but I couldn't wait. I was just crazy to get back home.

"I made inquiries and learned of an old tramp steamer, named the *Old Squaw,* making ready to leave for Honolulu on the following day with a cargo of hemp and stuff, and a bunch of Moros for some show in the States, and I booked passage on that.

"She was the worst old tub you ever saw. I didn't learn much about her, but I verily believe her to have been a condemned excursion boat. She wouldn't have been allowed to run to Coney Island.

"She was battered and unpainted, and she wallowed horribly. I don't believe she could have reached Honolulu much before the regular boat, but I couldn't wait, and I took her.

"I made myself as comfortable as possible, bribed the cook to insure myself against starvation, and swung a hammock on the forward deck as far as possible from the worst of the vile smells.

"But we hadn't lost sight of Manila Bay when I discovered that there was a dog aboard—and such a dog! I had never seen one that sent me into such a panic as this one, and he had free range of the ship. A Great Dane he was, named Gulliver, and he was the pride of the captain's rum-soaked heart.

"With all my fear, I realized he was a magnificent animal, but I looked on him as a gigantic devil. Without exception, he was the biggest dog I ever saw, and as muscular as a lion. He lacked some points that show judges set store by, but he had the size and the build.

"I had seen Vhol's Vulcan and the Württemberg breed, but they were fox-terriers compared with Gulliver. His tail was as big around as my arm, and the cook lived in terror of his getting into the galley and wagging it; and he had a mouth that looked to me like the crater of Mauna Loa, and a voice that shook the planking when he spoke.

"I first caught sight of him appearing from behind a huge

coil of cordage in the stern. He stretched and yawned, and I nearly died of fright.

"I caught up a belaying-pin, though little good that would have done me. I think he saw me do it, and doubtless he set me down for an enemy then and there.

"We were well out of the harbor, and there was no turning back, but I would have given my right hand to be off that boat. I fully expected him to eat me up, and I slept with that belaying-pin sticking into my ribs in the hammock, and with my revolver loaded and handy.

Great Danes

"Fortunately, Gulliver's dislike for me took the form of sublime contempt. He knew I was afraid of him, and he despised me for it. He was a great pet with the captain and crew, and even the Moros treated him with admiring respect when they were allowed on deck. I couldn't understand it. I would as soon have made a pet of a hungry boa-constrictor.

"On the third day out the poor old boiler burst and the *Old Squaw* caught fire. She was dry and rotten inside and she burned like tinder. No attempt was made to extinguish the flames, which got into the hemp in the hold in short order.

"The smoke was stifling, and in a jiffy all hands were struggling with the boats. The Moros came tumbling up from below and added to the confusion with their terrified yells.

"The davits were old and rusty, and the men were soon fighting among themselves. One boat dropped stern foremost, filled, and sank immediately, and the *Old Squaw* herself was visibly settling.

"I saw there was no chance of getting away in the boats, and I recalled a life-raft on the deck forward near my hammock. It was a sort of catamaran—a double platform on a pair of hollow, watertight, cylindrical buoys. It wasn't twenty feet long and about half as broad, but it would have to do. I fancy it was a forgotten relic of the old excursion-boat days.

"There was no time to lose, for the *Old Squaw* was bound to sink presently. Besides, I was aft with the rest, and the flames were licking up the deck and running-gear in the waist of the boat.

"The galley, which was amidships near the engine-room, had received the full force of the explosion, and the cook lay moaning in the lee scuppers with a small water-cask thumping against his chest. I couldn't stop to help the man, but I did kick the cask away.

"It seemed to be nearly full, and it occurred to me that I

should need it. I glanced quickly around, and luckily found a tin of biscuits that had also been blown out of the galley. I picked this up, and rolling the cask of water ahead of me as rapidly as I could, I made my way through the hot, stifling smoke to the bow of the boat.

"I kicked at the life-raft; it seemed to be sound, and I lashed the biscuits and water to it. I also threw on a coil of rope and a piece of sail-cloth. I saw nothing else about that could possibly be of any value to me. I abandoned my trunk for fear it would only prove troublesome.

"Then I hacked the raft loose with my knife and shoved it over the bulwark. Apparently no one had seen me, for there was no one else forward of the sheet of flame that now cut the boat in two.

"The raft was a mighty heavy affair, but I managed to raise one end to the rail. I don't believe I would ever have been able to heave it over under any circumstances, but I didn't have to.

"I felt a great upheavel, and the prow of the *Old Squaw* went up into the air. I grabbed the ropes that I had lashed the food on with and clung to the raft. The deck became almost perpendicular, and it was a miracle that the raft didn't slide down with me into the flames. Somehow it stuck where it was.

"Then the boat sank with a great roar, and for about a thousand years, it seemed to me, I was under water. I didn't do anything, I couldn't think.

"I was only conscious of a tremendous weight of water and a feeling that I would burst open. Instinct alone made me cling to the raft.

"When it finally brought me to the surface I was as nearly dead as I care to be. I lay there on the thing in a half-conscious condition for an endless time. If my life had depended on my doing something, I would have been lost.

"Then gradually I came to, and began to spit out salt

water and gasp for breath. I gathered my wits together and sat up. My hands were absolutely numb, and I had to loosen the grip of my fingers with the help of my toes. Odd sensation.

"Then I looked about me. My biscuits and water and rope were safe, but the sail-cloth had vanished. I remember that this annoyed me hugely at the time, though I don't know what earthly good it would have been.

"The sea was fairly calm, and I could see all about. Not a human being was visible, only a few floating bits of wreckage. Every man on board must have gone down with the ship and drowned, except myself.

"Then I caught sight of something that made my heart stand still. The huge head of Gulliver was coming rapidly toward me through the water!

"The dog was swimming strongly, and must have leaped from the *Old Squaw* before she sank. My raft was the only thing afloat large enough to hold him, and he knew it.

"I drew my revolver, but it was soaking wet and useless. Then I sat down on the cracker tin and gritted my teeth and waited. I had been alarmed, I must admit, when the boiler blew up and the panic began, but that was nothing to the terror that seized me now.

"Here I was all alone on the top of the Pacific Ocean with a horrible demon making for me as fast as he could swim. My mind was benumbed, and I could think of nothing to do. I trembled and my teeth rattled. I prayed for a shark, but no shark came.

"Soon Gulliver reached the raft and placed one of his forepaws on it and then the other. The top of it stood six or eight inches above the water, and it took a great effort for the dog to raise himself. I wanted to kick him back, but I didn't dare to move.

"Gulliver struggled mightily. Again and again he reared his great shoulders above the sea, only to be cast back, scratching and kicking, at a lurch of the raft.

"Finally a wave favored him, and he caught the edge of the under platform with one of his hind feet. With a stupendous effort he heaved his huge bulk over the edge and lay sprawling at my feet, panting and trembling."

Enderby paused and gazed out of the window with a big sigh, as though the recital of his story had brought back some of the horror of his remarkable experience.

Nubbins looked up inquiringly, and then snuggled closer to his friend, while Enderby smoothed the white head.

"Well," he continued, "there we were. You can't possibly imagine how I felt unless you, too, have been afflicted with dog-fear. It was awful. And I hated the brute so. I could have torn him limb from limb if I had had the strength. But he was vastly more powerful than I. I could only fear him.

"By and by he got up and shook himself. I cowered on my cracker-tin, but he only looked at me contemptuously, went to the other end of the raft, and lay down to wait patiently for deliverance.

"We remained this way until nightfall. The sea was comparatively calm, and we seemed to be drifting but slowly. We were in the path of ships likely to be passing one way or the other, and I would have been hopeful of the outcome if it had not been for my feared and hated companion.

"I began to feel faint, and opened the cracker-tin. The biscuits were wet with salt water, but I ate a couple, and left the tin open to dry them. Gulliver looked around, and I shut the tin hastily. But the dog never moved. He was not disposed to ask any favors. By kicking the sides of the cask and prying with my knife, I managed to get the bung out and took a drink. Then I settled myself on the raft with my back against the cask, and longed for a smoke.

"The gentle motion of the raft produced a lulling effect on my exhausted nerves, and I began to nod, only to awake with a start, with fear gripping at my heart. I dared not sleep. I don't know what I thought Gulliver would do to me, for I did not understand dogs, but I felt that I must watch him constantly. In the starlight I could see that his eyes were open. Gulliver was watchful too.

"All night long I kept up a running fight with drowsiness. I dozed at intervals, but never for long at a time. It was a horrible night, and I cannot tell you how I longed for day and welcomed it when it came.

"I must have slept toward dawn, for I suddenly became conscious of broad daylight. I roused myself, stood up, and swung my arms and legs to stir up circulation, for the night had been chilly. Gulliver arose, too, and stood silently watching me until I ceased for fear. When he had settled down again I got my breakfast out of the cracker-tin. Gulliver was restless, and was evidently interested.

" 'He must be hungry,' I thought, and then a new fear caught me. I had only to wait until he became very hungry and then he would surely attack me. I concluded that it would be wiser to feed him, and I tossed him a biscuit.

"I expected to see him grab it ravenously, and wondered as soon as I had thrown it if the taste of food would only serve to make him more ferocious. But at first he would not touch it. He only lay there with his great head on his paws and glowered at me. Distrust was plainly visible in his face. I had never realized before that a dog's face could express the subtler emotions.

"His gaze fascinated me, and I could not take my eyes from his. The bulk of him was tremendous as he lay there, and I noticed the big, swelling muscles of his jaw. At last he arose, sniffed suspiciously at the biscuit, and looked up at me again.

" 'It's all right; eat it!' I cried.

"The sound of my own voice frightened me. I had not intended to speak to him. But in spite of my strained tone he seemed somewhat reassured.

"He took a little nibble, and then swallowed the biscuit after one or two crunches, and looked up expectantly. I threw him another and he ate that.

" 'That's all,' said I. 'We must be sparing of them.'

"I was amazed to discover how perfectly he understood. He lay down again and licked his chops.

"Late in the afternoon I saw a line of smoke on the horizon, and soon a steamer hove into view. I stood up and waved my coat frantically, but to no purpose. Gulliver stood up and looked from me to the steamer, apparently much interested.

" 'Too far off,' I said to Gulliver. 'I hope the next one will come nearer.'

"At midday I dined, and fed Gulliver. This time he took the two biscuits quite without reserve and whacked his great tail against the raft. It seemed to me that his attitude was less hostile, and I wondered at it.

"When I took my drink from the cask, Gulliver showed signs of interest.

" 'I suppose dogs get thirsty, too,' I said aloud.

"Gulliver rapped with his tail. I looked about for some sort of receptacle, and finally pulled off my shoe, filled it with water, and shoved it toward him with my foot. He drank gratefully.

"During the afternoon I sighted another ship, but it was too distant to notice me. However, the sea remained calm and I did not despair.

"After we had had supper, I settled back against my cask, resolved to keep awake, for still I did not trust Gulliver. The sun set suddenly and the stars came out, and I found myself strangely lonesome. It seemed as though I had been alone out there on the Pacific for weeks. The miles and miles of heaving waters, almost on a level with my eye, were beginning to get on my nerves. I longed for someone to talk to, and wished I had dragged the half-breed cook along with me for company. I sighed loudly, and Gulliver raised his head.

" 'Lonesome out here, isn't it?' I said, simply to hear the sound of my own voice.

"Then for the first time Gulliver spoke. He made a deep sound in his throat, but it wasn't a growl, and with all my ignorance of dog language I knew it.

"Then I began to talk. I talked about everything the people back home and all that—and Gulliver listened. I know more about dogs now, and I know that the best way to make friends with a dog is to talk to him. He can't talk back, but he can understand a heap more than you think he can.

"Finally Gulliver, who had kept his distance all this time, arose and came toward me. My words died in my throat. What was he going to do? To my immense relief he did nothing but sink down at my feet with a grunt and curl his huge body into a semicircle. He had dignity, Gulliver had. He wanted to be friendly, but he would not presume. However, I had lost interest in conversation, and sat watching him and wondering.

"In spite of my firm resolution, I fell asleep at length from sheer exhaustion, and never woke until daybreak. The sky was clouded and our raft was pitching. Gulliver was standing in the middle of the raft, looking at me in evident alarm. I glanced over my shoulder, and the blackness of the horizon told me that a storm was coming, and coming soon.

"I made fast our slender provender, tied the end of a line about my own waist for safety, and waited.

"In a short time the storm struck us in all its tropical fury. The raft pitched and tossed, now high up at one end, and now at the other, and sometimes almost engulfed in the waves.

"Gulliver was having a desperate time to keep aboard. His blunt claws slipped on the wet deck of the raft, and he fell and slid about dangerously. The thought flashed across my mind that the storm might prove to be a blessing in disguise, and that I might soon be rid of the brute.

"As I clung there to the lashings, I saw him slip down to

the further end of the raft, his hind quarters actually over the edge. A wave swept over him, but still he clung, panting madly. Then the raft righted itself for a moment, and as he hung there he gave me a look I shall never forget—a look of fear, of pleading, of reproach, and yet of silent courage. And with all my stupidity I read that look. Somehow it told me that I was the master, after all, and he the dog. I could not resist it. Cautiously I raised myself and loosened the spare rope I had saved. As the raft tipped the other way Gulliver regained his footing and came sliding toward me.

"Quickly I passed the rope around his body, and as the raft dived again I hung on to the rope with one hand, retaining my own hold with the other. Gulliver's great weight nearly pulled my arm from its socket, but he helped mightily, and during the next moment of equilibrium I took another turn about his body and made the end of the rope fast.

"The storm passed as swiftly as it had come, and though it left us drenched and exhausted, we were both safe.

"That evening Gulliver crept close to me as I talked, and I let him. Loneliness will make a man do strange things.

"On the fifth day, when our provisions were nearly gone, and I had begun to feel the sinking dullness of despair, I sighted a steamer apparently coming directly toward us. Instantly I felt new life in my limbs and around my heart, and while the boat was yet miles away I began to shout and to wave my coat.

" 'I believe she's coming, old man!' I cried to Gulliver. 'I believe she's coming!'

"I soon wearied of this foolishness and sat down to wait. Gulliver came close and sat beside me, and for the first time I put my hand on him. He looked up at me and rapped furiously with his tail. I patted his head—a little gingerly, I must confess.

"It was a big, smooth head, and it felt solid and strong. I passed my hand down his neck, his back, his flanks. He seemed to quiver with joy. He leaned his huge body against me. Then he bowed his head and licked my shoe.

"A feeling of intense shame and unworthiness came over me, with the realization of how completely I had misunderstood him. Why should this great, powerful creature lick my shoe? It was incredible.

"Then, somehow, everything changed. Fear and distrust left me, and a feeling of comradeship and understanding took their place. We two had been through so much together. A dog was no longer a frightful beast to me; he was a dog! I cannot think of a nobler word. And Gulliver had licked my shoe! Doubtless it was only the fineness of his perception that had prevented him from licking my hand. I might have resented that. I put my arms suddenly around Gulliver's neck and hugged him, I loved that dog!

"Slowly, slowly, the steamer crawled along, but still kept to her course. When she was about a mile away, however, I saw that she would not pass as close to us as I had hoped; so I began once more my waving and yelling. She came nearer, nearer, but still showed no sign of observing us.

"She was abreast of us, and passing. I was in a frenzy!

"She was so near that I could make out the figure of the captain on the bridge, and other figures on the deck below. It seemed as though they must see us, though I realized how low in the water we stood, and how pitifully weak and hoarse my voice was. I had been a fool to waste it. Then an idea struck me.

" 'Speak!' I cried to Gulliver, who stood watching beside me. 'Speak, old man!'

"Gulliver needed no second bidding. A roar like that of all the bulls of Bashan rolled out over the blue Pacific. Again and again Gulliver gave voice, deep, full, powerful. His great side heaved with the mighty effort, his red, cavernous mouth open, and his head raised high.

" 'Good, old man!' I cried. 'Good!' And again that magnificent voice boomed forth.

"Then something happened on board the steamer. The figures came to the side. I waved my coat and danced. Then they saw us.

"I was pretty well done up when they took us aboard, and I slept for twenty-four hours straight. When I awoke there sat Gulliver by my bunk, and when I turned to look at him he lifted a great paw and put it on my arm."

Enderby ceased, and there was silence in the room save for the light snoring of Nubbins.

"You took him home with you, I suppose?" I asked.

Enderby nodded.

"And you have him still?" I certainly wanted to have a look at that dog.

But he did not answer. I saw an expression of great sadness come into his eyes as he gazed out of the window, and I knew that Jacob Enderby had finished his story.

Every Dog Should Own a Man

Corey Ford

EVERY DOG should have a man of his own. There is nothing like a well-behaved person around the house to spread the dog's blanket for him, or bring him his supper when he comes home man-tired at night.

For example, I happen to belong to an English setter who acquired me when he was about six months old and has been training me quite successfully ever since. He has taught me to shake hands with him and fetch his ball. I've learned not to tug at the leash when he takes me for a walk. I am completely housebroken, and I make him a devoted companion.

The first problem a dog faces is to pick out the right man—a gay and affectionate disposition is more important than an expensive pedigree. I do not happen to be registered but my setter is just as fond of me as though I came from a long line of blue bloods. Also, since a dog is judged by the man he leads, it is a good idea to walk the man up and down a couple of times to make sure his action is free and he has springy hindquarters.

The next question is whether the dog and man should share the house together. Some dogs prefer a kennel because it is more sanitary, but my setter decided at the start that he'd move right in the house with me. I can get into any of the chairs I want except the big overstuffed chair in the living room, which is his.

Training a man takes time. Some men are a little slow to respond, but a dog who makes allowances and tries to put himself in the man's place will be rewarded with a loyal pal. Men are apt to be high-strung and sensitive, and a dog who loses his temper will only break the man's spirit.

Punishment should be meted out sparingly—more can be accomplished by a reproachful look than by flying off the handle. My setter has never raised a paw to me, but he has cured me almost entirely of the habit of running away. When he sees me start to pack my suitcase he just lies down on the floor with his chin on his forepaws and gazes at me sadly. Usually I wind up by canceling my train reservations.

The first thing to teach a man is to stay at heel. For this lesson the dog should hook one end of a leash to his collar and loop the other end around the man's wrist so he cannot get away. Start down the street slowly, pausing at each telephone pole until the man realizes that he s under control. He may tug and yank at first, but this can be discouraged by slipping deftly between his legs and winding the leash around his ankles. If the man tries to run ahead, brace all four feet and halt suddenly, thus jerking him flat on his back. After a few such experiences the man will follow his dog with docility. Remember, however, that all such efforts at discipline must be treated as sport, and after a man has sprawled on the sidewalk the dog should lick his face to show him it was all in fun.

Every man should learn to retrieve a rubber ball. The way my setter taught me this trick was simple. He would lie in the center of the floor while I carried the ball to the far side of the room and rolled it toward him, uttering the word "Fetch!" He would watch the ball carefully as it rolled past him and under the sofa. I would then get the ball from under the sofa and roll it past him again, giving the same command, "Fetch!"

This lesson would be repeated until the setter was

47

asleep. After I got so I would retrieve the ball every time I said "Fetch!" my dog substituted other articles for me to pick up, such as an old marrow bone or a piece of paper he found in the wastebasket.

The matter of physical conditioning is important. A man whose carriage is faulty, and who slouches and droops his tail, is a reflection on the dog who owns him. The best way to keep him in shape is to work him constantly and never give him a chance to relax. Racing him up and down the street at the end of a leash is a great conditioner. If he attempts to slump into an easy chair when he gets back, the dog should leap into it ahead of him and force him to sit in a straight-backed chair to improve his posture. And be sure to get him up several times a night to go out for a walk, especially if it is raining.

Equally important is diet. Certain liquids such as beer have a tendency to bloat a man, and a dog should teach him restraint by jumping up at him and spilling his drink, or tactfully knocking the glass off the table with a sweep of his tail.

Not every dog who tries to bring up a man is as successful as my setter. The answer lies in understanding. The dog must be patient and not work himself into a tantrum if his man can't learn to chase rabbits or wriggle under fences as well as the dog does. After all, as my setter says, it's hard to teach an old man new tricks.

Your Dog's Medicine Chest

Arthur Trayford, D. V. M.
Gladys Hall

THERE ARE ANY number of items with which an owner can stock his dog's medicine chest and/or first-aid kit, but those most commonly required for home use are as follows:

A *Rectal Thermometer* of the kind that reads up to 108 degrees Fahrenheit is an important piece of puppy-care equipment and one that should be used at the first sign of sickness in a puppy or in a dog of any age. The best thermometers are the Stubbies that do not have the pear-shaped bulb and so are less likely to break (How to Take Your Dog's Temperature, page ?0?).

Milk of Magnesia is given as a laxative and also to cure acidity. The recommended dose is two teaspoonfuls for small dogs and one or two tablespoonfuls for large dogs. Milk of magnesia should not be mixed with the dog's dinner but given early in the morning or late at night.

Pepto-Bismol or Neo-Pectate are binding or tightening agents that help to check diarrhea. The recommended dosage is one teaspoonful to one tablespoonful for the average twenty- to forty-pound dog.

From *McCall's Complete Family Guide to Puppy & Dog Care* by Arthur Trayford with Gladys Hall. Copyright © 1971 by Arthur Trayford, D. V. M. and Gladys Hall. Published by E. P. Dutton & Co., Inc. (McCall's Publishing Co.) and used with their permission.

2% Boric Acid Solution for washing out the eyes.

1% Yellow Oxide Ointment for use when there is an injury to the eyes until such time as a veterinarian can be consulted.

B.F.1. Powder is a mild and dependable antiseptic for use in the ears, on minor skin irritations, and in open wounds.

Zonite is also a recommended antiseptic for bathing open wounds.

Cotton Bandages and Gauze are essential items in the medicine chest.

Aspirin or Bufferin are the best-known aids in reducing a high temperature and also for quieting a nervous dog. For the average twenty- to forty-pound dog, five to ten grains every four hours is the recommended dosage.

Suppositories are often useful as a means of regulating a puppy's bowel movements, particularly during the house-training period. They are also helpful in relieving constipation.

Tick and Lice Repellents, Flea Powder: During the spring, summer, and early autumn, you can make your dog much more comfortable (and very much more agreeable to have around) if you keep a supply of tick repellent, lice repellent, and flea powder on hand and use them according to the advice of your veterinarian or to the directions given on the manufacturers' labels. The important thing is to use them faithfully, otherwise the dog is apt to scratch itself raw. The consistent use of tick and lice repellents may also save a dog from a condition more serious than that of discomfort.

OTHER USEFUL ITEMS FOR PUPPY CARE

Bath Soap: Ivory soap, which is mild and pure, is as good as any soap on the market for a puppy's bath. It is preferable to use the soap in liquid form, since it rinses out more easily than if it is in cake form. If you want to spend a little more money, liquid Castile or any one of the various coconut oil soaps is very satisfactory. Containing oil, they do not dry the dog's coat but leave it supple, soft, and shining. It is generally advisable to bypass the advertised and high-priced "dog soaps," many of which contain caustics.

Brush for Grooming: The kind and size of brush to get depend upon the size and hair coat of the dog for which it is intended.

Nail Clippers: The toenails of a young puppy grow rapidly, and because a puppy usually walks on smooth surfaces, such as newspapers, they do not wear down to the proper length for comfort and safety or for the well-being of any fabric with which they come in contact. The points are often sharp enough to prick holes in hosiery, trouser legs, and upholstery, and as they grow they take on a curved shape which makes it difficult to extricate them from any fabric in which they are caught. Furthermore, in trying to pull itself loose, the puppy may injure itself. Long nails also make a dog's footing less secure. Periodically, therefore, the tips or points of the nails should be nipped off, taking care to merely blunt the nails rather than to shorten them appreciably. Great care must be taken not to cut into the "quick," which is quite sensitive and may bleed. Any type or make of clippers designed for cutting dogs' nails may be used. Nail clippers designed for humans should not be used, because they tend to crush a dog's nails rather than cut them.

Toys: A puppy needs toys to play with and these also serve to divert it from your more perishable possessions. As the disgruntled owner of a two-months-old Beagle complains: "I haven't had a whole sock, slipper, or shoe in the house since Bojangles came into it!"

The choice of toys that are safe for a puppy to play with is, however, extremely limited. All rubber toys (with the possible exception of the hard-rubber type) are strictly *verboten.* Puppies chew toys made of synthetic rubber. The bits of rubber get into the digestive tract, swell, and cause an obstruction that may require surgery in order to remove the offending bits and pieces.

All of the plastic and celluloid toys are literally for the birds, too, and not, if owners are wise, for their dogs. Especially lethal are the toys with gimmicks such as beads and bells inside of them. Bells make lovely sounds when they tinkle inside a toy, but inside a puppy they make trouble of, in some instances, a very serious nature. For example, if bits of a hard substance such as celluloid or metal get into the esophagus (the tube that leads from the pharynx to the stomach) and stay there, the pressure can cause a puncture or rupture of the tube. When this occurs, gangrene, or death of the tissue—and of the animal—often occurs.

Toys suitable for babies, such as calico animals stuffed with cotton, do not last long when puppies play with them. In no time at all the cotton is stuffing the puppy, which can also cause trouble of an obstructive nature.

The chemically treated so-called "indestructible" toys such as rubber balls so hard they can't be punctured by a puppy's teeth make the safest playthings for puppies, although we occasionally run into trouble with them, too. A pair of puppies can have a lot of fun playing tug of war with a burlap bag of a pair of stockings knotted together, but the game should be overseen, for the probability is that when the puppies tire of tugging they will take to chewing on what remains of the bag or the stockings.

In short, a great deal of trouble can be averted if a close watch is kept on any object given a puppy as a plaything in order to make sure it is being used as a plaything and not as a between-meals snack.

HOW TO TAKE YOUR DOG'S TEMPERATURE

Since it is not always possible or even necessary to take a dog to a veterinarian at the first sign of illness, it is advisable for an owner to know how to take his dog's temperature, the degree of the temperature being a pretty accurate gauge of the gravity or the relative inconsequence of the dog's condition.

Before taking a temperature, hold the thermometer firmly between the thumb and forefinger and shake it down with a sharp snapping motion until the mercury is driven down to at least 97°. Since you are using a rectal thermometer, the next step is to dip the bulb of the thermometer into Vaseline, petroleum jelly, or cold cream. You then lay the dog on its left side, insert the thermometer gently into the rectum, and hold it there for one or two minutes (most of the rectal thermometers register in one minute). After using the thermometer, wash it in soap and tepid water and immerse it in alcohol for an hour before drying and putting it away.

A dog's normal temperature is 101.8°. A healthy dog's temperature does not remain stationary, however, at the norm of 101.8° but is continually going up and down a point or two, depending on the time of day and on what the dog has been doing just prior to having its temperature taken. For example, the temperature of a perfectly healthy dog may go up a few tenths of a degree right after it has been playing or running or has been excited in some way. In most instances, a few tenths of a degree one way or the other is of little or no consequence. On the other hand, a rise of more than one degree should not be ignored, for it indicates that the body is fighting an infection of one kind or another. A sub-normal temperature of more than one degree is also cause for concern, since it may mean that the dog is suffering from some internal complications, such as hemorrhage, or is in shock, with the possibility of imminent collapse.

Usually the best times to take a temperature are in the early morning and late in the afternoon. But in order to determine whether a dog has a fever due to illness or as a consequence of exertion or excitement, it is advisable to take the temperature after the dog has been quiet and relaxed for an hour or more, irrespective of what time of day it may be.

HOW TO ADMINISTER MEDICINE

If your dog is eating normally, the tablet or pill can be enclosed in a piece of food and will probably be swallowed without ado. Otherwise—or when a dog is too ill to accept food—the technique of oral dosage must be followed. This consists of several maneuvers. First of all, it is necessary to open the dog's mouth. This should be accomplished with as much dexterity as possible on your part and as little excitement as possible for the dog, since pressure exerted on the mouth can be painful and there will be resistance to the administration of the medicine. The next maneuver is to place the left hand over the top of the dog's head with the thumb passing along its right cheek in front of the eye. The fingers of the left hand pass along the dog's left cheek and cover the left eye. In this manner the dog's head is restrained, and it may be encouraged to open its mouth by pressure of the finger tips on the opposite side of the face. The right hand should be free in order to place the tablet or capsule well down into the throat, after which the mouth should be closed and the jaws held gently but firmly together for a few seconds, or until the dog has swallowed the medication.

Liquid medication is usually administered without actually or fully opening the dog's mouth. Instead, a pocket is formed by pulling the lips to one side, and into this funnel-like pocket the liquid is poured, a few drops at a time, allowing time for the dog to swallow. The medicine can be administered by teaspoon, medicine dropper, small syringe, or by letting it dribble from the neck of a small bottle. If the dog is eating, liquid medicine can be mixed with its dinner, providing the odor is not such as to make the food unpalatable and that the dinner hour is the time prescribed for the dosage.

Depiction of a dog from a Boeotian amphora, 750 B.C.

An Old Man and His Dog

James Herriot

I LOOKED AGAIN at the slip of paper where I had written my visits. "Dean, 3, Thompson's Yard. Old dog ill."

There were a lot of these "yards" in Darrowby. They were, in fact, tiny streets, like pictures from a Dickens novel. Some of them opened off the market place and many more were scattered behind the main thoroughfares in the old part of the town. From the outside you could see only an archway and it was always a surprise to me to go down a narrow passage and come suddenly upon the uneven rows of little houses with no two alike, looking into each other's windows across eight feet of cobbles.

In front of some of the houses a strip of garden had been dug out and marigolds and nasturtiums straggled over the rough stones; but at the far end the houses were in a tumble-down condition and some were abandoned with their windows boarded up.

Number three was down at this end and looked as though it wouldn't be able to hold out much longer.

The flakes of paint quivered on the rotten wood of the door as I knocked; above, the outer wall bulged dangerously on either side of a long crack in the masonry.

A small, white-haired man answered. His face, pinched and lined, was enlivened by a pair of cheerful eyes; he wore a much-darned woollen cardigan, patched trousers and slippers.

From *All Creatures Great and Small* by James Herriot. Reprinted by permission of St. Martin's Press, Inc., Michael Joseph Ltd.

"I've come to see your dog," I said, and the old man smiled.

"Oh, I'm glad you've come, sir," he said. "I'm getting a bit worried about the old chap. Come inside, please."

He led me into the tiny living-room. "I'm alone now, sir. Lost my missus over a year ago. She used to think the world of the old dog."

The grim evidence of poverty was everywhere. In the worn out lino, the fireless hearth, the dank, musty smell of the place. The wallpaper hung away from the damp patches and on the table the old man's solitary dinner was laid; a fragment of bacon, a few fried potatoes and a cup of tea. This was life on the old age pension.

In the corner, on a blanket, lay my patient, a crossbred labrador. He must have been a big, powerful dog in his time, but the signs of age showed in the white hairs around his muzzle and the pale opacity in the depth of his eyes. He lay quietly and looked at me without hostility.

"Getting on a bit, isn't he, Mr. Dean?"

"Aye he is that. Nearly fourteen, but he's been like a pup galloping about until these last few weeks. Wonderful dog for his age, is old Bob and he's never offered to bite anybody in his life. Children can do anything with him. He's my only friend now—I hope you'll soon be able to put him right."

"Is he off his food, Mr. Dean?"

"Yes, clean off, and that's a strange thing because, by gum, he could eat. He always sat by me and put his head on my knee at meal times, but he hasn't been doing it lately."

I looked at the dog with growing uneasiness. The abdomen was grossly distended and I could read the telltale symptoms of pain; the catch in the respirations, the retracted commissures of the lips, the anxious, preoccupied expression in the eyes.

When his master spoke, the tail thumped twice on the

blankets and a momentary interest showed in the white old eyes; but it quickly disappeared and the blank, inward look returned.

I passed my hand carefully over the dog's abdomen. Ascites was pronounced and the dropsical fluid had gathered till the pressure was intense. "Come on, old chap," I said, "let's see if we can roll you over." The dog made no resistance as I eased him slowly on to his other side, but, just as the movement was completed, he whimpered and looked round. The cause of the trouble was now only too easy to find.

I palpated gently. Through the thin muscle of the flank I could feel a hard, corrugated mass; certainly a splenic or hepatic carcinoma, enormous and completely inoperable. I stroked the old dog's head as I tried to collect my thoughts. This wasn't going to be easy.

"Is he going to be ill for long?" the old man asked, and again came the thump, thump of the tail at the sound of the loved voice. "It's miserable when Bob isn't following me round the house when I'm doing my little jobs."

"I'm sorry, Mr. Dean, but I'm afraid this is something very serious. You see this large swelling. It is caused by an internal growth."

"You mean . . . cancer?" the little man said faintly.

"I'm afraid so, and it has progressed too far for anything to be done. I wish there was something I could do to help him, but there isn't."

The old man looked bewildered and his lips trembled. "Then he's going to die?"

I swallowed hard, "We really can't just leave him to die, can we? He's in some distress now, but it will soon be an awful lot worse. Don't you think it would be kindest to put him to sleep? After all, he's had a good, long innings." I always aimed at a brisk, matter-of-fact approach, but the old clichés had an empty ring.

The old man was silent, then he said, "Just a minute,"

and slowly and painfully knelt down by the side of the dog He did not speak, but ran his hand again and again over the grey old muzzle and the ears, while the tail thump, thump, thumped on the floor.

He knelt there a long time while I stood in the cheerless room, my eyes taking in the faded pictures on the walls, the frayed, grimy curtains, the broken-springed armchair.

At length the old man struggled to his feet and gulped once or twice. Without looking at me, he said huskily, "All right, will you do it now?"

I filled the syringe and said the things I always said. "You needn't worry, this is absolutely painless. Just an overdose of an anaesthetic. It is really an easy way out for the old fellow."

The dog did not move as the needle was inserted, and, as the barbiturate began to flow into the vein, the anxious expression left his face and the muscles began to relax. By the time the injection was finished, the breathing had stopped.

"Is that it?" the old man whispered.

"Yes, that's it," I said. "He is out of his pain now."

The old man stood motionless except for the clasping and unclasping of his hands. When he turned to face me his eyes were bright. "That's right, we couldn't let him suffer, and I'm grateful for what you've done. And now, what do I owe you for your services, sir?"

"Oh, that's all right, Mr. Dean," I said quickly. "It's nothing—nothing at all. I was passing right by here—it was no trouble."

The old man was astonished. "But you can't do that for nothing."

"Now please say no more about it, Mr. Dean. As I told you, I was passing right by your door." I said goodbye and went out of the house, through the passage and into the street. In the bustle of people and the bright sunshine, I could still see only the stark, little room, the old man and his dead dog.

As I walked towards my car, I heard a shout behind me. The old man was shuffling excitedly towards me in his slippers. His cheeks were streaked and wet, but he was smiling. In his hand he held a small, brown object.

"You've been very kind, sir. I've got something for you." He held out the object and I looked at it. It was tattered but just recognisable as a precious relic of a bygone celebration.

"Go on, it's for you," said the old man. "Have a cigar."

Deerhound

61

How to Name a Dog

James Thurber

EVERY FEW MONTHS somebody writes me and asks if I will give him a name for his dog. Several of these correspondents in the past year have wanted to know if I would mind the use of my own name for their spaniels. Spaniel-owners seem to have the notion that a person could sue for invasion of privacy or defamation of character if his name were applied to a cocker without written permission, and one gentleman even insisted that we conduct our correspondence in the matter through a notary public. I have a way of letting communications of this sort fall behind my roll-top desk, but it has recently occurred to me that this is an act of evasion, if not, indeed, of plain cowardice. I have therefore decided to come straight out with the simple truth that it is as hard for me to think up a name for a dog as it is for anybody else. The idea that I am an expert in the business is probably the outcome of a piece I wrote several years ago, incautiously revealing the fact that I have owned forty or more dogs in my life. This is true, but it is also deceptive. All but five or six of my dogs were disposed of when they were puppies, and I had not gone to the trouble of giving to these impermanent residents of my house any names at all except Shut Up! and Cut That Out! and Let Go!

Names of dogs end up in 176th place in the list of things that amaze and fascinate me. Canine cognomens should be designed to impinge on the ears of dogs and not to amuse neighbors, tradespeople, and casual visitors. I remember a few dogs from the past with a faint but lingering pleasure; a farm hound named Rain, a roving Airedale named Marco Polo, a female bull terrier known as Brody because she liked to jump from moving motor cars and second-story windows, and a Peke called Darien; but that's all.

Well, there is Poker, alias *Fantôme Noir,* a miniature black poodle I have come to know since I wrote the preceding paragraphs. Poker, familiarly known as Pokey, belongs to Mr. and Mrs. J. G. Gude, of White Plains, and when they registered him with the American Kennel Club they decided he needed a more dignified name. It wasn't easy to explain this to their youngest child David, and his parents never did quite clear it up for him. When he was only eight, David thought the problem over for a long while and then asked his father solemnly, "If he belongs to that club, why doesn't he ever go there?" Since I wrote this piece originally, I have also heard about a sheep dog named Jupiter, which used to belong to Jimmy Cannon, journalist, critic, and man about dog shows. He reported in a recent column of his that Jupiter used to eat geraniums. I have heard of other dogs that ate flowers, but I refuse to be astonished by this until I learn of one that's downed a nasturtium.

The only animals whose naming demands concentration, hard work, and ingenuity are the seeing-eye dogs. They have to be given unusual names because passers-by like to call to seeing-eyers—"Here, Sport" or "Yuh, Rags" or "Don't take any wooden nickels, Rin Tin Tin." A blind man's dog with an ordinary name would continually be distracted from its work. A tyro at naming these dogs might make the mistake of picking Durocher or Teeftallow. The former is too much like Rover and the latter could easily sound like "Here, fellow" to a dog. Ten years ago I met a

63

young man in his twenties who had been mysteriously blind for nearly five years and had been led about by a seeing-eye German shepherd during all of that time, which included several years of study at Yale. Then suddenly one night the dog's owner began to get his vision back, and within a few weeks was able to read the fine print of a telephone book. The effect on his dog was almost disastrous, and it went into a kind of nervous crack-up, since these animals are trained to the knowledge, or belief, that their owners are permanently blind. After the owner regained his vision he kept the dog, of course, not only because they had become attached to each other but because the average seeing-eye dog cannot be transferred from one person to another.

Speaking of puppies, as I was a while back, I feel that I should warn inexperienced dog-owners who have discovered to their surprise and dismay a dozen puppies in a hall closet or under the floor of the barn, not to give them away. Sell them or keep them, but don't give them away. Sixty per cent of persons who are given a dog for nothing bring him back sooner or later and plump him into the reluctant and unprepared lap of his former owner. The people say that they are going to Florida and can't take the dog, or that he doesn't want to go; or they point out that he eats first editions or lace curtains or spinets, or that he doesn't see eye to eye with them in the matter of house-breaking, or that he makes disparaging remarks under his breath about their friends. Anyway, they bring him back and you are stuck with him—and maybe six others. But if you charge ten or even five dollars for pups, the new owners don't dare return them. They are afraid to ask for their money back because they believe you might think they are hard up and need the five or ten dollars. Furthermore, when a mischievous puppy is returned to its former owner it invariably behaves beautifully, and the person who brought it back is likely to be regarded as an imbecile or a dog-hater or both.

How to Name a Dog

Names of dogs, to get back to our subject, have a range almost as wide as that of the violin. They run from such plain and simple names as Spot, Sport, Rex, Brownie to fancy appellations such as Prince Rudolph Hertenberg Gratzheim of Darndorf-Putzelhorst, and Darling Mist o' Love III of Heather-Light-Holyrood—names originated by adults, all of whom in every other way, I am told, have made a normal adjustment to life. In addition to the plain and fancy categories, there are the Cynical and the Coy. Cynical names are given by people who do not like dogs too much. The most popular cynical names during the war were Mussolini, Tojo, and Adolf. I never have been able to get very far in my exploration of the minds of people who call their dogs Mussolini, Tojo, and Adolf, and I suspect the reason is that I am unable to associate with them long enough to examine what goes on in their heads. I nod, and I tell them the time of day, if they ask, and that is all. I never vote for them or ask them to have a drink. The great Coy category is perhaps the largest. The Coy people call their pets Bubbles and Boggles and Sparkles and Twinkles and Doodles and Puffy and Lovums and Sweetums and Itsy-Bitsy and Betsy-Bye-Bye and Sugarkins. I pass these dog-owners at a dog-trot, wearing a horrible fixed grin.

There is a special subdivision of the Coys that is not quite so awful, but awful enough. These people, whom we will call the Wits, own two dogs, which they name Pitter and Patter, Willy and Nilly, Helter and Skelter, Namby and Pamby, Hugger and Mugger, and even Wishy and Washy, Ups and Daisy, Fitz and Startz, Fetch and Carrie, and Pro and Connie. Then there is the Cryptic category. These people select names for some private reason or for no reason at all—except perhaps to arouse a visitor's curiosity, so that he will exclaim, "Why in the world do you call your dog *that*?" The Cryptic name their dogs October, Bennett's Aunt, Three Fifteen, Doc Knows, Tuesday, Home Fried,

Opus 38, Ask Leslie, and Thanks for the Home Run, Emil. I make it a point simply to pat these unfortunate dogs on the head, ask no question of their owners, and go about my business.

This article has degenerated into a piece that properly should be entitled "How Not to Name a Dog." I was afraid it would. It seems only fair to make up for this by confessing a few of the names I have given my own dogs, with the considerable help, if not, indeed, the insistence, of their mistress. Most of my dogs have been females, and they have answered, with apparent gladness, to such names as Jennie, Tessa, Julie, and Sophie. I have never owned a dog named Pamela, Jennifer, Clarissa, Jacqueline, Guinevere, or Shelmerdene.

About fifteen years ago, when I was looking for a house to buy in Connecticut, I knocked on the front door of an attractive home whose owner, my real-estate agent had told me, wanted to sell it and go back to Iowa to live. The lady agent who escorted me around had informed me that the owner of this place was a man named Strong, but a few minutes after arriving at the house, I was having a drink in the living room with Phil Stong, for it was he. We went out into the yard after a while and I saw Mr. Stong's spaniel. I called to the dog and snapped my fingers, but he seemed curiously embarrassed, like his master. "What's his name?" I asked the latter. He was cornered and there was no way out of it. "Thurber," he said in a small frightened voice. Thurber and I shook hands, and he didn't seem to me any more depressed than any other spaniel I have met. He had, however, the expression of a bachelor on his way to a party he has tried in vain to get out of, and I think it must have been this cast of countenance that had reminded Mr. Stong of the dog I draw. The dog I draw is, to be sure, much larger than a spaniel and not so shaggy, but I confess, though I am not a spaniel man, that there are certain basic resemblances between my dog and all other dogs with long ears and troubled eyes.

Perhaps I should suggest at least one name for a dog, if only to justify the title of this piece. All right, then, what's the matter with Stong? It's a good name for a dog, short, firm, and effective. I recommend it to all those who have written to me for suggestions and to all those who may be at this very moment turning over in their minds the idea of asking my advice in this difficult and perplexing field of nomenclature.

Since I first set down these not too invaluable rules for naming dogs, I have heard of at least a dozen basset hounds named Thurber, a Newfoundland called Little Bears Thurber and a bloodhound named Tiffany's Thurber. This is all right with me, so long as the owners of Thurbers do not bring them to call on me at my house in Connecticut without making arrangements in advance. Christabel, my old and imperious poodle, does not like unannounced dog visitors, and tries to get them out of the house as fast as she can. Two years ago a Hartford dog got lost in my neighborhood and finally showed up at my house. He hadn't had much, if anything, to eat for several days, and we fed him twice within three hours, to the high dismay and indignation of Christabel, who only gets one big meal a day. The wanderer was returned to its owner, through a story in the Hartford *Courant,* and quiet descended on my home until a handsome young male collie showed up one night. We had quite a time getting him out of the house. Christabel kept telling him how wonderful it was outdoors and trotting to the door, but the collie wasn't interested. I tried to pick him up, but I am too old to pick up a full-grown collie. In the end Christabel solved the problem herself by leading him outside on the promise of letting him chew one of the bones she had buried. He still keeps coming back to visit us from time to time, but Christabel has hidden her bones in new places. She will romp with the young visitor for about twenty seconds, then show her teeth and send him home. I don't do anything about the situation. After all, my home has been in charge of Christabel for a great many years now, and I never interfere with a woman's ruling a household.

Poodles

The Coming of Riquet

Anatole France

SEATED AT HIS table one morning in front of the window, against which the leaves of the plane tree quivered, M. Bergeret, who was trying to discover how the ships of Aeneas had been changed into nymphs, heard a tap at the door, and forthwith his servant entered, carrying in front of her, opossum-like, a tiny creature whose black head peeped out from the folds of her apron, which she had turned up to form a pocket. With a look of anxiety and hope upon her face, she remained motionless for a moment, then she placed the little thing upon the carpet at her master's feet.

"What's that?" asked M. Bergeret.

It was a little dog of doubtful breed, having something of the terrier in him, and a well-set head, a short, smooth coat of a dark tan color, and a tiny little stump of a tail. His body retained its puppy-like softness, and he went sniffling at the carpet.

"Angélique," said M. Bergeret, "take this animal back to its owner."

"It has no owner, Monsieur."

M. Bergeret looked silently at the little creature, who had come to examine his slippers, and was giving little sniffs of approval. M. Bergeret was a philologist, which perhaps explains why at this juncture he asked a vain question.

"What is he called?"

From *The Amethyst Ring*, by Anatole France.

69

"Monsieur," replied Angélique, "he has no name."

M. Bergeret seemed put out at this answer: he looked at the dog sadly, with a disheartened air.

Then the little animal placed its two front paws on M. Bergeret's slipper, and, holding it thus, began innocently to nibble at it. With a sudden access of compassion M. Bergeret took the tiny nameless creature upon his knee. The dog looked at him intently, and M. Bergeret was pleased at his confiding expression.

"What beautiful eyes!" he cried.

The dog's eyes were indeed beautiful, the pupils of a golden-flecked chestnut set in warm white. And his gaze spoke of simple, mysterious thoughts, common alike to the thoughtful beasts and simple men of the earth.

Tired, perhaps, with the intellectual effort he had made for the purpose of entering into communication with a human being, he closed his beautiful eyes, and, yawning widely, revealed his pink mouth, his curled-up tongue, and his array of dazzling teeth.

M. Bergeret put his hand into the dog's mouth, and allowed him to lick it, at which old Angélique gave a smile of relief.

"A more affectionate little creature doesn't breathe," she said.

"The dog," said M. Bergeret, "is a religious animal. In his savage state he worships the moon and the lights that float upon the waters. These are his gods, to whom he appeals at night with long-drawn howls. In the domesticated state he seeks by his caresses to conciliate those powerful genii who dispense the good things of this world—to wit, men. He worships and honors men by the accomplishment of the rites passed down to him by his ancestors: he licks their hands, jumps against their legs, and when they show signs of anger towards him he approaches them crawling on his belly as a sign of humility, to appease their wrath."

"All dogs are not the friends of man," remarked Angélique. "Some of them bite the hand that feeds them."

"Those are the ungodly, blasphemous dogs," returned M. Bergeret, "insensate creatures like Ajax, the son of Telamon, who wounded the hand of the golden Aphrodite. These sacrilegious creatures die a dreadful death, or lead wandering and miserable lives. They are not to be confounded with those dogs who, espousing the quarrel of their own particular god, wage war upon his enemy, the neighboring god. They are heroes. Such, for example, is the dog of Lafolie, the butcher, who fixed his sharp teeth into the leg of the tramp Pied-d'Alouette. For it is a fact that dogs fight among themselves like men, and Turk, with his snub nose, serves his god Lafolie against the robber gods, in the same way that Israel helped Jehovah to destroy Chamos and Moloch."

The puppy, however, having decided that M. Bergeret's remarks were the reverse of interesting, curled up his feet and stretched out his head, ready to go to sleep upon the knees that harbored him.

"Where did you find him?" asked M. Bergeret.

"Well, Monsieur, it was M. Dellion's *chef* gave him to me."

"With the result," continued M. Bergeret, "that we now have this soul to care for."

"What soul?" asked Angélique.

"This canine soul. An animal is, properly speaking, a soul; I do not say an immortal soul. And yet, when I come to consider the positions this poor little beast and I myself occupy in the scheme of things, I recognize in both exactly the same right to immortality."

After considerable hesitation, old Angélique, with a painful effort that made her upper lip curl up and reveal her two remaining teeth, said:

"If Monsieur does not want a dog, I will return him to M. Dellion's *chef;* but you may safely keep him, I assure you. You won't see or hear him."

She had hardly finished her sentence when the puppy,

hearing a heavy van rolling down the street, sat bolt upright on M. Bergeret's knees, and began to bark both loud and long, so that the windowpanes resounded with the noise.

M. Bergeret smiled.

"He's a watch-dog," said Angélique, by way of excuse. "They are by far the most faithful."

"Have you given him anything to eat?" asked M. Bergeret.

"Of course," returned Angélique.

"What does he eat?"

"Monsieur must be aware that dogs eat bread and meat."

Somewhat piqued, M. Bergeret retorted that in her eagerness she might very likely have taken him away from his mother before he was old enough to leave her, upon which he was lifted up again and re-examined, only to make sure of the fact that he was at least six months old.

M. Bergeret put him down on the carpet, and regarded him with interest.

"Isn't he pretty?" said the servant.

"No, he is not pretty," replied M. Bergeret. "But he is engaging, and has beautiful eyes. That is what people used to say about me," added the professor, "when I was three times as old, and not half as intelligent. Since then I have no doubt acquired an outlook upon the universe, which he will never attain. But, in comparison with the Absolute, I may say that my knowledge equals his in the smallness of its extent. Like his, it is a geometrical point in the infinite." Then, addressing the little creature who was sniffing the waste-paper basket, he went on: "Smell it out, sniff it well, take from the outside world all the knowledge that can reach your simple brain through the medium of that black truffle-like nose of yours. And what though I at the same time observe, and compare, and study? We shall never know, neither the one nor the other of us, why we have been put into this world, and what we are doing in it. What are we here for, eh?"

As he had spoken rather loudly, the puppy looked at him anxiously, and M. Bergeret, returning to the thought which had first filled his mind, said to the servant:

"We must give him a name."

With her hands folded in front of her she replied laughingly that would not be a difficult matter.

Upon which M. Bergeret made the private reflection that to the simple all things are simple, but that clear-sighted souls, who look upon things from many and divers aspects, invisible to the vulgar mind, experience the greatest difficulty in coming to a decision about even the most trivial matters. And he cudgelled his brains, trying to hit upon a name for the little living thing that was busily engaged in nibbling the fringe of the carpet.

"All the names of dogs," thought he, "preserved in the ancient treatises of the huntsmen of old, such as Fouilloux, and in the verses of our sylvan poets such as La Fontaine— Finaud, Miraut, Briffaut, Ravaud, and such-like names, are given to sporting dogs, who are the aristocracy of the kennel, the chivalry of the canine race. The dog of Ulysses was called Argos, and he was a hunter too, so Homer tells us. 'In his youth he hunted the little hares of Ithaca, but now he was old and hunted no more.' What we require is something quite different. The names given by old maids to their lap-dogs would be more suitable, were they not usually pretentious and absurd. Azor, for instance, is ridiculous!"

So M. Bergeret ruminated, calling to memory many a dog name, without being able to decide, however, on one that pleased him. He would have liked to invent a name, but lacked the imagination.

"What day is it?" he asked at last.

"The ninth," replied Angélique. "Thursday, the ninth."

"Well, then!" said M. Bergeret, "can't we call the dog Thursday, like Robinson Crusoe who called his man Friday, for the same reason?"

73

"As Monsieur pleases," said Angélique. "But it isn't very pretty."

"Very well," said M. Bergeret, "find a name for the creature yourself, for, after all, you brought him here."

"Oh, no," said the servant. "I couldn't find a name for him; I'm not clever enough. When I saw him lying on the straw in the kitchen, I called him Riquet, and he came up and played about under my skirts."

"You called him Riquet, did you?" cried M. Bergeret. "Why didn't you say so before? Riquet he is and Riquet he shall remain; that's settled. Now be off with you, and take Riquet with you. I want to work."

"Monsieur," returned Angélique, "I am going to leave the puppy with you; I will come for him when I get back from market."

"You could quite well take him to market with you," retorted M. Bergeret.

"Monsieur, I am going to church as well."

It was quite true that she really was going to church at Saint-Exupère, to ask for a Mass to be said for the repose of her husband's soul. She did that regularly once a year, not that she had even been informed of the decease of Borniche, who had never communicated with her since his desertion, but it was a settled thing in the good woman's mind that Borniche was dead. She had therefore no fear of his coming to rob her of the little she had, and did her best to fix things up to his advantage in the other world, so long as he left her in peace in this one.

"Eh!" ejaculated M. Bergeret. "Shut him up in the kitchen or some other convenient place, and do not wor——"

He did not finish his sentence, for Angélique had vanished, purposely pretending not to hear, that she might leave Riquet with his master. She wanted them to grow used to one another, and she also wanted to give poor, friendless M.

Bergeret a companion. Having closed the door behind her, she went along the corridor and down the steps.

M. Bergeret set to work again and plunged head foremost into his *Virgilius nauticus*. He loved the work; it rested his thoughts, and became a kind of game that suited him, for he played it all by himself. On the table beside him were several boxes filled with pegs, which he fixed into little squares of cardboard to represent the fleet of Aeneas. Now while he was thus occupied he felt something like tiny fists tapping at his legs. Riquet, whom he had quite forgotten, was standing on his hind legs patting his master's knees, and wagging his little stump of a tail. When he tired of this, he let his paws slide down the trouser leg, then got up and began his coaxing over again. And M. Bergeret, turning away from the printed lore before him, saw two brown eyes gazing up at him lovingly.

"What gives a human beauty to the gaze of this dog," he thought, "is probably that it varies unceasingly, being by turns bright and vivacious, or serious and sorrowful; because through these eyes his little dumb soul finds expression for thought that lacks nothing in depth nor sequence. My father was very fond of cats, and, consequently, I liked them too. He used to declare that cats are the wise man's best companions, for they respect his studious hours. Bajazet, his Persian cat, would sit at night for hours at a stretch, motionless and majestic, perched on a corner of his table. I still remember the agate eyes of Bajazet, but those jewel-like orbs concealed all thought, that owl-like stare was cold, and hard, and wicked. How much do I prefer the melting gaze of the dog!"

Riquet, however, was agitating his paws in frantic fashion, and M. Bergeret, who was anxious to return to his philological amusements, said kindly, but shortly:

"Lie down, Riquet!"

Upon which Riquet went and thrust his nose against the door through which Angélique had passed out. And there he remained, uttering from time to time plaintive, meek little cries. After a while he began to scratch, making a gentle rasping noise on the polished floor with his nails. Then the whining began again followed by more scratching. Disturbed by these sounds, M. Bergeret sternly bade him keep still.

Riquet peered at him sorrowfully with his brown eyes, then, sitting down, he looked at M. Bergeret again, rose, returned to the door, sniffed underneath it, and wailed afresh.

"Do you want to go out?" asked M. Bergeret.

Putting down his pen, he went to the door, which he held a few inches open. After making sure that he was running no risk of hurting himself on the way out, Riquet slipped through the doorway and marched off with a composure that was scarcely polite. On returning to his table, M. Bergeret, sensitive man that he was, pondered over the dog's action. He said to himself:

"I was on the point of reproaching the animal for going without saying either good-bye or thank you, and expecting him to apologize for leaving me. It was the beautiful human expression of his eyes that made me so foolish. I was beginning to look upon him as one of my own kind."

After making this reflection M. Bergeret applied himself anew to the metamorphosis of the ships of Aeneas, a legend both pretty and popular, but perhaps a trifle too simple in itself for expression in such noble language. M. Bergeret, however, saw nothing incongruous in it. He knew that the nursery tales have furnished material for nearly all epics, and that Virgil had carefully collected together in his poem the riddles, the puns, the uncouth stories, and the puerile imaginings of his forefathers; that Homer, his master and the master of all the bards, had done little more than tell over again what the good wives of Ionia and the fishermen of the islands had been narrating for more than a thousand years before him. Besides, for the time being, this was the least of his worries; he had another far more important preoccupation. An expression, met with in the course of the charming story of the metamorphosis, did not appear sufficiently plain to him. That was what was worrying him.

"Bergeret, my friend," he said to himself, "this is where you must open your eyes and show your sense. Remember that Virgil always expresses himself with extreme precision when writing on the technique of the arts; remember that he went yachting at Baïae, that he was an expert in naval construction, and that therefore his language, in this passage, must have a precise and definite signification."

And M. Bergeret carefully consulted a great number of texts, in order to throw a light upon the word which he could not understand, and which he had to explain. He was almost on the point of grasping the solution, or, at any rate, he had caught a glimpse of it, when he heard a noise like the rattling of chains at his door, a noise which, although not alarming, struck him as curious. The disturbance was presently accompanied by a shrill whining, and M. Bergeret, interrupted in his philological investigations, immediately concluded that these importunate wails must emanate from Riquet.

As a matter of fact, after having looked vainly all over the house for Angélique, Riquet had been seized with a desire to see M. Bergeret again. Solitude was as painful to him as human society was dear. In order to put an end to the noise, and also because he had a secret desire to see Riquet again, M. Bergeret got up from his arm-chair and opened the door, and Riquet re-entered the study with the same coolness with which he had quitted it, but as soon as he saw the door close behind him he assumed a melancholy expression, and began to wander up and down the room like a soul in torment.

He had a sudden way of appearing to find something of interest beneath the chairs and tables, and would sniff long and noisily; then he would walk aimlessly about or sit down in a corner with an air of great humility, like the beggars who are to be seen in church porches. Finally he began to bark at a cast of Hermes which stood upon the mantel-shelf, whereupon M. Bergeret addressed him in words full of just reproach.

"Riquet! such vain agitation, such sniffing and barking were better suited to a stable than to the study of a professor, and they lead one to suppose that your ancestors lived with those horses whose straw litters they shared. I do not reproach you with that. It is only natural you should have inherited their habits, manners, and tendencies as well as their close-cropped coat, their sausage-like body, and their long, thin nose. I do not speak of your beautiful eyes, for there are few men, few dogs even, who can open such beauties to the light of day. But, leaving all that aside, you are a mongrel, my friend, a mongrel from your short, bandy legs to your head. Again I am far from despising you for that. What I want you to understand is that if you desire to live with me, you will have to drop your mongrel manners and behave like a *scholar*, in other words, to remain silent and quiet, to respect work, after the manner of Bajazet, who of a night would sit for hours without stirring, and watch my father's pen skimming over the paper. He was a silent and tactful creature. How different is your own character, my friend! Since you came into this chamber of study your hoarse voice, your unseemly snufflings and your whines, that sound like steam whistles, have constantly confused my thoughts and interrupted my reflections. And now you have made me lose the drift of an important passage in Servius, referring to the construction of one of the ships of Aeneas. Know then, Riquet, my friend, that this is the house of silence and the abode of meditation, and that if you are anxious to stay here you must become literary. Be quiet!"

Thus spoke M. Bergeret. Riquet, who had listened to

him with mute astonishment, approached his master, and with suppliant gesture placed a timid paw upon the knee, which he seemed to revere in a fashion that savored of long ago. Then a kind thought struck M. Bergeret. He picked him up by the scruff of his neck, and put him upon the cushions of the ample easy chair in which he was sitting. Turning himself round three times, Riquet lay down, and then remained perfectly still and silent. He was quite happy. M. Bergeret was grateful to him, and as he ran through Servius he occasionally stroked the close-cropped coat, which, without being soft, was smooth and very pleasant to the touch. Riquet fell into a gentle doze, and communicated to his master the generous warmth of his body, the subtle, gentle heat of a living, breathing thing. And from that moment M. Bergeret found more pleasure in his *Virgilius nauticus.*

From floor to ceiling his study was lined with deal shelves, bearing books arranged in methodical order. One glance, and all that remains to us of Latin thought was ready to his hand. The Greeks lay halfway up. In a quiet corner, easy to access, were Rabelais, the excellent story-tellers of the *Cent nouvelles nouvelles,* Bonaventure des Périers, Guillaume Bouchet, and all the old French "conteurs," whom M. Bergeret considered better adapted to humanity than writings in the more heroic style, and who were the favorite reading of his leisure. He possessed them in cheap modern editions only, but he had discovered a poor bookbinder in the town who covered his volumes with leaves from a book of anthems, and it gave M. Bergeret the keenest pleasure to see these free-spoken gentlemen thus clad in Requiems and Misereres. This was the sole luxury and the only peculiarity of his austere library. The other books were paper-backed or bound in poor and worn-out bindings. The gentle friendly manner in which they were handled by their owner gave them the look of tools set out in a busy man's workshop. The books of archaeology and art found a resting-place on the highest shelves, not by any means out of contempt, but because they were not so often used.

Now, while M. Bergeret worked at his *Virgilius nauticus* and shared his chair with Riquet, he found, as chance would have it, that it was necessary to consult Ottfried Müller's little *Manual*, which happened to be on one of the topmost shelves.

There was no need of one of those tall ladders on wheels topped by railings and a shelf, to enable him to reach the book; there were ladders of this description in the town library, and they had been used by all the great book-lovers of the eighteenth and nineteenth centuries; indeed, several of the latter had fallen from them, and thus died honorable deaths, in the manner spoken of in the pamphlet entitled: *Des bibliophiles qui moururent en tombant de leur échelle.* No, indeed! M. Bergeret had no need of anything of the sort. A small pair of folding steps would have served his purpose excellently well, and he had once seen some in the shop of Clérambaut, the cabinet-maker, in the Rue de Josde. They folded up, and looked just the thing, with their bevelled uprights each pierced with a trefoil as a grip for the hand. M. Bergeret would have given anything to possess them, but the state of his finances, which were somewhat involved, forced him to abandon the idea. No one knew better than he did that financial ills are not mortal, but, for all that, he had no steps in his study.

In place of such a pair of steps he used an old cane-bottomed chair, the back of which had been broken, leaving only two horns or antennae, which had shown themselves to be more dangerous than useful. So they had been cut to the level of the seat, and the chair had become a stool. There were two reasons why this stool was ill-fitted to the use to which M. Bergeret was wont to put it. In the first place the woven-cane seat had grown slack with long use, and now contained a large hollow, making one's foothold precarious. In the second place the stool was too low, and it was hardly possible when standing upon it to reach the books on the highest shelf, even with the finger-tips. What generally happened was that in the endeavor to grasp one book, several others fell out; and it depended upon their being bound or paper-covered whether they lay with broken corners, or sprawled with leaves spread like a fan or a concertina.

Now, with the intention of getting down the *Manual* of Ottfried Müller, M. Bergeret quitted the chair he was sharing with Riquet, who, rolled into a ball with his head tight pressed to his body, lay in warm comfort, opening one voluptuous eye, which he re-closed as quickly. Then M. Bergeret drew the stool from the dark corner where it was hidden and placed it where it was required, hoisted himself upon it, and managed, by making his arm as long as possible, and straining upon tiptoe, to touch, first with one, then with two fingers, the back of a book which he judged to be the one he was needing. As for the thumb, it remained below the shelf and rendered no assistance whatever. M. Bergeret, who found it therefore exceedingly difficult to draw out the book, made the reflection that the reason why the hand is a precious implement is on account of the position of the thumb, and that no being could rise to be an artist who had four feet and no hands.

"It is to the hand," he reflected, "that men owe their power of becoming engineers, painters, writers, and manipulators of all kinds of things. If they had no thumb as well as their other fingers, they would be as incapable as I am at this moment, and they could never have changed the face of the earth as they have done. Beyond a doubt it is the shape of the hand that has assured to man the conquest of the world."

Then, almost simultaneously, M. Bergeret remembered that monkeys, who possess four hands, have not, for all that, created the arts, nor disposed that earth to their use, and he erased from his mind the theory upon which he had just embarked. However, he did the best he could with his four fingers. It must be known that Ottfried Müller's *Manual* is composed of three volumes and an atlas. M. Bergeret wanted volume one. He pulled out first the second volume, then the atlas, then volume three, and finally the book that he required. At last he held it in his hands. All that now remained for him to do was to descend, and this he was about to do when the cane seat gave way beneath his foot, which passed through it. He lost his balance and fell to the ground, not as heavily as might have been feared, for he broke his fall by grasping at one of the uprights of the bookshelf.

He was on the ground, however, full of astonishment, and wearing on one leg the broken chair; his whole body was permeated and as though constricted by a pain that spread all over it, and that presently settled itself more particularly in the region of the left elbow and hip upon which he had fallen. But, as his anatomy was not seriously damaged, he gathered his wits together; he had got so far as to realize that he must draw his right leg out of the stool in which it had so unfortunately become entangled, and that he must be careful to raise himself up on his right side, which was unhurt. He was even trying to put this into execution when he felt a warm breath upon his cheek, and turning his eyes, which fright and pain had for the moment fixed, he saw close to his cheek Riquet's little face.

At the sound of the fall Riquet had jumped down from the chair and run to his unfortunate master; he was now standing near him in a state of great excitement; then he commenced to run round him. First he came near out of sympathy, then he retreated out of fear of some mysterious danger. He understood perfectly well that a misfortune had taken place, but he was neither thoughtful nor clever enough to discover what it was; hence his anxiety. His fidelity drew him to his suffering friend, and his prudence stopped him on the very brink of the fatal spot. Encouraged at length by the calm and silence which eventually reigned, he licked M. Bergeret's neck and looked at him with eyes of fear and of love. The fallen master smiled, and the dog licked the end of his nose. It was a great comfort to M. Bergeret, who freed his right leg, stood erect, and limped good-humoredly back to his chair.

Riquet was there before him. All that could be seen of his eyes was a gleam between the narrow slit of the half-closed lids. He seemed to have forgotten all about the adventure that a moment before had so stirred them both. The little creature lived in the present, with no thought of time that had run its course; not that he was wanting in memory, inasmuch as he could remember, not his own past alone, but the faraway past of his ancestors, and his little head was a rich storehouse of useful knowledge; but he took no pleasure in remembrance, and memory was not for him, as it was for M. Bergeret, a divine muse.

Gently stroking the short, smooth coat of his companion, M. Bergeret addressed him in the following affectionate terms:

"Dog! at the price of the repose which is dear to your heart, you came to me when I was dismayed and brought low. You did not laugh, as any young person of my own species would have done. It is true that however joyous or terrible nature may appear to you at times, she never inspires you with a sense of the ridiculous. And it is for that very reason, because of your innocent gravity, that you are the surest friend a man can have. In the first instance I inspired confidence and admiration in you, and now you show me pity.

"Dog! when we first met on the highway of life, we came from the two poles of creation; we belong to different species. I refer to this with no desire to take advantage of it, but rather with a strong sense of universal brotherhood. We have hardly been acquainted two hours, and my hand has never yet fed you. What can be the meaning of the obscure love for me that has sprung up in your little heart? The sympathy you bestow on me is a charming mystery, and I accept it. Sleep, friend, in the place that you have chosen!"

Having thus spoken, M. Bergeret turned over the leaves of Ottfried Müller's *Manual*, which with marvelous instinct he had kept in his hand both during and after his fall. He turned over the pages, and could not find what he sought.

Every moment, however, seemed to increase the pain he was feeling.

"I believe," he thought, "that the whole of my left side is bruised and my hip swollen. I have a suspicion that my right leg is grazed all over and my left elbow aches and burns, but shall I cavil at pain that has led me to the discovery of a friend?"

His reflections were running thus when old Angélique, breathless and perspiring, entered the study. She first opened the door, and then she knocked, for she never permitted herself to enter without knocking. If she had not done so before she opened the door, she did it after, for she had good manners, and knew what was expected of her. She went in therefore, knocked, and said:

"Monsieur, I have come to relieve you of the dog."

M. Bergeret heard these words with decided annoyance. He had not as yet inquired into his claims to Riquet, and now realized that he had none. The thought that Madame Borniche might take the animal away from him filled him with sadness, yet, after all, Riquet did belong to her. Affecting indifference, he replied:

"He's asleep; let him sleep!"

"Where is he? I don't see him," remarked old Angélique.

"Here he is," answered M. Bergeret. "In my chair."

With her two hands clasped over her portly figure, old Angélique smiled, and, in a tone of gentle mockery, ventured:

"I wonder what pleasure the creature can find in sleeping there behind Monsieur!"

"That," retorted M. Bergeret, "is his business."

Then, as he was of inquiring mind, he immediately sought of Riquet his reasons for the selection of his resting-place, and lighting on them, replied with his accustomed candor:

"I keep him warm, and my presence affords a sense of security; my comrade is a chilly and homely little animal." Then he added: "Do you know, Angélique? I will go out presently and buy him a collar."

Bloodhound

How Much to Feed Your Dog

Leon F. Whitney

THERE ARE SOME general principles of feeding which are important to the health of every dog regardless of breed. Next to our consideration of what to do when the end comes, this is the most ticklish subject we have to tackle.

Nobody should have any difficulty understanding the fundamental rule: *In feeding mature pets, the less they eat,* compatible with keeping them in sound condition, *the healthier they'll be and the longer they'll live.* It goes without saying, of course, that they should have a complete and balanced diet. They should not be allowed to get too fat or too thin. If you try to keep them too thin, they may get too little of some essential ingredient; if you permit them to get too fat, you will shorten their lives.

In growing pets, the faster they grow the cheaper it is to raise them. Yes, *but*—will they live longer, be healthier? Probably the best rule for sound health and longevity is to grow them moderately fast, but not to force them.

Nearly everyone overfeeds. And almost every animal will eat 20 per cent more than it needs. There are some animals, like some people, which never get fat even though they are chronically overfed. The way to feed—the way people who are good feeders feed their pets—is to find just the amount which will maintain your pet's weight and feed no more. No rule in feeding is as important as this one.

Your dog is happier if not burdened with unnecessary fat.

If only Mrs. Jones and all others who allow pets to become obese knew a few truths about food storage in the body and something about fasting—which some people call starvation—how much better off their pets would be.

Starvation is the long-continued deprivation of food.

Fasting is total or partial abstinence from food.

Starvation is forced; fasting is voluntary. A sick animal fasts; an obese animal must be starved but not necessarily deprived of all food. When an animal is too fat he won't really starve, even though he takes no food until his fat is consumed. We say "he lives on his fat." In the winter the raccoon fasts. Not that he reasons what he is doing. He lazily lives on his fat. He has stored sufficient vitamins and minerals along with the fat and moves about very little except during the warm spells of winter. No one need be sorry for raccoons. Why, then, pity our fat dogs when they have to forego the habit of overeating for a while?

Most of this feeling sorry for pets which are reducing stems from the idea that starvation is painful. But it is not, so long as there is a reservoir of food in the stored fat of the body. If a little protein and a little carbohydrate is fed —say a slice of bread a day—to help burn the fat, there is no danger of acidosis developing. If a vitamin-mineral supplement is added, there is no danger of starvation at all.

Anyone who thinks starvation is painful need only try it. I once lost forty-two pounds in less than two months and smaller amounts on many other occasions, and I have never felt a pang of anything but hunger. Hunger pangs are habit pangs—not pain at all.

Starvation is painless until it reaches the point of emaciation, so humans tell us. There are many instances of dogs living with only water for two months. One dog lived 117 days. So don't think your pet is going to die if he doesn't eat for a few days while you are accustoming him to what is good for him. His taste can become re-educated so he will like the diet you choose, and he will thrive on it if it is complete.

Clients whom I have advised to feed a certain diet ask if a dog doesn't need variety. How can a certain canned food or meal-type food which is fed day after day still be palatable? The reason is that our pets can smell each ingredient in a food. You and I smell hash. The dog smells separately each of the ingredients of which hash is composed. If you doubt this, watch a finicky pet trying to separate finely ground ingredients from each other in a mixture of foods. It isn't difficult to understand this ability if one thinks about it for a moment. My bloodhounds can smell a man's track a day after he has walked down a path, even when that track has been trampled all over by many other people. Why should we doubt that it is as simple a matter for any dog to smell the ingredients of a dog food and to enjoy its various components?

It is far more cruel to overfeed than to reduce. It is a discredit to the owner. It shortens the life of the animal to be obese, and makes him sluggish and no longer fun to have around. It often brings great misery and suffering to pet and owner alike, because of the paralysis which so frequently sets in as the pet grows older.

Loss of weight can be accomplished in two ways: by reducing the amount of food or by exercising the pet. With most pets a decrease in food consumption is the more practical and effective means. With dogs, however, the close personal feeling between the master and the dog sometimes makes it difficult for the owner to reduce feeding sufficiently to achieve the purpose. Admittedly this is a vexing problem which is too much for some weak-willed persons to surmount. With dogs, obesity is a serious matter, and if the owner cannot bring himself to limit the amount of food

How Much to Feed Your Dog

the animal gets, he should certainly be willing to exercise
the pet enough to prevent its becoming dangerously fat.

"He's fond of table scraps."

89

Dogs can be exercised in many ways without great inconvenience to the owner. There is no problem with the hunting breeds. Their love of hunting makes it necessary only to turn them out and their energy expenditure "melts the fat away." With other dogs, going for increasingly longer walks does wonders. Swimming is fine exercise. Retrieving is best of all. Nearly any dog can be taught to retrieve. Have you ever thought how many miles a dog can be made to run while you stand in one spot and exercise only your arm and back? You take Darwin, your spaniel, to the park. There you throw a ball fifty yards. He races and retrieves it. That's one hundred yards. Repeat it seventeen times and Darwin has run a mile. A hundred times and he has run over five miles. Perhaps at first he will become tired, but gradually you'll have him retrieving by the hour.

Or, to exercise Darwin *and* yourself, teach him to retrieve a golf ball. Go to a golf links after the playing is over and pretend to throw a ball into the rough. Darwin will dash in, sniff around for the golf-ball odor, and bring one out. I know a man whose dog retrieved forty-two in one trip around a course. Such exercise puts and keeps a dog in tiptop condition.

The Dog As Guard

Henry Davis

SINCE THE prehistoric beginnings of man's relationship with *canis familiaris*, the dog has served not only as his pal but as his guardian, a trait which has proven of inestimable value. To this day, once a dog has accepted a person or family as his master, he immediately develops a well-defined sense of proprietorship and is ready to defend them, their home and possessions against all intruders. This sense of guardianship is present in almost all dogs, regardless of the breed, although it naturally asserts itself more in bolder or more aggressive animals.

This guardian trait, now recognized by science and canine authorities as a definite instinct, may be traced back to the era before the dog became domesticated, to the times when it defended its lair in self-preservation and tolerated no encroachment upon its hunting areas.

Although the larger breeds have generally been used for protective purposes and after generations of breeding and training for this purpose might be termed "specialists" in this sort of work, many of the smaller types, such as the terriers, also possess the same highly developed instinct to guard and protect. The first dogs used exclusively for guarding were called "bandogs," i.e., dogs tied up with a band or chain. This name was used for a long time, but after the Norman conquest of England in 1066 the word "mastiff,"

From *The New Dog Encyclopedia* by Henry Davis, published by Stackpole Books, Harrisburg, Pa.

said to be a corruption of "master of thief," came into common use. The custom of keeping "bandogs" chained up arose because it was believed that keeping them confined by chains during the day made them fiercer at night.

The "mastive or bandogge" was described by Abraham Fleming as "vast, huge, stubborn, eager, of a heavy and burdensome body, and therefore but of little swiftness," and it "took fast hold with its teeth and held on beyond all credit." The description suggests that the "bandog" was more likely to have been the Bulldog rather than the Mastiff, as we know the breeds today.

In 1641, Barnaby Goode, translating the work of Conrad Heresbach, described "The Bandog for the House" as follows:

> Of first the Mastie that keepeth the house: for this purpose you must provide you such a one, as hath a large and mightie body, a great and shrill voyce, that both with his barking he mat discover and with his sight dismay the Theefe, yea, being not scene, with the horror of his voice put him to flight. His stature must neither be long nor fiery, either browne or grey, his lippes blackish, neither turning up, nor hanging too much downe, his mouth blacke and wide, his neather-jawe fat, and comming out of it on either side a fang, appearing more outward than his other teeth; his upper teeth even with his neather, not hanging too much over, sharpe, and hidden with his lippes; his countenance like a Lion, his brest great and shagayard, his shoulders broad, his legges big, his tayle short, his feet very great, his disposition must neither be too gentle, nor too curst, that he neither fawne upon a theefe, nor lavish of his mouth, barking without cause, neither maketh it any matter though he be not swift; for he is but to fight at home, and to give warning of the enemie.

The Dog As Guard

Linnaeus described the Mastiff and his uses in *The Animal Kingdom* (1792):

> MASTIFF—*Canis Anglicus*. Of very large size, having a robust body, and the lips are pendulous at the sides, or chops.
>
> Is very thick-set and strongly made, having a large head, and great lips, which hang down on each side. This dog is peculiar to England, and grows to a great size, being used principally as a watch dog, which duty he fulfills with great fidelity, and even judgement. Some will permit a stranger to come into the yard, or place which he is appointed to guard, and will go peaceably along with him through every part of it, so long as he touches nothing, but the moment he attempts to meddle with any of the goods, or endeavours to leave the place, he informs him, first by gentle growling, neither do mischief nor go away; and never uses violence unless resisted; will even, in this case, seize the person, throw him down, and hold him there for hours, or until relieved, without biting.

Mastiff

In the Middle Ages travel was exceedingly dangerous, and the man who ventured abroad was taking his life in his own hands unless accompanied by one or more faithful guard dogs. Carriages were invariably accompanied by dogs, some of which ran ahead to give warning. The use of "carriage dogs" continued even after travel became no longer dangerous, and developed into a fashion.

The value of the dog as a guard and protector has always been recognized and his services so utilized. The same applies to his capacity to track down highwaymen and criminals. Bloodhounds, as we know them today, were sometimes called "slough-dogs," for they were used to follow offenders through the sloughs, bogs, and mosses. They were also later called "Sleuth hounds," for obvious reasons. In Holinshed's *Chronicles* (1577) there is mention of a law to the effect that "whoso denieth entrance or sute to a Sleuth hound is persuit made after fellons and stollen goods, shall be holden as accessarie unto the theft."

Robberies and thefts became so prevalent in some sections of England that "Sleuth hounds" were ordered kept and cared for by the inhabitants. A warrant of 1616 reads:

> . . . Whereas upon due consideration of the increase of stealths daily growing both in deed and report among you on the borders, we formerly conclude and agree, that for reformation therefore watches should be set, and slough dogs provided and kept, according to the contents of His Majesty's directions to us in that behalf prescribed.

Time has in no way diminished the value of the dog as a protector. With the rise of crime throughout the world in our day and age, the guard dog is playing an increasingly important role, and this protective trait of his is being more highly developed and utilized than ever before.

Bloodhound

THE DOG AND INDUSTRIAL SECURITY

Night watchmen around warehouses and factories are aided many times over by the service of a dog, especially in smaller operations which cannot afford elaborate protection services. Jewelry shops and liquor stores are similarly protected. Often delivery trucks carry a guard dog, as does an occasional taxi driver in large cities where holdups are constant. The dog sits in the front seat beside the driver and God help the hand, other than the master's, that reaches for the cash box.

Another interesting phase of guard dog work is that used by department stores. For example, Macy's in New York City, has had canine guards since October, 1952 when the store purchased four Doberman Pinschers to patrol the store after hours in an effort to control the heavy losses inflicted by "sleep-ins." These are burglars who enter the store shortly before closing, remain overnight stealing merchandise and packing it, then leave early the next morning soon after the store opens.

Since their introduction at Macy's, the Dobermans have been directly responsible for the apprehension of numerous thieves who attempted to stay in the store overnight. The Dobermans have also prevented serious damage to the store by discovering machines that had been left on at store closing and also by discovering fire-smoldering and waterflows. On several occasions they have found runaway chil-

The four original Dobermans were purchased fully trained. All subsequent Dobermans have been trained by Macy detectives assigned to the canine corps. Training classes are held on the roof where the kennels are located, and on the selling and reserve floors. The training is extensive and includes basic obedience exercises, searching, finding, flushing and attacking a prowler on instructions. The Dobermans are also trained to discover smoke, fire and waterflows.

THE DOG IN POLICE WORK

Still another increasingly important use of guard dogs is in police work. In the areas of searching, patrolling, tracking and deterrence of crime they have proven to be a definite asset. Particularly outstanding has been their night work, and as policing becomes more expensive as well as dangerous, they are playing an ever widening role. Among the cities which currently employ dogs are St. Louis, Boston, Baltimore, Winston-Salem, Providence, Cincinnati, Norfolk, and the Transit and Park Police of Philadelphia, to name but a few.

The dogs are particularly effective in flushing out a thief

cornered in a store or building or alley, and in almost every instance a man running away from the scene of a crime will stop quicker for a dog than for a patrolman, regardless of the circumstances.

For this work one officer and his dogs are generally assigned to a patrol car instead of the usual two men, thus spreading out the effectiveness of the police force. Whenever the patrolman investigates a suspicious situation, the dog goes with him. The animal can readily be sent up dark alleys, and when the officer captures and frisks a suspect, the dog sits at heel ready to defend upon command should the suspect suddenly attack the officer, as sometimes happens. The dogs are also trained to jump through an open car window and stop the driver if he attempts to escape in that manner.

German Shepherds are nearly always used for police work. They are fed, housed and trained by the patrolmen who handle them. The officers must have the approval of their wives for this, for they also must agree to keep the dogs kenneled at home. They must be fond of dogs and possess a level-headed temperament, and not be subject to hasty decisions or actions.

Describing the first contingent of police dogs used by the Winston-Salem Police Department, Philip Warner said in *The German Shepherd Dog Review:*

> The program of training started with the testing of all dogs for gun soundness and agitation; the willingness to attack, if necessary. The patrolmen were schooled in safety procedures, rules of the training area and care of their dogs' health. The men instructed their dogs in fifteen basic obedience commands by voice, signal and a combination of signal-voice commands. From the basic obedience work they advanced to attack work, on and off leash, with and without command. Tracking work was studied and carefully

learned; patrol work and the very important building search was taught. During the course of training the men and dogs were developing a very close relationship and a deep affection for each other. Each dog learned that his first duty was to his master and to attack any aggressive move toward him, and that everything learned, other than this, was secondary. The key to all training was control, the handler's complete control over his dog.

. . . The public relations value of the K-9 Unit (of the Winston-Salem Police Department) has been immeasurable and the public acceptance of these German Shepherds has been overwhelming. During the first year of operation the dogs and their handlers made appearances before a total audience of approximately 10,000 persons . . . the unit made 355 arrests, answered 577 calls, assisted other personnel 612 times, and apprehended a total of 32 suspects from building searches or while fleeing.

DON'T TRAIN PETS AS POLICE DOGS

Trained dogs under the charge of trained men have added to the efficiency of those police forces throughout the country which have seen fit to acquire them. But Arthur Frederick Jones, editor of the *American Kennel Gazette*, official magazine for the American Kennel Club, quickly points out that police dog training is not for house pets. It is highly technical work involving an attack dog that must be kept under constant control by its master. "Most decidedly," he says, "they are not suited to private ownership in the capacity of pets." For if a child, in jest or by accident, gives the trained attack dog the wrong command, the consequences could be serious.

The protective instinct is present in almost all dogs. The

fact that it can easily be encouraged and, in many cases, trained to a high degree of efficiency for special application, is making the guard dog more effective than ever before. Its role in our modern, high-powered society is assured.

Attack dog employed against cavalry in 14th century.

A Letter from John Steinbeck

Explaining Why He Could Not Write an Introduction for Ted Patrick's Book, "The Thinking Dog's Man"

DEAR TED:

Of course I was happy to get your dog book and flattered that you should ask me to write an introduction to it. I must refuse for two reasons.

First, I never write introductions. I have enough trouble just writing my own books.

Second, this book of yours is quite an expert job. I am no expert where dogs are concerned. It is true I have owned a number of dogs, have associated with many more, and have observed myriads. But to say I am expert would be like considering a man who hung around bars and knew a lot of people an expert psychologist.

At present, I have no dog. Our house is still raw from Charley's death last spring. But Charley never considered hmiself a dog. He was Charley. Surely I will have another dog. Hearing that Charley had died, kind people all over the country and many in Europe have written offering to give me a dog, the best dog in the world. This is so friendly and so generous that it is hard to refuse. But I don't want to shop for a dog. My next dog will just have to happen to me and I to him. I can wait for that.

I found your book refreshing in its refutations of a number of dog myths. Dogs are remarkable enough, so that there is no reason to make up lies about them. And I was interested in what you had to say about a dog's mental processes. Is it true that there is a silly school which holds that a dog has no memory? I wonder how they arrived at that staggering generality. If they said it about me, it would be more to the point. I have also heard that a dog has no distance vision. I once had a dog who used to watch sea gulls flying almost beyond my vision. There was no question about his seeing them. His head, as well as his eyes, followed their progress. On the other hand, I once had a dog who saw things that were not there, or if they were, neither I nor my family or friends could see them. He was a large and dreamy English setter named Toby, the White Flower of the Mountain. Sometimes, when the moon was full, he would stand and bark monotonously at an oak tree for an hour at a time. Again, lying in front of an open fire, he would awaken, look at the front door and with his eyes and nose follow something across the room, sometimes watching it exit through another door and sometimes move to a chair. Toby thumped his tail in greeting to some of these things he saw, while he greeted others with a low growl of dislike. All right, Ted, so he was crazy, but he was so convinced he saw things that we could almost see them too. Toby had other odd qualities too, but I won't go into those.

Now that's another reason for not writing an introduction. I might trap myself into telling dog stories.

But how about a man story! In Pacific Grove, I had a friend—an artist—gentle soul—a man of peace and quiet. There was no anger nor violence in him, nor for that matter was there any tendency toward crime either against persons or property. Then, how would you account for the attested fact that all dogs hated him and bit him on sight and without warning? He liked dogs and tried to make friends with them, but no dog ever accepted him. Of course, my friend was poor, but no poorer than the rest of us. And if he set off anthropophobia in dogs, he had an equally unfortunate effect on policemen. It was rare for him to go out without being picked up and questioned by the police. It went even farther. If he tried to cash a check, bank tellers told him to wait, while they subjected his paper to extreme scrutiny. And in this case, both dogs and cops were wrong. How do you explain that? If you ascribe it to a subtle odor beyond the olefactory range of man, you would have to credit policemen with bloodhound virtues they do not have.

I have always disliked people who talk baby talk to dogs, but my feeling is nothing to what dogs feel. I have watched the cold contempt in a dog's eyes when he was being addressed as "itty bitty, sweety foo!"

On the other hand, I distrust people who believe that dogs are better than we are. Dogs are not better. They are just different from us. Surely they can do some things better, but I have yet to see a dog balance a checkbook, or make an omelette or compose a sonnet.

I believe that a smart man is probably superior to a smart dog. A case in point was told me by one of the leaders of the Danish underground during the German occupation. The Danish fishing boats had to go out for food supply, and yet the Germans knew those same boats were smuggling refugees to Sweden. So the Gestapo devised a plan. Before each boat sailed, all hands were ordered ashore. Then highly efficient tracking dogs were sent aboard to smell out any secret hiding place or hidden stowaway. The dogs never found anyone.

"It was very simple," my informant told me. "I'm surprised the Germans never figured it out. You see, we issued salt shakers of crystal cocaine to the boatman. They sprinkilled it on the gangplanks. And by the time the dogs had sniffed their way aboard, their noses were so numb they couldn't have smelled an antisocial skunk." Then he sighed. "I'm afraid some of those dogs came out of the war cocaine addicts."

A Letter from John Steinbeck

You know, Ted, the human—imperfect and deeply aware of his frailties—is prone to find the virtues he wishes he had in other species—courage in the lion, memory in the elephant, gentleness in the lamb, and oddly enough, both loyalty and honesty in the dog. These are myths, which have little basis in fact. It is my belief that a dog in virtue at least is little better than we are. Once I was neighbor to a cynical old homosexual aunty of a dog, an unkempt long-haired rascally sex deviate who introduced pederasty to every young and gallant male on the block. I don't know how he attracted them. Perhaps his deviation was so glandular as to inflame the randy and random impulses of all the young and ignorant dogs of our neighborhood.

I have know glutton dogs, swinish dogs, dogs of incredible vanity. And then, there are fools—just plain, clumsy, stupid fools. And as for dishonesty, how about a dog I once knew in Truckee? He was an Airedale, if you will pardon the expression, Ted, and he lived at a gambling house called the Silver Mirror. I don't know how he learned his hustle, but he not only mastered it, but worked it to the limit. It is well known that when a man makes a killing at gambling, he must give something to the first bum who puts the bee on him. Well, at the Silver Mirror, that first bum was Omar, the Airedale. Maybe he learned to detect the exultant tone of voice of a winner, but with twenty tables working, let one man make a decent win at craps or blackjack and there was Omar beside him, sitting up with a wet-eyed look of utter starvation. And Omar invariably got a steak. On a good night, Omar made as many as six or seven sirloins. He operated for several years, and died of overeating, but I swear even in his obese old age, when Omar put the arm on a winner, you'd swear he hadn't eaten for a week—a born, blowed-in-the-glass hustler he was.

Believe me, Ted, I am not running dogs down. I just want to put them in their proper perspective. If all dogs were

"Why can't he beg the way other dogs do?"

the noble beasts we pretend, how would we know a real hero when we see one? And real hero dogs there are.

There are real rules of conduct among dogs also. You have said that male dogs practically never fight females. Have you noticed another rule?

Let's say there's a fight and one dog gets the worst of it and wants to call it quits. Well, if he turns his back, it usually works and if he puts his head in a corner, it always works. No dog will bite another in the rear, unless the other dog is running away; no dog, that is, except one. I won't even mention his breed, because you and I have always been friends

—well, hell, I might as well admit it—he was an Airedale, and he was mine and he wasn't as good a fighter as he thought he was. Maybe I am guilty of irreverence, or *lèse-majesté,* but this Airedale was a bit of a coward. I was living in the mountains, and once a week I walked about six miles to a little combination grocery and post office for supplies and mail. The boss dog of that place was a no-good shepherd, setter, coyote-looking thing, but he knew his way around. Every week, my dog fought this grisly creature and every week, he got licked. He showed he was licked by putting his head in a corner. Then, he was safe—licked, but safe. Came a day when something went haywire with the boss dog. Maybe he'd been out all night or had a hangover, or perhaps he was overconfident from having won too many fights. Anyway, my dog beat the tar out of him, really licked him until the boss dog yelled "uncle" and turned his back and put his head in the loser's corner. Perhaps my dog was smarting from too many beatings, or it's possible he just wasn't a gentleman. But I ask you to believe that he bit the boss dog twice on the behind and then clamped down on his testicles. When we pried him loose, the boss dog was retired both as a fighter and as a stud. So you see, Ted, there can be dogs without honor, too, even as with us.

When I read your book, I was afraid I might get to reminiscing. But I won't allow myself that luxury. However, I do recall one strange happening.

Living alone, a man gets to using his dog or dogs as extra senses. They tell him when someone is coming, and sometimes they can even forecast weather. I had one experience where the absence of a dog reaction gave me a really nasty scare. Again, it was in the mountains, and the winter had come and it was deep snow. I had two dogs: an A---d--e and an Irish terrier. They were a comfort to me—gave me someone to talk to. You get lonely and sometimes, alone, you get scared for no reason. There wasn't any danger there, except breaking a leg and freezing to death for lack of help.

There were a few timber wolves in the country, but they had too much game to be dangerous to men. Now and then, I heard them howling at night and then the dogs would raise hell. I think they were scared of the wolves and were protesting too much. And once in the snow, I came on a trampled place where a young deer had got cornered and pulled down and eaten. The record was all there in the snow to see. The dogs barked stupidly and pretended to find tracks, but they didn't go far from me and my rifle.

Well, one week there came a whizzer of a blizzard, hard dry snow spouting along parallel to the ground and drifting up against anything in its way. It was so cold it stung your face like gritty sand. The wind whooped and gusted and threshed around in the firs and pines and tamaracks. It was a real wild one that continued for three days.

For me, it was a lovely time. My little house was warm. I had plenty of cut wood and canned and dried food and kerosene. I loved to sit warm, hearing the gusts and the ping of the driven sleet on the windows. Outside, my wood pile and wheelbarrow were great big mounds of drifted snow. The trees were all aproned on one side with drift.

Night came down early. I cooked a good dinner and fed the dogs and let them out and then they came in and went to sleep. The kerosene lamps looked pretty and comfortable and actually kept the cabin warm; it was that small and tight. I washed up and tossed my garbage out the door to pick up later. Besides, it sometimes attacted coons and both the dogs and I liked a young roast coon. The old ones were too tough.

It was pitch-black outside in the raging, gusting wind. I was just drying the last dishes when I heard a sound from outside that raised the hair on my head. If you can imagine the scream of a baritone woman being strangled—well, it was half that and half mountain lion scream, which I heard once in my life—a horrible, thick, gurgling screech. Then silence.

I put the dish down and stepped to the rack for my rifle —an old heavy Winchester 38-56 that carried a slug half as long as your little finger. I had the gun in my hand when that scream came again. I glanced at the dogs and *they were sound asleep!*

I don't know, Ted, whether you've ever felt that panic that makes you suddenly wet all over and sick to your stomach. I remember sitting on my bed with a big old rifle in my lap, levered down to throw a shell into the chamber. And I remember thinking, "If the dogs didn't hear it, it isn't outside; it's in my head. I'm going nuts."

And then, the scream came again. I thought, I can't sit here; I'll go over the edge. I have to go outside.

I remember it in slow motion. I got my flashlight, bounced the dogs awake and pulled on the inward opening door. The wind howled into the house and brought the piled snow with it. The dogs went pumping through the deep drift, each one about his business. I flashed my light around. Nothing.

And then, in a roar of wind, it came again—that horrid low scream. And do you know what it was? A three-pound coffee can upright on a snowdrift. I'd thrown it out and the wind was mouthing it like a mountain man playing a jug.

Do you see what I mean? If the dogs had reacted, I might have killed me a coffee can. As it was, I was sick all over with fear.

So you see, Ted—I can't write an introduction for your dog book. If I did—what would it be, nothing but some observations and some dog stories. I like your book fine, but let's forget the introduction, shall we?

Yours,
John

January 9, 1964

Instincts and Behavior

J. J. McCoy

Smell

First of all, your dog lives in a world of smells. His nose is an intricate organ, telling him many things about people, animals and objects. He can detect hundreds of odors that are missed by us. No matter where those odors are—in the air, on the ground, on objects, hands or clothing—the dog easily picks them out and sorts them. He has a vast range of smells—all unconsciously classified and available for quick identification.

The Bloodhound, for example, has such a keen sense of smell that he can select one scent from among hundreds in the same area. And he can do this even though the one scent he is searching for is several days old or mixed with many others. Scientists studying the olfactory sense have learned that dogs can detect the difference between natural and artificial musk. Even to a human being with an unusual sense of smell, natural and artificial musk have identical odors.

Your dog's nose, therefore, is his guide to the identification of people, objects and other animals. Regardless of how many times your dog sees people or animals, he will not accept them until he puts his nose to work. Then—and only then—will he be satisfied.

But for the dog to bring his sense of smell into play, he

must be within range. If he is too far away or the wind is blowing away from him, he will be unable to identify a person or animal. There is a classical experiment for this. Put on an old coat and hat. Pull the hat down over your ears and turn up the coat collar. Now get downwind from the dog, so that he cannot pick up your scent. Crawl toward him or approach him in an apelike walk. Watch his reaction. He'll either bark and run off, or stand still. If he stands still, he'll growl and the hairs on the back of his neck will rise. The chances are he'll assume an attack position: body rigid, tail lowered and teeth bared. Don't push this experiment too far. When you see that he doesn't recognize you, straighten up, take off the hat and coat, and call out to him. Then let him approach and sniff you.

Vary the experiment and approach the dog upwind with the same costume and stance, and you'll get a different reaction. Once he whiffs your scent, he'll bound toward you with tail-wags and yelps of recognition. No doubt, if he could talk, he'd say, "Come on, take off the disguise. I know you!"

Sight

Most dogs have poor eyesight. There are exceptions notably the sight hunters or gaze hounds. These gaze hounds, such as the Saluki, Afghan and Greyhound, are lean, speedy dogs that hunt with their eyes fixed on the quarry. They have good vision and are farsighted. But the majority of dogs are nearsighted. The Bloodhound, keen-nosed though he may be, is one of the most myopic of all dogs.

Despite his nearsightedness, your dog will react to motion. In fact, he has a high degree of sensitivity to motion. And this is a main reason why many dogs recoil from a hand that is suddenly thrust at them. The dog's ability to see motion can be likened to a similar reaction in human beings. We can notice motion that is outside the direct line of vision. We may be looking ahead and at the same time notice something moving to the right or left and slightly behind us. We refer to this as seeing something move "out of the corner of our eye."

While your dog may not be able to identify a person or animal by sight, he can tell in which direction they are moving. That is, he can tell a clockwise or counterclockwise movement. He also has the ability to see at night and a facility known as eyeshine or *tapetum lucidum*. Eyeshine can be seen at night when your headlights or flashlight are focused on the dog's eyes. It is caused by the light bouncing off a layer of cells at the back of the dog's eyes. The facility of eyeshine is also present in some other animals, such as the cat and raccoon. Human beings do not have eyeshine.

When it comes to color vision, your dog has a low score. His color range is limited to black and white, possibly gray. Interestingly enough, dogs do make choices between colors. Or so it seems. They do not select green over red, or blue over yellow. But if given a choice of three colored toys—one bright red, one dull green and one black—your dog will probably pick the red one. He'll make this choice because of the difference in brilliance among the three toys. In short, he'll pick the red toy because it is *bright* red. But in the final analysis, your dog's color vision is very weak, and it can become confused when the shape or position of an object is changed or altered.

To sum up, your dog's eyesight is poor and he has an undeveloped color-vision range. Nature, to compensate for these two weaknesses, has given him a highly developed sense of smell and sound. And in these two senses, your dog has no peer.

Sound

Dogs have exceptionally keen hearing and can pick up sounds too faint for human ears. They can also detect sounds of a higher pitch. The silent dog whistle is designed on the principle of your dog being able to hear the high-pitched sounds. Blow on one of these silent whistles and *you* hear nothing, except maybe some expelled air. But if the dog is nearby and he's well trained, he'll dash over to you in short order.

Dogs are very responsive to the human voice. By changing your inflections and tones, you can get a variety of reactions from your dog. An encouraging word will set off a barrage of joyful barks or a series of frenzied tail-wags. Speak harshly to him, and he'll become depressed, perhaps slinking away or cringing before you. You may have noticed how some dogs back away from a loud or harsh-voiced person. Some dogs may even run off and hide if a voice "hits" them the wrong way.

Your voice and how you use it are the most important factors in communicating with your dog. Remember, it will be the tone, inflection and shading in your voice that will provoke a response, not the words. But more about this in the chapter on training your dog.

Taste

Your dog's sense of taste is closely related to his sense of smell. What he will not accept with his nose, he'll rarely, if ever, eat. Some dogs have acquired unusual tastes and will eat foods that border on the exotic. But the majority of dogs have plain tastes and will stick to standard foods.

Touch

What we're referring to here, of course, is the dog's degree of sensitivity to *being* touched.

Dogs react in various ways when touched by the human hand. Most dogs don't mind being petted. In fact, they will almost beam with pleasure while you scratch behind their ears or massage their stomachs. Many of us have met the old house dog that, after he's sniffed and checked you out as a friend, thrusts his rear end at you to be scratched.

But there are dogs that violently object to being touched. This touchy-type dog will quickly let you know that he doesn't want to be petted. He may cringe, pull back, run off or snap at anyone who tries to pet him. This is especially true when you suddenly thrust your hand at his head.

Unfortunately, people get bitten because they either ignore a dog's objection to being touched or are unaware of it. Many people assume that *all* dogs like to be petted and just can't resist stopping to pat every dog they meet. Considering what we've just learned about the dog's poor eyesight, need to identify everything with his nose, and a possible objection to being touched—we can understand why some dogs snap at people.

A dog's objection to being touched may be an inherited or acquired trait. Genetics, environment and state of health all have a bearing on the dog's degree of sensitivity to being touched. But regardless of the cause, you and others will have to respect the dog's dislike of being petted.

Protective Instinct

Most dogs have an innate sense of protection for the people with whom they live. This protective sense is stronger in some dogs than others. But once your dog gets accustomed to the house and occupants, he will assume a guardianship over the household. He will bark a warning, possibly launch an attack when danger threatens his charges. Now, he may not be able to do this with the dash and skill of Rin-Tin-Tin or Lassie, but his concern is genuine. He will, if necessary, risk bodily harm or death to protect you.

Dog teams fighting

Your dog will also show an instinct to guard property. This is a deep-rooted instinct that is dominant in the wild, as well as domestic, dogs. Wolves and coyotes carefully stake out property lines and defend them against all aggressors, canine and otherwise. They do this by urinating on trees, rocks and bushes around the perimeter of their domain. The domestic male dog's habit of lifting his leg and urinating against trees, poles and fireplugs is a remnant of this powerful instinct. But your dog doesn't have to "stake a property claim." Your home is well defined—fences, shrubbery and so forth—and the dog gets to know the boundaries. And once he is familiar with the property, he will defend it. (Even though this "defense" consists of barking shrilly from the safety of the porch or house!)

Individual dogs with a strong protective instinct and a tendency toward overaggressiveness, are trained as guard dogs. But there is a big difference between the average watchdog and guard dog. The guard dog is taught to be hostile to everyone except his master, and is always a potential hazard. Such a dog is not for the average person.

Intelligence

Finally, we come to the matter of intelligence in the dog. Much has been written about how smart or dumb dogs are when faced with various psychological tests. Unquestionably, the dog doesn't measure up to man or the great apes in intelligence. He does rank high above most of the other animals below the primates.

Some dogs are more intelligent than others. Similarly, certain breeds have a higher intelligence quotient. The German Shepherd Dog and Collie, for example, are two breeds with high I.Q.s. For practical purposes, your dog's I.Q. should be based on two factors: 1) his *readiness to learn* and 2) the degree to which he *remembers and uses what he learns*. There's no point in hoping for a dog whose intelligence matches that of a highly inventive chimpanzee.

CHIHUAHUA

**GERMAN
SHEPHERD**

**DOBERMAN
PINSCHER**

115

BULL DOG

DACHSHUND

116

The Dog Who Came in from the Cold

William Iversen

"Go HOME, BOY!" I told him, after he had trailed me for three whole blocks. "That's a good dog—go home!"

He was hardly more than a shivering shadow sitting there in the icy dusk, waiting for me to turn around so he could continue following me. He *was* going home, as it turned out. But I didn't know it yet.

"Shoo! Beat it! Go home!" I sternly commanded from the front step. Then the door opened and Lois, my wife, put her head out.

"What's going on?" she asked.

"Nothing," I said. "It's just some dog. He's lost and won't go away."

She peered at my newfound friend. He was a scraggly, scrawny mutt with a rough brown coat, a too-long tail, and eyes that were more mournfully soulful than any two eyes had a right to be.

"Poor thing," she pouted. "He's cold and he's hungry." In a matter of minutes, "Patrick" (he arrived on March 17, so . . .) was inside the house, and Lois was briskly rubbing him down with a large bath towel marked HIS.

"Why don't you hang up your coat and get ready for dinner?" she said, handing me back my soggy towel. "Meanwhile, I'll fix Patrick a plate of scraps from the table."

The "scraps," I discovered, were four or five choice

slices of fresh-roasted sirloin, cut up in bite-size pieces and smothered in hot gravy.

"Do you think he would like a few 'scraps' of that lemon meringue pie?" I inquired as Patrick sat in the dinette doorway, contentedly licking his whiskers.

"This is no time for joking," Lois informed me. "The first thing we ought to do is check the lost-and-found column in this evening's paper. Then we have to decide where he can spend the night."

"You're right," I agreed. "How about the garage? I'll put an old blanket in a box, and he can sleep out there." No dog ever got a look like the one that Lois gave me. "You're not serious are you? Why, he'd freeze out there."

"Well, then, let's see." I pretended to ponder, now that I was fairly certain where Patrick was going to spend the night. "There's that new motel at the interchange . . ."

Later, as I sat reading the lost-and-found ads, Patrick's now-dry tail would wag and thump whenever I glanced in his direction. "Too bad you're not a tan cat with white paws or a French poodle named Gigi," I told him, tossing the paper aside. "But no one seems to be missing a dog like you."

He looked apologetic. Then Lois came in from the kitchen, and he stood up to greet her. A perfect gentleman.

"We'll have to keep checking," she said, switching on the TV. "Remind me to get a copy of the local paper when it comes out next week."

"Next *week*?" I echoed, as the TV picture began to emerge on the screen. "You knew it would end this way," an actress whispered, in smiling closeup. "You knew from the very beginning, didn't you?"

"Yes," I mumbled, "I guess I did."

In less than a week I had got used to Patrick—even to his habit of sleeping in our bed, with his head resting on my legs. (His former owner must have had cast-iron shins.) I got used to having him run to greet me when I came home, to the long evening walks we took—and also to checking the lost-and-found ads.

"Nothing?" Lois would ask hopefully, when I came in with the paper. "Nothing," I would report. Her smile of relief would flash from me to Patrick—whose tail would then throw a big celebration.

Though I may not have been as demonstrative as Patrick and Lois, I was every bit as relieved. For, even in that short time, I had discovered that Patrick was no ordinary dog. Despite all his sociable wags and woofs, there was a sobriety about him that made him the kind of dog a man could really talk to. Sometimes, while I was working in the den, he would drop in for a chat. No matter what we discussed—politics, sports, taxes or just life in general—his views and mine were always identical.

"He's got a good head on his shoulders," I told Lois. "That more than makes up for his little quirks."

Patrick's quirks began to show up the day after he found me. "He did an odd thing this afternoon," Lois said as we sat down to dinner. "I let him out in the yard, and he brought in the milk bottles."

"How's that again?" I asked.

"He brought in the two empty milk bottles that I had put out by the back door. He insisted upon it."

"Did you do that?" I asked Patrick, who was sitting down at my left foot, taking this all in. He gave a small, uncertain wag, as if to say that he guessed he had.

"It must be something he's been trained to do," I theorized. But during the next few days the theory had to be extended to account for the fact that Patrick would bring in anything we left in the yard: gardening gloves, a trowel, a length of rope—even a plastic bag full of rubbish. "And who," Lois asked, "would train a dog to bring in rubbish?"

There were other quirks. On Saturday I drove to the hardware store to pick up some paint. Before starting out,

I checked to see if there was room for the cans in the car trunk. No sooner did I raise the lid than Patrick jumped into the truck and settled down.

"Patrick, old man," I said to him, "I'm not one to pry, you understand. But what's the secret of your past? Are you a fugitive from a life of crime—a former milk-bottle snatcher who's used to making his get-away in open car trunks?"

Patrick blinked and looked away, as if to say that the past was the past, and he would rather not talk about it. Someday, perhaps. But in the meantime, I'd just have to trust him.

So I did, and as the days went by, Patrick gradually became *our* dog, complete with license, shots, favorite ball— and a larger place in our lives than I would have thought possible.

Sometimes I still wake up at night, surprised to find that I can move my legs without dislodging Patrick's head from my shins. For a moment, I wonder where he is. But only for a moment. Because then I remember the June evening when we were coming home from a walk, and this big, cheery workman jammed on the brakes of his pickup and whooped, *"He-e-y-y, Buster!"*

I remember how Patrick froze—and then, when the memory hit him, how he leaped out to the end of his leash, yelping a joyous greeting. He was—you guessed it—the man's dog. Or, rather, he belonged to the man's four kids. It was the kids who had named him Buster.

The man's name was Charlie Taylor, and he and his family lived less than a mile away. Lacking papers to prove that Patrick was his dog, he came around later that evening with a batch of snapshots that showed our Patrick—his Buster—at all stages.

"Here he is, bringing the kids' toys in from the yard," Charlie Taylor said, proudly. "Trained him to do that when he was hardly more than a pup. And here he is again, all set to go for a ride in my pickup truck." The truck served as the family car, and Patrick always rode in back.

Well, at least his quirks were explained. And there was no denying he belonged to the Taylors. His happy grin, one which Lois and I had seldom seen, became his main expression the minute the four young Taylors trooped up the front walk. The only time it disappeared was when he was finally out in the truck, and Lois and I reached up to give him one last pat. For those few seconds he was *our* dog once again, and his eyes begged for understanding.

As the truck moved off, he looked back once or twice, but it was too dark to see his expression. Just his head bobbing over the tailgate.

I'd rather not dwell on the rest of that night, or the days and weeks that followed. Patrick's absence filled the house.

At Christmas we had a card from the Taylors, which the whole family signed under the printed business address: "Charles E. Taylor, Home Improvements & Alterations." Then, just a week ago Sunday morning, Charlie dropped by the house. I was upstairs shaving when I heard him say to Lois, "You don't *have* to take him. We can give him to somebody else." Then I heard Lois say, "Oh, no. We'd love to have him!"

It's Patrick, I thought. The Taylors were giving him back! With my face half lathered, I followed the voices into the kitchen. "Look," Lois said, holding up a small, fuzzy armful of something that had a too-long tail. "One of Patrick's pups!"

"We bred him to Tammy next door," Charlie explained. "She's part collie, with spaniel ears—but this pup turned out pretty good."

"He certainly did," Lois said, setting the pup down on the floor. "He looks just like Patrick, and he wags his tail like Patrick, too!"

Patrick Two is the name we gave him, and he's every

inch his father's son. He'll have to grow some before he can pick up a milk bottle, or jump up on my bed. And if you try to talk to him seriously on any topic at all, he just rolls over on his back to have his belly scratched. But I would say that he is, without question or doubt, the single greatest home improvement Charlie Taylor ever made.

Setter

Just a Joke, Sir!

ONE EVENING a man entered a bar and, after a brief glance around the room, his eye was caught by a dog sitting on a barstool. His master, sitting next to him on another stool, was deep in thought, studying the checkerboard which lay on the bar between them.

The dog suddenly lifted his paw and moved a black counter from one square to another.

The newcomer gaped in astonishment, approached the players and, unable to conceal his wonderment, said to the dog's owner, "Gee, that dog's pretty smart."

"Oh, he's not so smart," answered the owner. "I beat him two out of three."

Two dogs met in the street one afternoon for their usual romp. "Say, Terry, what's wrong with you?" asked the little poodle. "You look terrible today."

"I feel terrible," the terrier replied. "I'm on edge, I can't sleep, and I have no appetite."

"Then you should see a good vet."

"I've seen a half dozen already, and they all say I'm in fine shape."

"Maybe what you really need is a good psychiatrist."

"That's impossible," the terrier sighed, "I'm not allowed on couches."

A gentleman purchased a collie puppy and decided to train him to "speak" for his meals. He would hold the dog's food dish just out of reach of the dog, and then bark a few times before placing the bowl down, in the hope that the pup would associate barking with his food and begin to "speak" for himself.

After a few weeks of such training, the man again held the food just out of the dog's reach, and waited for the pup to bark. When the collie only stared back blankly, as usual, the owner gave up and put the dish before the dog anyway. Still the collie refused to eat—until his master barked.

Some Sunnybank Dogs

Albert Payson Terhune

A SCHOOLTEACHER, looking back over his experiences with more than a thousand pupils, would find himself dwelling with special interest in recollections of at least nine or ten of them; nine or ten personalities so outstanding, for one reason or another, that they will not let themselves be forgotten or grouped with the vast majority.

It is so with my memories of the long line of Sunnybank dogs.

Soon or late, every dog master's memory becomes a graveyard; peopled by wistful little furry ghosts that creep back unbidden, at times, to a semblance of their olden lives. To outsiders, the past deeds and misdeeds of these loved canine wraiths may hold no great interest.

With this somewhat windy apology, which really is no apology at all, let's go:

Lad stands out as foremost of the dogs of Sunnybank. I have written his life saga; stretching its exploits through no fewer than three "Lad" books. So I need not go in for a wearisome retelling of his biography. A few episodes and characteristics, and then we'll pass on to the next cage.

He was a big and incredibly powerful collie, with a massive coat of burnished mahogany-and-snow and with absurdly small forepaws (which he spent at least an hour a

125

day in washing) and with deepset dark eyes that seemed to have a soul behind them. So much for the outer dog. For the inner: he had a heart that did not know the meaning of fear or of disloyalty or of meanness.

But it was his personality, apart from all these things, which made—and still makes—him so impossible to forget. As I have tried clumsily to bring out in my three books about him.

He was immeasurably more than a professionally loyal and heroic collie. He had the most elfin sense of fun and the most humanlike reasoning powers I have found in any dog.

Suppose we talk about those traits for a minute or two.

The Mistress and I went to pay a call of sympathy on a lachrymose old woman whose arm had been broken. The fracture had knit. The victim was almost as well as ever. But she reveled in giving dramatic recitals of her mishap to anyone and everyone who would listen.

We took Lad along with us when we dropped in on the invalid-emeritus. Before we had been there five minutes, we had every reason to wish we had left him at home.

Not that he failed to behave with entire outward decorum. But he took much uncalled-for part in the conversation. The woman launched forth on a detailed report of her accident. She sprinkled the lamentable recital thickly with moans and groans and belching sighs.

Lad was enormously pleased with the performance. So much so that he elected to turn the dolorous solo into a still more doleful duet. Every time our hostess gave forth one of the many successive sounds of grief, Lad copied it with startling realism and in precisely the same key. In perfect imitation, he moaned and whimpered and sighed and emitted ghastly groanings.

Throughout, he was lying demurely at the Mistress's

feet. But his eyes were a-dance. The plumed tip of his tail twitched uncontrollably. Lad was having a beautiful time. The Mistress and I were not.

We sought to keep our faces straight, as the woman's narrative waxed in noisy intensity and as Lad's accompaniment swelled to a crescendo.

Groan for groan he gave her and moan for moan. Carried away by his own brilliant enactment, his ululations increased in volume until they all but drowned out the sufferer's performance. It was a horrible duel of emotional expression. And Lad won it. For the woman paused in her jeremiad, and stared down at the statuesquely couchant collie in tearful admiration.

"Oh, he's wonderful!" she exclaimed. "Just *wonderful!* He understands all the agonies I've been through! And it almost breaks his heart. I wish some people were half as sympathetic as this poor dumb beast."

Lad, who for five minutes had been anything but dumb, eyed her in happy expectation; waiting for her to strike the next imitable note of grief, and yearning for a chance to resume his own performance. But there was no opening. The lament had shifted to clamorous praise of the dog's unbelievable comprehension and sympathy. And in the hymn of praise there were no alluring groans to copy.

We got away as soon as we could. If ever a dog merited rebuke for disgraceful impudence, Lad was that dog. But neither the Mistress nor myself had the heart to scold him for it.

With uncanny wisdom the collie had realized from the outset that the old lady was in no pain, in no real distress, that she was just airing her past trouble in maudlin quest for sympathy and in an orgy of self-pity. And he had joined blithely in the scene; in a spirit of straight ridicule.

In cases of genuine human distress or pain or misfortune, Lad's sympathy was ever eager and heartsick. But he had a whole-souled disgust for any form of faking; a disgust he took pleasure in showing most unmistakably.

Sometimes his guying took a subtler form. As when a man came here to see me on business—a man Lad disliked and distrusted as much as did I. The day was hot. The visitor took off his new pongee coat and laid it on the edge of the veranda. Then he began to talk.

He had an unpleasant manner and he was saying unpleasant things. I was hard put to it to remember I was his host, and to behave civilly to him. I found the effort more and more difficult as the talk went on.

Lad was lying beside my chair. As always, he sensed my mood.

With a collie's odd psychic powers he knew I was increasingly angry and that I yearned to kick the visitor off my land. The dog looked worriedly up into my face. Then he eyed my caller, and the tip of one of his long white eye-teeth peeped from under the lip that had begun to curl ever so slightly.

I could see the tiger muscles go taut beneath Lad's coat. I laid my hand on his head and whispered sharply:

"*Quiet*, Lad. Let him *alone!*"

All his adult life the dog had known the meaning of both those commands and the stark necessity of obeying them. Yet the Master was pestered by this obnoxious stranger. And, with Lad, that was not on the free list. Glumly he lay down, his eyes fixed alertly on the guest.

Then, stealthily, he got to his feet. With catlike softness of foot he crossed to the veranda edge where was draped the visitor's imported white coat—a garment of much value, even if not of many colors. To my shame I admit I saw the collie's progress without checking it. I had used up my whole day's stock of hospitality.

Lad lifted the snowy and costly coat from its place. He carried it out onto the muddy gravel of the driveway as tenderly as though it were a sick puppy. The owner was too busy orating to notice the rape of the garment. And I had not the good breeding to call Lad back.

On the driveway, Lad sought out a spot where was a smear of surface mud and silt as wide as a dining-room table—the effluvia of that morning's heavy rain.

With the same exaggerated tenderness he laid the coat atop the area of mud. Then, in very evident relish, he proceeded to roll on it, back and forth, several times. After which he proceeded to rub one of his heavy shoulders into the muddily crumpled British imported pongee, and then the other shoulder. He ended the desecration by rolling once more upon it.

Now to an outsider this shoulder rubbing and rolling might have had no significance, apart from crass mischief. A dogman would have understood the unspeakable black insult implied. For only into carrion—liquescent and putrescent carrion—does a dog roll and rub his body in that fashion. It is the foulest affront he can offer.

It was when Lad had completed his task of defilement as I have told it and was pacing back in majestic dignity to his place beside my chair, that the visitor's eye chanced to rest—first inquisitively and then in swift horror—upon his treasured white coat; or at the befouled bunch of muddy cloth which had been that coat.

Again I should have reprimanded Lad ferociously. Again I did not.

In October of 1912 the Mistress was stricken with a long and perilous attack of pneumonia. It was a time of horror which even yet I don't like to recall. Through the endless days and the interminable nights Lad crouched against the door of her sickroom. He would not eat. If he were put out of the house, he would smash a cellar window, and, two minutes later, he would be back at his post outside the shut door.

Day and night he lay there, shivering, moaning softly under his breath. Doctor and nurse, coming or going, would tread accidentally on his sensitive body a dozen times a day.

Outside, the October woods were full of chaseable rabbits and squirrels: Lad's lifelong pacemakers in wild-forest chases. But the dog paid no heed. Miserable and sick with dread, he lay there.

Then, of a glorious Sunday morning, the death danger was past. I called Lad into the sickroom. Trembling, ecstatic, he made his way to the side of the bed, moving as softly as any nurse or mother. The Mistress was told of his long vigil. And she patted his classic head and told him what a grand dog he was.

Then I told him to go outdoors. He obeyed.

Once outside, he proceeded to comport himself in a manner unworthy of a three-months puppy.

For the next ten hours complaints came pouring in on me: complaints ranging from tearful to blasphemous; complaints I was too happy to heed.

Lad had broken into the dairy, by hammering open its door with his head. There he had pulled, one by one, every milk or cream pan from the shelves, and had left the stone floor deep in a white covering.

Lad had chased the Mistress's cat up a tree. And the poor little feline was stranded out on the end of a wabbly bough whence only a long ladder could rescue her.

Lad had gushed forth among the cows and had driven them into stampede flight. One of them, tethered to a long chain, he had chased in a circle till the chasee was too exhausted to stand.

Lad had cantered up to the gate lodge. There he had slipped into the kitchen and had yanked from the open cover a ten-pound leg of mutton designed for the Sunday dinner

of my superintendent and his family. This hotly savory
trophy he had been burying deep in a flowerbed when the
superintendent's wife rescued it in sorry plight.

Lad had nipped the heels of an elderly horse which
drew a carryall wherein his owner and the latter's children
were driving to church. The horse had run away, more in
conscientiousness than in terror, for several yards, before the
driver could rein him in.

Meantime, Lad had sprung upward and had caught
between his teeth the corner of an elaborate laprobe. He had
dragged this for a quarter mile, and at last had deposited it
in the dead center of a half-impenetrable berry patch.

Lad had hunted up three neighbors' dogs and had
routed them out of their kennels and had bestowed on them
a series of terrific thrashings.

Lad had ripped the nurse's best newly starched uniform
from the clothesline (he hated the antiseptic-smelling and
abhorredly efficient nurse from the first) and had deposited
it in the black lakeside mud.

In brief, Lad had misbehaved as never before in all his
stately life had he dreamed of misbehaving. He had been,
for ten hours, a Scourge, a neighborhood Pest.

Fast and furious poured in the complaints from everywhere. To my lasting discredit, I must say I made the same
reply to every weeping or cursing complainant:

"Let him alone. Send me the bill and I'll settle it. Lad
and I have been through the red flames of hell, this past
fortnight. Today he's doing the things *I'd* do if I had the
nerve. We're celebrating, he and I."

(I don't need to point out to any of you that this was
an inanely drunken speech for any grown man to keep on
repeating as I repeated it on that golden Day of Deliverance.)

A year later, Lad took upon himself, of his own accord,
a man's size job. Namely, the task of shaping his harum-

scarum young son, Wolf, into a decent canine citizen. Patiently, the big dog wrought at this chore. At first the results were slow and uncertain.

For one thing, Wolf's inborn sense of mischief made his sedate sire's life a burden. The worst form of plaguing was the stealing by Wolf of Lad's most cherished meat bones.

At first the older collie suffered these thefts without resentment or punishment. Lad could thrash (and *did* thrash) every dog of his size, or much larger, which attacked him. But against a silly half-grown pup he would not employ his fearsome punitive powers. He hit on a better trick for keeping his beloved bones from Wolf's thieving teeth. I was lucky enough to be on hand, at a distance, to see this ruse carried out more than once. And, to me, it savors, not of blind atavistic canine instinct, but of true human sense of reasoning.

Lad received, as part of his dinner, a gorgeously meatful beef bone. He had eaten to repletion. Thus he planned to bury this delicious two-pound morsel for future exhuming and knawing. First, he took preliminary steps.

Then with no show of caution at all he carried the red-streaked bone to a sheltered spot in a flower border. There he laid it down and proceeded to dig a hole in the soft loam —a hole deeper than he usually dug.

In the bottom of this pit he placed the bone. With his nose, he shoved an inch or so of earth atop the buried treasure. (A dog digs holes with his forepaws, you know. But he uses his nose, never his paws, for filling such holes. I don't know why.)

After the bone was comfortably if lightly covered, Lad dived into a clump of shrubbery hard by, and reappeared carrying a bare and sterile bone he had hidden there—a bone which long ago had lost its last iota of dog appeal and which had been bleached white by many rains.

This forlorn relic he dropped into the cavity. Then he

proceeded to push back all the displaced dirt, up to the level of the rest of the ground; and walked unconcernedly away, not once turning to glance back at the cache.

Wolf had been watching from a safe distance, and with avid interest. As soon as Lad left the scene of interment, the puppy danced over to it and began to dig. Thus, often, he had rifled his sire's underground bone-repositories. Presently, Wolf had dug down to the first bone.

In disgust he sniffed at its meatless aridity. Then he turned away. Apparently he had had all his toils for nothing, for less than nothing, for a bone a starving coyote would have turned up its nose at. Off trotted the baffled puppy without the faintest suspicion that a right toothsome meat-fringed bone was lying less than two inches beneath the decoy bone he had disinterred.

Now, unless I am more in error than usual, that ruse of old Lad's called for something like human reasoning and powers of logic. Assuredly it was not based on mere instinct. Every move was thought out and executed in crafty sequence.

I have heard of two other dogs, since then, whose owners saw them do the same thing.

Let's go back to an aftermath of Lad's crazy spree of relief when he knew the Mistress was out of danger. A week or so later, the convalescent was carried downstairs, one Indian summer morning, and ensconced in a porch hammock. Lad, as always, lay on the veranda floor beside her.

During the forenoon, two or three neighbors came to see the Mistress, to congratulate her on her recovery and to bring her gifts of flowers and candy and fruit and the like. These presents they placed in her lap for inspection. Lad watched interestedly. Soon he got up and loped away toward the woods.

Somewhere far back in the forests he found—much more likely *re*found—the carcass of an excessively dead horse.

From it he wrenched part of a rib. Then, dragging his heavy burden, he made his way home.

None of us noticed the collie's approach; the wind blowing from the wrong direction. Our first knowledge of his return to the porch was when he came alongside the hammock and dropped his awful gift across the Mistress' lap.

And why not? To a dog, such far-gone carrion is a rare delicacy. Not for food, but to roll in. To him the odor must seem delicious, if one may judge by his joy in transferring it to his own coat.

Lad had followed the example of the morning's visitors by bringing his dear deity a present—the choicest he could find.

After all, the reek of carrion cannot be much more offensive to us than is the smell of tobacco and of booze and of costly imported perfumes, to dogs. Yet for the incomprehensible pleasure of being near us, our dogs endure those rank smells; while we banish from the house any dog whose fur has even the faintest reek of carrion.

Collie

Some Sunnybank Dogs

Of all my countless ignorances of dog nature, the densest is his yearning to be near his master or mistress.

I don't know why my collies will leave their dozing in front of the living-room hearth for the privilege of following me out into a torrent of winter rain. They hate rain.

I don't know why all folk's dogs risk gladly a scolding or a whipping by breaking out of a room or a kennel into which they have been shut, and galloping down the street or over the fields to catch up with the master who purposely has left them behind.

Today (for another and non-thrilling instance) I am writing at my hammock desk, a hundred yards or more from the house. Seven dogs are with me. It is a cool, brilliant afternoon; just the weather for a romp. The lawns and the woods and the lake all offer allurement to my collies.

What are the seven doing? Each and every one of them is lounging on the ground, close to the hammock.

Even crippled and ancient Sandy (Sunnybank Sandstorm) has left the veranda mat where he was so comfortable. To him all movement nowadays is a source of more or less keen discomfort. Yet he limped painfully down the six steps from the veranda to the driveway, and came slowly over to me, as soon as he found I was here; stretching himself at my feet, on bumpy ground much less comfortable than his porch bed. And here for the past two hours he has been drowsing with the others.

Why? *I* don't know. There must be some mysterious lure in the presence of their human gods which gives dogs that silly yearning to stay at their sides; rather than to do more amusing and interesting things.

When I chance to go from the house toward the stables, a cloud of the white doves of Sunnybank fly to meet me and to escort me in winnowing flight to my destination. There is no mystery about this semblance of devotion. They know their food box is in a shed there.

The same cause was assignable to the welcoming whinnies of my horses (when I still kept horses) that greeted me as I passed in through the stable doors in the early mornings.

It is the same with the goldfish, when a hundred of them converge in fiery streams to where I halt at the curb of the wide lily pool; and when they wriggle fearlessly in and out among my dabbling fingers. They know—or hope—I am there to feed them.

No, none of those phenomena holds a single half-grain of mystery, any more than does human fawning on a rich relative. But the dogs—mine and everyone's—stick around where we are and go where we go, through no graft motive at all.

They are absurd enough to want to be with us, and with no hope of reward. That is an impulse I have sought hard and vainly to explain to myself.

In the bunch of Sunnybank collies, as they lie around me here on the grass, there is no trace of the flattering attention they show toward the maids, who love to feed them surreptitiously from the kitchen windows; none of the still more rapt interest they bestow on my superintendent as he prepares their one ample daily meal.

There is no such patently self-seeking tinge in their attitude toward me as they lie here on the lawn. There was none of it in the canine procession which followed me to the house, three minutes ago, when I went to my study for a new supply of typewriter paper, and which waited at the door for me and then convoyed me back here to the hammock.

No, it is a trait I can't figure out. As I think I have said several times in the past page or two.

Which is a long digression from our story. I like to hope it hasn't bored you overmuch. And now let's get back to Lad:

I have dealt here only with a few of the queerly human and mischievous and logic-guided happenings in Laddie's life. Not with his actual history.

His death battle with two younger and stronger dogs in the snow-choked forests back of Sunnybank, his deeds of dashingly worshipful service to the Mistress and to myself during his full sixteen years of life, the series of stark adventures that starred his long career—are not these chronicled to perhaps tiresome length in my three books about him?

Foremost among the Sunnybank dogs of my childhood and young boyhood was my father's oversized pointer, Shot. He is worth your notice. Naturally, in my modern dog show Shot would be "gated" most unmercifully.

He was of royally pure blood. But his head lacked the so-styled refinement of today's show pointer. His mighty chest and shoulders and hindquarters that carried him tirelessly for ten hours a day through the stiffest kinds of shooting country, and the harsh coat and thick skin which served as armor against briar and bramble and kept him unscathed through the thorniest copses—these were at laughable variance with the silken skin and dainty narrow-chested body lines of the show-type pointer of nowadays.

At "laughable" variance. But to me the laugh would not be on Shot. For, to me, he still is, in memory, the grandest pointer of my rather long experience.

My mother's health broke. My father took her and all of us to Europe, in the hope of curing her. (The cure was made. She lived more than forty healthy years longer.)

Sunnybank was rented during our two-year absence from America. Shot was sent to one of my uncles to be cared for until we should come back for him.

This uncle, Colonel G. P. Hawes, Sr., was an ideal sportsman. He understood dogs as it is given to few men to understand them. He and Shot had been good friends, since the pointer came to us as a just-weaned puppy. The dog could not have had a better home and a more congenial guardian.

Yet Colonel Hawes wrote my father that the usually gay dog had grown sullen and mopey and spiritless. Shot went through his duties in the hunting field as honestly as ever, but with no interest. He was grieving sorely for his absent master and for Sunnybank.

After our two-year exile we came back to America. One of my father's first moves was to go to my uncle's home and bring Shot to Sunnybank. He took me along on this errand. Its details are as clear in my memory as if they had occurred last month.

As soon as we were seated, Colonel Hawes sent a man to bring Shot into the house. The dog was kenneled some distance away and had not seen or scented our arrival. Into the living room plodded the pointer, at my uncle's summons.

He was thinner, much thinner, than I remembered him. His gait and his every line and motion were listless. He seemed wholly without spirit and devoid of any interest in life. My father had arranged the scene beforehand. He had told me what to do. I did it.

He and I sat motionless and without speaking. We were at the end of the room farthest from the door, and we were seated perhaps ten feet from each other.

Lifelessly, Shot came through the doorway. Just inside the threshold he halted. Up went his splendid head. His eyes sought out my father's mute and moveless figure. For a second or more the dog stood so.

Then he began to creep toward my father, hesitantly, one slow step at a time, crouching low and shuddering as with ague. Never did his dazed eyes leave my father's face. Inch by inch he continued that strangely crawling advance.

He did not so much as glance toward where I was sitting. His whole mind was focussed on the unmoving and

138

unspeaking man in the chair ahead of him. So might a human move toward the ghost of a loved one; incredulous, hypno-tized, awed. Then my father spoke the one word:

"*Shot!*"

The dog screamed; as though he had been run over. He hurled himself on his long-lost master, sobbing and shrieking, insane with joy. Then the sedate pointer whirled around him in galloping circles, and ended the performance by dropping to my father's feet; lying his head athwart his shoe and chattering and sobbing.

I drew a shaky breath. At the sound Shot raised his head from its place of adoration.

He dashed over to me and accorded me a welcome which ordinarily would have seemed tumultuous, but which was almost indifferent, compared to the greeting he had accorded my father. Then, all at once, he was back to his master again, lying his head on the man's knee and still sobbing in that queerly human fashion.

(Yet not long ago I read a solemn scientific preachment to the effect that no dog could remember a lost master's face and scent for the space of eighteen months! Shot beat that record by half a year. And I believe he could have beaten it by a decade.)

To Sunnybank we came; Shot with us. The dog's sullen apathy was gone—gone for all time. He was jubilantly happy at his return to the home of his earliest memories. But for weeks he would not willingly let my father out of his sight. He seemed to fear he would lose his master again.

My father taught me to shoot. A few years after our return to America he and I went out quail-hunting with Shot. At the base of a steep hill there was a brambly meadow. The meadow was cut midway by a railroad track. As he neared the track, the dog came to a dead point. He was facing a clump of low bushes on the far side of the rails.

Statue-still, Shot stood, at point, waiting my father's

signal to move forward toward the clump. Before that signal could be spoken, an express train came whizzing around the curve at the foot of the hill, and bore down toward us. Under its wheels and in its wake was a fog of dust and of flying hit cinders.

Shot stood, rocklike, on his point. The train roared past, not ten inches from his nose. The dog did not stir or falter, though he was peppered with burning cinders and choked by the whirlwind of dust and soot.

Pointer

Some Sunnybank Dogs

After the train had rattled its ill-smelling length out of the way, my father signaled Shot to move forward. The pointer took two stealthy steps ahead: steps that carried him to the center of the railroad track. From the clump just in front of him three quail whirred upward like a trio of fluffy little bombs. I suppose they had been too scared by the passage of the train to break cover until then.

Shot dropped to the ground, tense and waiting. My father brought down two of the birds in one of his customary brilliant left-and-right volleys.

I missed the third.

I was too shaky over the dog's peril and his plucky ignoring of it to do any creditable shooting just then. Shot lived to a ripe—an over-ripe—old age. We buried him in a strip of lakeside land a furlong or more from the house: a strip where sleep the Sunnybank dogs of almost eight decades. He was interred next to a grave whose little marble headstone's blurred lettering still may be deciphered as

FRANK Our Dog. For Thirteen Years
Our Faithful Friend. Died 1876.

Frank was Shot's immediate predecessor as my father's hunting companion.

Frank bit me when I was at the ago of two. I had tried to bite off one of his floppy ears. It was a punitive nip Frank gave me rather than a real incision. I am told I wept loudly at the scare and hurt of it.

(If "when a man bites a dog, that's *news*," I wonder if it is tabloid news when a two-year-old boy chews a dog's ear.)

It was long before my birth that my father bought Frank. The dog was just past puppyhood. The time was winter. So my parents were at Newark, where my father was pastor of the old First Reformed Church. Not at Sunnybank.

(Even as, to my sorrow, I was not born at Sunnybank like three of my nephews, but at Newark; because my birth date fell on December 21st—my mother's forty-second birthday.)

Young Frank was restless in his new home. On the day after his arrival he ran away. My father and my mother and my two elder sisters and the servants went to look for him. All in different directions.

My mother wandered about for an hour, calling the pointer's name from time to time. At last, just in front of her, in the twilight, she saw him emerge from an alleyway. She called to him. He paid no heed, but walked away. She gave chase and overhauled him. The dog showed his teeth as she grabbed him by the collar. This though he had seemed to take a genuine liking to her after his arrival at our home.

She ripped a flounce or something from an underskirt—women wore a labyrinth of underskirts and petticoats in those prehistoric days—and fastened it to his collar. Then she proceeded to drag him homeward.

"Drag" is the right word. For the pointer fought and held back every step of the way. A small but enthusiastic crowd formed, and followed the pair with shouts of gay encouragement. After a mile of hard going they reached our house, at 476 High Street.

In triumph, if in much weariness, my mother hauled the snappingly protesting dog indoors and into the firelit living room.

There, in front of the hearth, lounged my father. Frank was asleep on the rug at his feet.

The runaway dog had tired of his roamings and, half an hour earlier, had come back home of his own accord; just as my father was returning from a fruitless search for him.

The dog my mother had kidnapped was enough like him to have been Frank's twin brother. They never knew who the other pointer belonged to. But when they let him escape into the night he bounded off as with some evident destination of view. For weeks thereafter my mother dreaded arrest on a charge of dog stealing.

Never again did Frank run away, throughout the thirteen happy years of his life. Every winter he stayed on at Sunnybank when the family returned to Newark. There, in the absence of his gods, he made himself a member of the superintendent's family at the gate lodge; waiting in weary impatience for the family's return home.

When in early spring our carriage and the baggage wagon turned in at the gate, Frank would follow them down the winding furlong driveway to Sunnybank House. Here, till our departure in late autumn, he remained. And he would bark harrowingly at the superintendent or at anyone of the gate-lodge household who might venture to come near our door.

He was a peerless field dog and a peerless watchdog. To the inch, he knew the boundaries of our land. No unauthorized outsider might pass those boundaries without instant challenge and assault from Frank. He treed several innocent (if any of their foul breed can merit the term, "innocent") sightseers. He was a Neighborhood Terror.

Nightly, at stated intervals, he would leave his porch mat and would patrol the outside of the house and every part of Sunnybank's home tract. He was perhaps the best of all the great Sunnybank watchdogs we have had over a period of nearly eighty years.

I never liked him. And he didn't like me. Thus, my praise of his worth comes from my brain and from my conscience, not from my heart. He was bitterly and justly resentful, too, when in his old age young Shot came here to take his place in the field work he no longer had the strength or endurance to perform. I can't blame the ancient dog for that.

It was soon after Frank's death that someone gave my mother a miniature black-and-tan terrier. She named her "Jip," after Dora Copperfield's tiny dog. Though Jip nominally was my mother's, yet the little terrier chose my father as her only god. Her devotion to him was all-engrossing. She insisted on going everywhere with him. Sometimes this was not wholly pleasant.

As when, one Sunday, she was locked safely at home in his study while the rest of us went to church. My father was in the midst of his sermon when Jip came strutting proudly up the aisle.

A servant had gone into the study to replenish its fire. Jip had sneaked out, unseen. Somehow she had made her way to the street. There she had had no trouble at all in picking up my father's trail and following it.

Happy at the reunion with her adored master, Jip eluded easily the grabbing hands of the sexton and of one or two of the worshipers whose pews she went past. Up the pulpit steps she bounded, and leaped to the pulpit itself, landing squarely if scramblingly on the open Bible.

My father did not so much as pause in the delivery of his sermon, nor did he heed the snickers of the congregation. Which showed fairly good self-control, I think, as he had not noticed the terrier's progress up the aisle, and as his first intimation of her presence was when she appeared, wagging her tail and wriggling with joy, on the top of the pulpit's Bible.

Without checking his discourse, my father picked up the little morsel of caninity very gently and thrust her into one of the flowing sleeves of his black clerical gown.

From that exalted position, her beady eyes surveyed the congregation in triumph. Throughout the rest of the long church service she did not stir. She just cuddled deep in the folds of her master's silken sleeve, her alert head alone visible to the grinning onlookers.

Some Sunnybank Dogs

If she shamed us on that day, she more than atoned for her sin a few nights later.

Always she slept on the foot of my father's bed. He woke to hear her growling with falsetto intensity far down in her throat. Then she sprang to the floor and scampered out of the room and downstairs.

A moment later, the house re-echoed to her furious barking. My father went down to investigate. For never before had the good little dog done such a thing as to disturb the slumbers of the family. Others of the household also went downstairs to find what it was all about. As a result, a burglar was nabbed and jailed. In his cell, later, the man gave this testimony:

"The thing we're most scared of in a house is a small dog that barks and keeps backing away, like that black cur at Dominie Terhune's last night. You can't make them shut up and you can't get close enough to them to land a kick. They wake up everybody."

So much for gallant and adoring Jip. I don't remember what became of her. And now, a good deal more than a half-century later, there is nobody I can ask. Peace to her, anyhow! She stood patiently for a godless lot of mauling from my grubby childish hands. I recall that much, very distinctly.

Jock and Jean were son and mother. Both were children of my great collie, Bruce, "The Dog without a Fault"; the hero of my book that bears his name.

Usually a mother dog loses all special interest in her pups soon after she has weaned them. That was what Jean did, in regard to most of her many offspring. But never with Jock.

To the day of Jock's death he was still her cherished baby. Daily—though he grew to be almost twice her size—she would make him lie down, first on one side and then on the

145

other, while with her untiring pink tongue she washed him from nose to tail tip.

She superintended his eating. Daintily she would transfer from her own food dish to his the choicest tidbits of her dinner.

It was pretty: this love and care of the little brown collie mother for her brown collie son. And Jock reciprocated it all to the utmost. He and Jean were wretchedly unhappy when either was forced to be away from the comradeship of the other for more than an hour at a time.

Jock was one of the best collies, from a show point, I have bred. Close he was to complete perfection. In his only dog show he cleaned up everything in his classes against strong competition; and he was beaten for "Best of Breed" only by his own peerless sire, Bruce.

This meant immeasurably less to me than did my success in breeding into him a clever and gay and courageous spirit and a flavor of wise "folksiness" which made him an ideal companion. Mentally, spiritually, in disposition, he was a replica of Bruce. I asked (and ask) better of no dog on earth. As to his jolly pluck:

From the time he could leave the brood nest, Jock feared nothing. He would tackle any peril, any adversary, with a queerly happy and defiant high-pitched bark whose duplicate I have yet to hear.

That queer bark of glad defiance was ever his war cry.

On a day, while I sat writing in my outdoor hammock, young Jock lounged at my feet. He leaped up, suddenly, with that jocund challenge bark of his.

I looked behind me. There I saw on the lawn a big and thick-girthed copperhead snake. The serpent had been gliding through the grass toward the hammock and toward my unheeding ankles, when Jock either had sighted him or else had become aware of the nauseous viperine odor—a stench as of stale cucumbers—which clings to such venomous snakes.

In some occult way, Jock had seemed to divine my possible peril. He had sprung up from his doze and had rushed at the copperhead, sounding his glad battle cry. The snake checked its own slithery advance. It coiled, and prepared itself to face this plangent new adversary.

Many a fool dog would have plunged forward to death. Many a more prudent dog would have avoided the issue. Jock was neither a fool nor prudent.

It was a new experience to me to watch his duel with the copperhead. Never before, I think, had he encountered a snake. Yet he fought with consummate skill. In and out he flashed, tempting the copperhead to strike, and than dodging back, barely an inch out of reach of the death-dealing fangs; and immediately flashing in with an effort to slay the serpent before it could coil afresh.

Each combatant was a shade too swift for the other. Back and forth for some seconds waged the death duel. Neither adversary scored the fatal bite, though more than once each was within a hair's breadth of it. And ever rang forth that odd battle bark of my young collie.

Then I had sense enough to realize that I was allowing an untried paragon to put his skill, for life or for death, against the most deady type of viper in this region. And I went to his help.

I smashed the copperhead's ugly triangular skull under my heel.

This with no zest at all. For I was wearing low shoes of canvas at the time. And if I had missed, the snake might well have scored on my unprotected ankle. I had a twinge of mental nausea as I gauged the distance and the required speed and accuracy for my head blow.

(There is little of the hero and a goodly modicum of the coward in my make-up. I detest danger and all its by-products. But Jock was my chum. And he was risking his life for me.)

The heel came down fatally on the fat copperhead. The fight was ended. So was the snake's life. And for two days thereafter Jock would have nothing whatever to do with me. I had spoiled his jolly life battle by butting in on it and by slaying his very entertaining opponent. He viewed me with cold aversion, until his youth and his inborn love for me overcame his disapproval.

But we were chums, he and I, for a pitifully short time after that.

For, a week later, like the fool I was, I took him to the dog show I have mentioned. He had been inoculated twice against distemper, and I used every other preventive and safeguard I knew of. (Doses of Delcreo in advance, a sponging of mouth and of pads with grain alcohol directly after the show, followed by the rubbing of flaked naphthaline into his luxuriant coat and a liberal dosage of castor oil.)

But a distemper-sickening chow had touched noses with him briefly at the big show. And that was enough. Jock was the more delicate because he was so closely inbred. He was infected. Ten days afterward he developed a dry cough and a wet nose.

The disease had set in. The malady which kills more pure-bred dogs than do all other diseases put together; the malady which took horrible toll from that same show and which has killed more than a thousand dogs a month, in its flood tide, after other shows.

Distemper practically never kills a mongrel (cross-breed is a better term) which it assails. The afflicted dog crawls under the barn or into some other cool and dark hiding place. Thence he emerges a few days later, bone thin and weak, but cured. But it slays at least fifty per cent of the thoroughbreds it attacks. Sometimes more.

It is a disease which, like typhoid, its human counterpart, calls for twenty-four hours a day of nursing. And, as in typhoid, nursing is 90 per cent of the cure.

Not often does actual distemper kill its victims. Oftener they die of its sequel illnesses: pneumonia or pleurisy or chorea. Chorea is a form of St. Vitus's dance. With dogs, almost always it is fatal.

Jock weathered the distemper itself. I nursed him, twenty-four hours a day, through the pneumonia which followed upon it. Then through the long siege of Chorea which came after pneumonia. I cured him of each successive one of these scourges, though I waxed dead on my feet from sleeplessness and from eternal vigilance during every one of them.

I gave up all attempt to work. And I spent my days and my eternally long nights in the wide box stall that was Jock's sickroom. Then, just as success seemed ahead, the youngster somehow acquired "re-infection." At least that is what the two vets named it.

At gray dawn of one November morning I sat on the floor in a dim corner of the box stall, with Jock's head and shoulders pillowed on my aching knees. I had had seven weeks of the conflict, with not one night's rest. Yet I was thrilled at the idea I gradually was winning the battle for the good collie comrade I loved.

Jock had been sleeping peacefully for hours. Suddenly he lurched to his feet. His fevered eyes were fixed on something in the black shadows at the far opposite corner of the wide stall; something my own gross human gaze could not see.

Forward he sprang, voicing that same strange high challenge bark of his. Then he fell dead, across my outstretched feet.

What did he see—if anything—lurking there in the stall's far corner? Probably nothing. Perhaps "the Arch Fear in visible shape." Whatever It was, brave young Jock had no dread of It. With his olden glad bark of defiance he had staggered forward to meet It.

Perhaps some of us soul-possessing humans may die a less valiant death.

At sunrise I had my men dig a grave for Jock, far from the house, and in the center of the line of Sunnybank dogs' graves I have spoken of, at the lake edge and on the border of the more distant woods. There we buried the fearless young collie; buried him almost six feet deep, before we fumigated his box-stall sickroom.

For the past weeks Jean had been shut up in her own spacious kennel yard. That day I let her out, for the first time since her loved son had fallen ill. Eagerly, unwearingly, the little she-collie searched every inch of the forty-acre Place. Back and forth and in narrowing circles she coursed and cast, in quest of Jock.

After several hours she came to the grave of her puppy. There she halted; first sniffing about, then waving happily her plumed tail and nestling down beside the mound of new earth.

There was nothing sad or hopeless in her attitude and aspect. It was as if, after long search, she had arrived by chance at a spot nearer her precious son than she had been for weeks.

Presently she got up and ran to find me. Then she led me joyously to the grave; and once more she snuggled down to it, with waving tail and happy, smiling eyes. There she stayed all day. Not mournfully, but in pleasant expectation.

There was no taint of exhibitionism or of the role of professional mourner, or even of grief, in her bearing. She had missed her dear son all these weeks. Now at last she was nearer to him than she had been throughout that long time of waiting. Her sense of smell told her that.

Several times before settling down there she circled the ground, nose to earth, for a radius of perhaps thirty feet, as if in search of some newer trail to follow. There was none. She realized she was closer to him, at his grave, than anywhere else. Presumably she believed Jock would come back to her, there, in course of time. So she waited, in happy eagerness.

She did not establish a senseless twenty-four-hour-a-day vigil. But every morning, as soon as she was let out of her kennel yard, she would canter to Jock's grave in that same blithe expectation of finding he had returned. There she would stand or lie for a few minutes before going back to the day's usual routine.

She was a strangely lovable little collie, was Sunnybank Jean; with a hundred pretty ways that were all her own. The Mistress, whose property she was, used to say:

"Any burglar could steal Jean if only he'd pat her while he was doing it."

Unlike most of our collies, she loved petting, even from strangers. And she delighted in the arrival of guests.

At sight or sound of a car coming down the furlong of winding wooded driveway from the highroad above, Jean would run to the foot of the drive at the veranda's edge and stand wriggling with jolly anticipation, thrusting forward one of her white fore paws in an effort to shake hands with the approaching visitors—even while their car still was many yards away.

Two minor mishaps were forever befalling Jean. One was the wedging of some fragment of bone into the hinges of her jaw at the very back of her mouth. This propped her jaws wide apart and she could not close them or get rid of the obstacle. The other was throwing her shoulder out of joint during a gallop or a romp.

Both these things happened again and again. But they did not bother her. Invariably she would come straight to me with a flatteringly trustful expression on her visage; an aspect which said as plainly as could any shouted words:

"Boss, I'm in a jam again. But it's all right, now that you're here. *You'll* fix it for me. You always do."

With plumed tail awag, she would stand patiently and even gaily while I pried loose the lump of knuckle-bone from between her jaw hinges, or pulled the dislocated shoulder joint back into place.

One morning, when she was let out for a run, she went as always to Jock's grave. On her way back to the house she heard a car starting down the drive from the highroad. In her role of Reception Committee, she raced to her usual place of welcome and stood with fore paw outthrust in a handshaking gesture.

The car, laden with sightseeing strangers from far away, had crashed the gates at the lodge and had sped down the drive at perhaps forty miles an hour. This with the customary sweet disregard for the several "Please Drive Slowly" signs which disfigure our trees along the way.

Perhaps the driver did not notice the beautiful little collie near the veranda; the canine Reception Committee with waving tail and politely extended fore paw, waiting so happily to welcome the newcomers.

The car went over Jean, disemboweling her and breaking most of her bones.

She must have been in hideous agony during the few minutes before she died. But not so much as a whimper escaped her. She was as plucky as they make them.

When I ran out of the house, toward her, Jean lifted her head and turned it toward me with the same flatteringly trustful expression that always had been hers when her jaw hinge was blocked by a bone or when her shoulder was out of joint; the expression that said:

"It's all right, now that *you're* here. *You'll* fix it for me."

A large woman in bright blue was among the tourists who debarked tumultuously from the killer car. Breezing over to where I knelt beside my dead little collie friend she made graceful amends for everything by assuring me with a gay smile:

"I am really VERY sorry this has happened."

(What a heaven-sent gift it must be, to know how to say just the right thing at just the right time! Hers was a talent to be envied. Yet for the only time in my life I replied to a woman's words with a torrent of indescribably foul blasphemy.)

A local magistrate fined the head of the party one hundred dollars for trespass and for malicious mischief or for some such fault. He wanted to make the sum much larger. I persuaded him not to. I told him the mischief had not been malicious, but idiotic. Which was far worse, but not so heinous in the eyes of the law. Also that if he should fine every unwarranted sightseer motorist who trespasses on Sunnybank's posted grounds the national debt could be wiped out in no time at all.

I told him to divide the hundred dollars between two village charities. Which he did. I wanted no part of the blood money that he imposed for my collie chum's killing.

As far as I was concerned I thought the rotten incident was closed. It was not.

A syndicated newspaper column's space, two days later, was devoted to the affair and to denouncing me venomously for my boorishness in penalizing a party of "kindly meaning hero worshippers who had traveled so far to see me." Several papers throughout the country—one of them a religious weekly—printed editorials along the same general line of invective.

Thus I lost not only good little Jean, but much popular approval and, doubtless, many readers.

A Gallery of Stone Lithographs

H. von Reichert

THE WONDERFUL PRINTS which appear on these pages were originally published in a book entitled *Naturgeschichte*, brought out in Vienna in 1837. This two-volume work was comprised of a text by V. Pröphan, which occupied the first volume, and drawings engraved on stone by H. von Reichert, which occupied the second volume. Rarely has an artist captured the activities of the dog so well.

Water spaniel and pups

Spaniel

Pointer

Dachshunds

English spaniel

White Griffon Terriers

Italian Greyhounds

Griffon

Pointers

158

Mastiff

Pointers

Why Does Your Dog Do That?

Göran Bergman

WHY DOES YOUR DOG SPEAK?

ONE DOES NOT have to have a great deal of experience to interpret most dog vocalisations in the right way. The central rôle which barking and other vocalisations play in a dog, however, indicate that they should be gone into fairly thoroughly, despite their easy comprehension. In addition, the vocalisations of dogs in certain cases are not so simply interpreted as one might think. The use of sounds not only varies individually very greatly, but also sometimes appears in a dog as displacement activity. A dog has at its command all the sounds which occur in a wolf. The differences between the sounds of a wolf and a dog are no greater than that they are due only to extensive selection carried out by man, which has led to the rise of different breeds. On the other hand, a dog's vocalisations are very different from those of both the jackal and the fox.

Barking

In most breeds, barking is the most common vocalisation. A dog barks primarily in situations which put the dog into a

Reprinted from *Why Does Your Dog Do That?* by Göran Bergman, © Popular Dogs Publishing Co., Ltd. 1970, by permission of Howell Book House Inc., publisher.

mood dominated by a combination of alertness-fear-aggression. Barking can appear as an intention movement, as just a weak, soundless expelling of breath. At high intensity, barking can become almost a continuous howling. The more aggression dominates, the more hollow the bark; the more the dog shows fear, the higher and more shrill becomes the bark. A dog which is not in the slightest worried only barks as a displacement activity at pleasure or if it finds itself in some special mood which is connected with sounds of the barking type, for instance at a drive or when it points game, or if it has learnt to use its bark in some special situation, for instance to draw attention to itself.

Barking in alert situations of different kinds has a clear social warning function, which man can also find useful. But a dog barks quite independently of whether it is thus warning another individual. The nuances of a bark—from strong aggression to preparation for flight—are heard by a listening dog even if it cannot see the dog that is barking, or even if the barking dog is a complete stranger. In addition the note and ring of the bark clearly tell other dogs quite a lot about the size of the barker. A small timid dog is often afraid of a deep bark, even if the barker is a long way away. A dog which knows another dog, also recognises its bark and it uses this experience on strange dogs' barks. However, it is not known whether a little dog without previous experience reacts more obviously to a large dog's bark than to a small dog's bark. This is probably unlikely; in a wolf-pack there are no drastic variations in voice and size.

Barking as an expression of joy, of expectation in face of a pleasure-denoting situation which the dog has learnt to meet, is very common. This sort of barking can sometimes be regarded as a kind of displacement activity and often also as a challenge.

Barking on drives can be regarded as a social signal, but at the same time a displacement activity. Selection has evi-

161

dently greatly influenced the inclination to bark in situations relevant to hunting. In certain cases a dog barks in a situation which in natural circumstances would not give it an advantage—for instance barking at a guinea-fowl sitting high up in a tree, quite out of reach of the dog.

Although a dog's inclination to bark is usually very great, barking in an alert situation can quite easily be emphasised by training. In some examples of breeds whose bark is usually easily released, the inclination to bark in alert situations is abnormally small. Such dogs are often more aggressive and fearless than other examples of the same breed and consequently also bark less—fear is one of the most important mainsprings of barking. The popular conception that a dog which barks a lot does not bite is thus not entirely incorrect, ethologically speaking. Barking is an activity which a dog can easily learn to carry out to order, wholly independent of any innate releasing stimulus.

A dog has an inclination to bark or make itself heard in some other way when it is hindered from carrying out some worthwhile activity. This behaviour can possibly be explained by the theory of displacement activity. If the vocalisation is followed by success in the activity striven for, then the dog quickly associates its vocalisation with that success. This is, amongst other things, the reason why dogs so easily begin to bark to be given titbits.

Growling

A dog that growls deeply is demonstrating an aggressive mood which has no direct element of fear in it. But the growl does not really mean that a dog will attack. On the contrary, a dog usually growls most loudly in situations in which it is dominated by aggression, but social inhibitions stop it from attacking or biting. In this way, growling becomes a kind of demonstration of power, and it is primarily directed against enemies close to a dog and of which the dog is not afraid. At the actual moment of attack—if there is an attack—the growling usually becomes a more obvious roar. At increased intensity, growling can be stopped by short suppressed barks, without an attack following.

Another type of growling is the rather obvious intention of ordinary barking. This kind of growling easily becomes a whining or squealing sound. Naturally, there is no sharp dividing line between different types of growls. Aggressive growling can perhaps be called an intention to bark of an extreme aggressive type, which has a free-standing function and its own resonance.

Whining

A dog which has experienced some unpleasantness whines. A corresponding situation occurs if a dog is in an atmosphere in which some behaviour is strongly activated but cannot be realised. Thus one can say that both mental dissatisfaction and physically unpleasant situatons cause whining. At extreme intensity, whining can easily become a sound of a barking type, and sometimes also howling. In the latter case, the reason is obviously usually discomfort of a non-physical nature.

Yelping

This sound, often a short and shrill vocalisation, is a very characteristic reaction to pain and experiences causing shock. Many dogs yelp if they are frightened by a sudden loud or unexpected noise, or something which very suddenly appears in its field of vision quite near it. Dogs with bad-tempered natures, however, do not react with any obvious yelping, but with some kind of swift flight movement, simultaneously showing signs of aggression. Dogs do no usually react to olfactory sensations with yelps, but sometimes with aggressive behaviour. Olfactory sensations hardly ever seem to appear so suddenly that they cause such a shocked reaction which, for instance, bangs or other unusual noises do. Dogs yelp if, for instance, their tails are trodden on, and often at this, in many very gentle dogs, a certain aggressive mood is released which is usually expressed by it raising its back hairs or in that it snaps quickly.

A dog's inclination to be frightened in situations of surprise varies individually a great deal. Rough dogs are not afraid, but just slightly aggressive; dogs with especially timid natures are easily frightened and cannot shake off the mood easily.

Squealing

At extreme delight and surprise, a number of dogs react by letting out a high, vibrating squealing noise. This sound appears to be released only with happiness which does not involve expectation, but satisfaction. In face of the prospect of receiving a titbit, a dog does not squeal, but when a member of the family who has been away a long times comes home, squealing occurs in an intensive greeting ceremony. A young dog occasionally squeals when it greets its mother, but the mother does not greet her pup with this sound. One gets the impression that individual dogs which seldom squeal make this sound only when they greet people or other dogs by whom they have been affected when they were pups. But there are also dogs which squeal at a quite low 'joy intensity' —or which become very happy from very insignificant causes.

Howling

In wolves, howling occurs in several different situations, but in a dog this vocalisation is not nearly so common. A wolf uses howling primarily as a kind of gathering signal in hunting. A corresponding situation is hard to find in dogs, which are, after all, not usually allowed to hunt in packs in extensive hunting areas in which contact between the pack's individuals is not easy to keep. In both dogs and wolves, however, howling occurs as an indication of some kind of pack feeling of affinity, the content of which has not really been closely analysed. One animal begins to howl and the others soon follow suit. It is often easy to get a dog to howl quite loudly by using this reaction. Humming and playing music of different kinds releases howling in some dogs. Dogs used to music hardly react at all, while dogs who have never heard music are considerably more sensitive. One can cause howling most easily by directly imitating the howl of a dog. Presumably dogs can show some kind of emotion which corresponds to grief, but that they should then howl is unlikely. On the other hand, it is more likely that desertion and loneliness release howling as a kind of gathering signal. Also, a hunting wolf which loses contact with members of the pack naturally also falls into such a mood and starts howling. According to this argument, howling would not really be a gathering signal, but in certain situations it might acquire this significance. There are also examples of very sudden joy giving rist to short but intensive howling.

Other Vocalisations

The vocalisations of dogs are far from stereotyped and variations on their use occur very often. *Intermediate forms be-*

tween two or more vocalisations are in a number of dogs more usual than vocalisations which indicate a 'pure' mood. Dogs also have a very great capacity for reacting to each other's vocalisations according to the mood content that such a mixed vocalisation has. It is quite common that a dog barking at something makes another dog bark at something quite different. Under the influence of the bark from the other dog, a dog may believe, if one may use a somewhat anthropomorphic expression, that some object which is in reality quite harmless is dangerous. One can express roughly the same thing more scientifically: the bark releases a mood which lowers the threshold value for the stimuli that can release reactions of fear or make the dog look for reasons in its environment for the barking of the other dog.

"He's my dog. I'm a Shakespearean actor."

Growling is associated with marked facial expressions which presumably at close quarters are more effective signals than the sound itself. I shall return to facial expressions in another context later. Also, growling can in another dog release reactions of fear of quite harmless sounds or objects. But growling is primarily directed at another dog nearby which in its turn does not misunderstand this vocalisation. But it can happen that the *nasal sounds* unnatural to a dog, which a number of pug-type dogs make when they are happy or excited, are misunderstood by dogs which have not previously come into contact with these strange and incomprehensible vocalisations of mood. These sounds have caused clear suspicious-aggressive behaviour in my dachshunds, amongst others. Naturally these nasal sounds have no clear ethological significance. Their mood content is quite unknown to other dogs, and possibly even to them themselves.

Many dogs make a *weak crooning* sound when in a friendly mood. Since her infant days, my old dachshund bitch has 'cooed' at each indrawn breath when she is very happy, especially when she is calmly moving around out of doors. Indoors, she only makes this sound now and again when in a satisfied mood. The inclination to make this sound, which is not part of instinctive behaviour, is to some extent hereditary. Of my dachshund's ten pups, two have had the same inclination, though rather weak. It is in all probability caused by some unimportant anatomical anomaly. The sound occurs in roughly the same way as a snore. The way the muscles in the region of the larynx and throat tighten and loosen in different moods leads to the sound occurring in certain moods, while it does not occur in other moods.

Dogs can *sigh* very markedly. A dog which has settled down sighs when after much scratching and turning it has at last got comfortable. Dogs sigh when, after having great expectations, they finally give up hope that the expected will happen. Dogs which are very contented but not excited often sigh, provided they are sitting still or lying down, preferably on someone's knee. A dog's inclination to sigh is especially evident if a member of the family who has been away a long time allows the dog uninhibitedly to greet him and then sit on his lap. The dog's facial expression in this situation is one of 'bliss'. One cannot say that sighing has any real ethological function. It is clear, however, that dogs and people sigh in rather similar moods. Physiologically the sigh can be called a deep compensatory inspiration of breath after a strain that may lower the breathing tempo, or directly increase the need for oxygen, through mental strain.

Dogs begin to *sneeze* if they lie on their backs with their noses pointing upward. Evidently a fluid from the breathing tubes in the nostrils irritates the scent membranes.

Coughing is common in dogs, sometimes in the form of short spurts of air much like our own cough, but also another kind which causes a hooting sound on inspiration, which is repeated with a number of cramp-like breaths following one another, then slowly dying down. In breathing of this kind, expiration occurs swiftly and without coughing interruptions. The dog appears sick and it all looks very unpleasant, but the coughing spell vanishes quickly by itself. The cause of this cramp-like breathing appears to be irritants in the bronchial tubes. My dachshunds usually have this trouble when they have been digging in loose dry soil. Sneezing, on the other hand, does not result from this kind of digging. It can be mentioned that these reflex-released sounds have no social function and are not noticed much by surrounding dogs.

Dogs often *snore* very loudly, and older dogs snore more than younger ones. Not even the loudest snore releases reactions in other dogs except, at the most, a feeble passing surprise.

WHAT IS YOUR DOG'S MOOD?

Other moods besides those connected with aggression or fear are also expressed in a dog's facial expression. A number of such moods, however, are reflected so weakly that they may be hard to see in dogs you do not know well. It can, for instance, be a question of a combination of an alert mood and friendliness, or an alert mood with no trace of the insecurity which is most often found when the dog is alerted to events slightly further away. Eyes, ear position, facial features, tail movements, breathing and posture change very sensitively, and the spectator cannot in only one of these indicators see all the changes in a dog's mood, even in calm domestic conditions. Two moods under normal domestic circumstances, however, have easily described characteristics, and they are the extremely contented and calm mood, and the challenge to play.

The calm satisfied mood in a number of dogs has a special sign which can here be called *a smile*. When it is calm and contented and satisfied with all and sundry, a dog with sufficiently mobile skin at the corners of its mouth then gets a small crease just by or above the angle of the mouth. In alert situations, this smile vanishes at once, but if the dog likes being stroked, the smile increases at calm stroking of the head and back, or scratching of the neck or stomach. The slightest sign of social insecurity makes the smile vanish, as does the slightest anxiety or expectation, even if the latter is something emphatically positive. In a weak joyful mood, for instance when its owner comes into the room and the dog wags its tail once or twice, the smile may remain or even become more obvious. A dog that smiles is clearly a very happy dog, but it is not excited or prepared to play. My dachshunds show clear smiles when they first have wildly greeted the homecoming member of the family and are then allowed to sit on the person's knee. This smile is then combined with flattened ears, eyes half-open and fixed on the object of their delight so that the whites show in the corners. The nose points slightly upwards and sighs complete the mood expressions. Another situation when a smile appears in my dachshunds is the extremely friendly and slightly expectant mood aimed at getting someone to go out into the kitchen to cook the food. Thus in this mood, too, the most important factor is a very great satisfaction, especially if the reason for that satisfaction is something which will happen after a while. In this situation, however, the ears are not laid back, but demonstratively held outwards and the forehead is slightly wrinkled. Thus this behaviour shows very clear features of invitation.

Dachshunds

A dog's general posture and manner of carrying out different movements is also an expression of different moods. A dog performs a kind of display activity, which consists of carrying out different movements a trifle more powerfully, more slowly and more definitively than usual. In this way, a dog demonstrates its strength and size to its antagonist. In fighting, this demonstration can become complete immobility, at which a dog holds its muscles at full tension, growls, and, if it is the stronger, stares at its opponent. Stiffening into a position which includes a demonstration of inferiority (head turned aside) also occurs. These ceremonies will be dealt with more fully in connection with the rank order behaviour of dogs.

Both in fully grown dogs, young dogs and older pups, behaviour occurs which quite rightly is called play. Dogs' manner of inviting one another to this behaviour is easily recognized and is part aggressive and part submissive, paraded with great attention. Dogs' games will be dealt with in connection with the development of pups. All that need be said here is that a dog which invites another smaller or weaker dog than itself to play, usually holds its ears even nearer to each other than in a purely aggressive mood, and included in a subordinate dog's play invitation is often the 'frightened' ear position paraded with a quite fearless tail position and no fear in the eyes. But it does happen that a dominant dog when inviting to play emphasises its goodwill to a weaker partner by holding its ears well back.

Yawning has already been mentioned in connection with stretching movements. When a dog has just found out that something pleasant is to happen, it often yawns especially pronouncedly, and quite often lets out a long-drawn-out, usually rising sound. This type of yawning is obviously an anticipatory activity even more common than shaking movements. Naturally, a possible explanation of this might be that yawning could be a kind of preparation for in-

171

creased physical activity, ventilation of the lungs being improved by deep breathing.

When a dog yawns as anticipatory activity to whoever happens to be there, it often opens its mouth over its master's hand. Why it does so is not known, but a possible explanation is that the opening of the mouth is so strongly linked with the sphere of function to which biting belongs that when opening its mouth the dog also carries out an action from the aggressive sphere of function—moving its jaws over an object which is just in front of its nose. A yawning dog never bites, however, at least not in association with yawning.

WHY DOES YOUR DOG MARK HIS TERRITORY?

The marking of territory occurs in canines either with urine or excrement, or with both, and neither wolves nor dogs are exceptions to this rule. They mark their territories with both urine and excrement, but with most emphasis on urine-marking. A dog, however, has well-developed anal-glands which give its excrement an individual scent. A surplus of fluid in these glands sometimes gives a dog briefly a strong smell of anchovies, which infallibly releases an intensive licking of the anal region to remove the scent. Beyond its direct function in territory-marking, urinating is important as a pure display action. A male dog urinates when it meets almost any strange dog, regardless of its sex. The more a male dog's urinating has the character of display action, the higher the dog places its scent-marking. If the urination is only carried out to empty the bladder, after a too long spell indoors for instance, then it may happen that a male dog doesn't cock its leg and urinates without choosing a place. It then stands with its feet apart, its hindlegs well back and hind regions lowered. It is cruelty to animals to walk a dog so seldom that it urinates in this way! In normal cases, a male dog urinates in small, then very small spurts, so if an unexpected display situation arises towards the end of the walk, a dog is still usually able to manage a few drops against a tree or some other suitable, or indeed unsuitable, object.

A male dog's choice of place for urinating is normally decided primarily by the scent world of the territory. A dog which is regularly walked through territory where other male dogs are walked, seeks out as many of the other dogs' scent-markings as possible and tries to cover them. A dog recognises scent-markings which the territory's other dogs have made. The scent-marking alone makes a dog aggressive, if the dog who has left it is an 'enemy'. Dogs which are good friends, on the other hand, do not react much to each other's markings, both in relations between bitches and relations between male dogs. It has sometimes been maintained that dogs are able to establish from the height of the marking whether a male dog who has made the marking is 'dangerous'. Naturally it may be that among equal-sized dogs, the male dog which happens to be the most disposed to display on an average always marks highest. But the marking does not occur with such great precision that it would be easy for other dogs to interpret this scent-mark's mood-content in detail. A dog stems from the wolf, which has nowhere near such a variation in size as the dog, with its many breeds, so it is highly unlikely that a dog could use the height of a marking as a sign of how dangerous the dog that had made it might be. A small dog may regard a large dog as its friend, but has real enemies among the territory's smallest dogs.

Bitches thoroughly inspect male dogs' markings, but do not usually place their urine on a male dog's. It is very difficult to fathom all the different factors which decide where a bitch urinates. She seeks out a place with much greater care than a male dog, if the circumstances are such that she can peacefully devote herself to this innate behaviour. Often the urine is placed close to some male dog's scent-mark. The main impression one gets is that the placing is done so that the male dog can easily find the marking, but that the marking should not be covered by male dogs' incessantly repeated markings on posts, etc., round about. In extreme cold, or in rain, or if the bitch is very much taken up by some preparation, for a hunting trip, for instance, she urinates clearly only so thát it shall quickly be over, without choosing a place at all, even if the need to urinate is not great. In special situations she also learns to urinate to order on an indicated place. On the other hand, male dogs can in such cases seldom overcome the impulse to seek out some suitable place for their scent-markings.

Just as male dogs cover up other male dogs' markings, so does a bitch very often place her urine on or just beside other bitches' urine. If you take two bitches out for a walk, the dominant one usually urinates first, and then the subordinate one places her scent-marking on the dominant one's or just beside it. This is also so among male dogs when they meet each other; the dominant one urinates first and the weaker one afterwards, if the opportunity arises to attempt to cover the marking as far as is possible.

Dogs on a visit in strange homes sometimes have a strong inclination to leave a urine 'visiting-card' behind them. Male dogs on a visit in homes where there is a bitch do this very easily. On later visits, they then go to the 'visiting card' place and investigate to see if it has been covered by another dog. Male dogs are especially inclined to do this if there is a bitch in season in the house. The visit may well strain human relations—so in these circumstances leave your male dog at home if it has no mission to accomplish! Bitches, too, on a visit to a strange house may leave their visiting cards behind them, and this can happen even in houses where there is no dog at all. Punishment is no use against this behaviour. A bitch which has this tendency attempts to make her marking even if it is quite clear that it is forbidden. My first dachshund bitch had a habit of placing a few drops on the hall mat at the end of a visit. But this behaviour is much rarer in bitches than in male dogs.

Some bitches, during the long periods when they are sexually inactive, may show covering behaviour which is approximate to a male dog's. They may even lift one hindleg slightly when they urinate and they sometimes urinate in smaller portions than normally. In all bitches, however, interest in male dogs' markings is greatest just before they come into season or during the first few days. During this time, a bitch normally often has a very clear tendency to divide up her urinating into many portions, in that way marking her presence and her physiological condition for the male dogs in the area.

Dogs usually place their excrement to one side of paths they generally use themselves. What the significance of this is is not known for certain. Carolus Linnaeus says in his short though in many ways extremely acute book on dogs, that a dog preferably places its excrement on some insignificant elevation. In Linnaeus' day hardly any dogs were kept on a lead, so one can presume that the choice of place then was not noticeably influenced by where man might wish his dog to open its bowels. Nowadays, however, it is often hard to trace any tendency to place excrement on elevations, but the fox has a strong inclination to place its excrement on stones, for instance. The anal glands give dogs' excrement an individual scent, which makes the excrement very suitable for territorial marking.

The actual choosing of a place is done with very great care in a dog. But it is difficult to understand which scents are then decisive. The place is chosen just as carefully, even if no other dog has visited the place for perhaps years. I think that when searching for a place for its excrement, a dog, strives to accomplish this on a place where it already finds its own scent. A dog completes its toilet more quickly if you do not let it walk on while it is seeking a place. Then it willingly walks back, largely in its own tracks, turns and goes back and forth across the tracks and then decides on a place.

Dogs of both sexes *scratch with both forelegs and hindlegs* after opening their bowels. A number of dogs also do this after marking with urine in association with pronounced display. This action never results in the excrement or the urine being covered over. It is thought that this behaviour may increase the spread of the scent and thus make the marking more effective. This explanation, however, is a little forced. This behaviour often occurs quite pronouncedly, irrespective of whether other dogs are around, and also in places where no other dogs have been for a very long time, even several years. In general, an alert observer can see from his dog whether after opening its bowels it will scratch with its legs or not. If the dog is activated and content, or if it is in a display mood, then it makes the scratching movements, otherwise it usually does not. In addition, different individuals vary a great deal when it comes to this action's intensity and occurrence. My male Scottie only scratched after urinating if other male dogs were nearby, but sometimes after opening its bowels irrespective of other dogs, though far from after every bowel-opening. My dachshund bitches scratch only if they are excited in some way, but only very seldom after urinating.

WHY DOES YOUR PUPPY ACT LIKE THAT?

A newly born pup, blind, deaf and smelling of carrots, is a completely helpless creature, its movements and reactions purely reflexes. When warm, a pup is quite quiet and immobile. Pups lie close together and keep each other sufficiently warm in this way, but if it is cold, a pup grows uneasy, creeps forward and whines. When something touches the pup's nose, it swings its head from side to side, in this way finding its mother's dugs. When suckling, the pup pushes itself forward with its hindlegs and presses on the milk gland with its forepaws. So a pup has all the essential reflexes typical of all mammals. From the very beginning, sucking is efficient and the tongue and gum together form a sucking funnel. During suckling, the pup holds its tail in the same somewhat lowered position as an adult dog does when eating.

Investigations into electrical activity in the cortex of the brain in pups show that higher brain functions are quite absent during the first ten days. The cortex is equally inactive when the pup is awake, as when it is asleep. Not until the pup is about twenty days old does any marked increase in brain activity appear when it is awake and moving. What a pup does during the first fifteen to twenty days is directed without the involvement of cortex centra. During the first ten days, the pup is a 'reflex animal' entirely, then follows a kind of transition period and at the same time the pup grows rapidly stronger. At birth, a pup's eyes are more or less closed, and they open gradually during the infant period's latter half. At about ten days, the pup begins to react to light, and within a few days to mildly contrasting visual impressions. The pupil reflex, however, is already in existence at birth. At first the cornea is semi-opaquely bluish, and becomes fully transparent within about five weeks.

During the infant and transition period pups normally urinate only when the mother licks their bellies. She does this very intensively and often rolls them over on to their backs so that no urine soils the bed. The mother's movements are swift and powerful and one has the impression that she does not carry out the actions until she senses the smell of urine. Excrement is also consumed very thoroughly. If the mother carries out normal tending actions, the pups' bed is kept very clean during the first two weeks, although the pups never leave it.

When the pup is twenty to twenty-two days old it begins to react to sounds. The first sign of this is when the pup starts at loud bangs or when the mother barks. At about the same time it also shows the first signs that it is going to be able to prick up its ears.

From the time when both sight and hearing have come into function onwards, the pup develops swiftly both physically and mentally. Deviations from a wolf-cub's development are insignificant and different dog breeds show roughly the same speed of development, but at the same time there are individual variations. Many of the differences which characterise the temperament of different breeds also appear before the pup is four weeks old. Wolf-cubs suckle their mothers until the thirty-eighth or thirty-ninth day. Pups can if necessary manage without their mother or bottle-feeding from about four weeks. At this age they can drink, or rather lick up fluid food, and try to chew and swallow very small pieces of more solid food. The sharp milk-teeth of a pup make the mother reluctant to fulfil larger pups' clamouring demands for milk. It may happen, however, that some bitches allow pups to suckle at least occasionally up to seventy days. When the pups are scarcely four weeks old, they often jump up towards the mother, who begins to suckle them sitting, and later also standing.

In a wolf, the female stops cleaning and licking her cubs when they are four weeks old. Before that, the pups have grown sufficiently to move around on their own outside their bed. A two-week-old pup can walk wobblingly and slowly, a four-week-old already wanders about on its own in a room and looks for its mother if she is in the room, if only mostly in the form of erratic straying. At this age, the pups whine with slight indications of barking if they are cold, or if they have lost contact for a few minutes with the mother, or a person, or the other pups. During the whole of the pup's growing period, the mother reacts intensively if she hears the pups whine or cry out. To some extent a bitch can tell what has happened from the type of whine. She gets very worried at cries and becomes aggressive, but at whines she lies down with the pups. Other bitches which have no pups are also strongly attracted by the cries and whining of pups.

As soon as a pup actively starts moving about outside the bed, it also starts moving away from the bed to urinate. But the bitch usually cleans up after her pups even after they begin to move round a room. This reaction of licking the pup and getting it to urinate thus gradually disappears. During the fourth week, the first traces of what becomes play appear and at the same time the first attempts at aggressive barking are heard. These are, however, only very short, small, and apparently spontaneous outbreaks of these moods. It also happens that impressions which later have no play-releasing effects at all make a pup growl and bark or even rush forward, only to ignore completely at once whatever released this behaviour. The first clear tail-wagging may sometimes appear in pups that are only about two weeks old. At five weeks tail-wagging is usually quite common. As soon as the pup can walk, it can also swim, although its paws cannot give it sufficient speed for swimming to be of any practical use for the first five weeks. My younger dachshund bitch jumped into the water and swam out after us when she was only six weeks old. At four to five weeks the pup reacts with swimming motions if you hold it out over water, in a bath, for instance, even if it has never before been in contact with water.

A bitch's behaviour towards her growing pups entails only a few types of actions. Guarding behaviour is not so fixed as during the first days. Grooming behaviour decreases rapidly, suckling gradually becomes more and more spasmodic, and occurs mostly in places other than the bed. A bitch's ability to entice her pups to her is weak. The pups go to the mother because they are hungry or cold or are in a playful mood or because they are afraid, but not because the mother entices them to her. I have never heard any sounds which the pups would react to and which only have the function of enticing the pups to the mother. Instead, the pup begins to react to all the mother's sounds, her steps and the sight of her. When they are six to seven weeks old, pups are already able to move together with the mother, and follow her. At the same time the inclination to play increases greatly.

How to Meet a Strange Dog

J. J. McCoy

FOR THE SAKE of simplicity, we'll divide dogs into friendly and unfriendly dogs. You can usually tell the friendly dog by the way he approaches you. He'll come up to you openly, his nose sniffing for your scent, his tail wagging and held high, and he may give out with a friendly bark. His whole approach is, you might say, aboveboard.

Most of us would say that any dog that bars our path with a growl or show of teeth is an unfriendly one. This may be an injustice to the dog, since he may merely be guarding his master or property. But until you know he is just being protective and is a friendly dog when "off duty," treat him as an unfriendly dog. And consider unfriendly dogs as unsafe.

Recognizing the Unsafe Dog

Proceed with caution if you meet a dog that fits any of the following qualifications:

Standing with body rigid, tail stiff and held at "half-mast."

Barking shrilly or hysterically.

Going into a slink or crouch, with his body and tail rigid, teeth bared.

Coming at you with head lowered, nose held close to the ground.

Standing with a staring expression, ears laid flat.

Attempting to circle and get behind you.

Safety Rules for Meeting a Strange Dog

When a strange dog approaches you, STOP.

Stand still and do not move your hands or body.

Speak softly. Always speak to any dog that has not seen you approach. Make sure the dog knows you are around.

Wait to see what the dog is going to do. Look for signs of an unsafe dog.

If the dog tries to circle and get behind you, *pivot slowly,* so that you are always facing him. Do not move your arms, legs (except to pivot) or make any threatening gesture.

Never turn your back on a dog that is moving toward you. *Do not panic and run.* Admittedly, it takes courage to stand still, but it is your best defense tactic. Wait until the dog stops moving before you move, and then move slowly. *Stop* when he moves again.

Never touch any strange dog. And never strike or kick at any dog.

Do not hand a person a package or shake hands when that person's dog is close by. The dog may misinterpret your move as an attack on his master.

Finally, never accept a dog owner's suggestion that you "make friends" with his dog by touching or feeding the animal. Remember, the dog should make the first overture of friendship, not you. And he will not do this until he smells you.

What to Do If Attacked by a Dog

The safety rules will help you to avoid being bitten in most situations. Study and remember them. Pass them along to your family and neighbors. However, there may come a time when it is too late to apply the safety rules. This will be when you've reached the point of no return. For example, you might stumble over a dog asleep in the bushes, or a dog suddenly leaps at you before you can stop or back away. These are serious situations and the most you can do is to protect yourself from being severely bitten.

If a Large Dog Attacks You

Quickly fold your arms and hold them across your face. Twist your body to the right or left (depending from which direction the dog leaps) as the dog jumps at you. The upper arm or shoulder should strike the dog and knock him off balance. Repeat this maneuver if he attacks again. Call for help. If the dog tries to get behind you, pivot with him. Stand still when he stops attacking and move only when he has retreated to a safe distance. You may get bitten, but your defensive tactics will reduce the severity of the attack and save your life.

If a Small Dog Attacks You

Lift one knee as the dog leaps. The knee will perform the same function as the arm and shoulder block on the big dog. Life your knee *straight* up, not forward and up. If properly executed, the lifted knee will knock the small dog off balance. Repeat if he tries to attack again. Call for help. Pivot with the dog if he tries to circle and get behind you. Stand still when he stops attacking and move only when he's gone off.

Some Common Sense

In any meeting with a strange or hostile dog, remember

that dogs instinctively chase motion. Stand still. Don't turn and run, although your knees are shaking and you want to get away fast. Your entire plan of defense against a possibly dangerous dog is to eliminate motion until the dog wanders off.

There are some situations in which no safety rules or defensive tactics will work. These are usually the result of ignorance of the nature of dogs and the dangers involved. For example, many people do not know that dogs are very protective about their food. Many dogs will snap or attack anyone trying to take away their food. Yet people still try to do this and are severely bitten. Children should be warned not to touch a strange dog's food or try to offer him any. Very often, a child will hold out a piece of candy and when the dog moves to take it, the child pulls back. This is extremely dangerous.

Man Bites Dog Foods and Finds Some Are to His Liking

Raymond A. Sokolov

EVERY NIGHT in this country, 32,600,000 dogs eat dinner. So do about 20,000,000 cats. And more and more of them every year are eating commercial pet food. Americans will spend $1.5-billion for 6 billion pounds of pellets and kibble and dog biscuits—much more than the $390-million spent on baby food—without having the slightest idea of what is in that miserable-looking slop or how it tastes.

Not to worry. Veterinary researchers insist that more is known about dog and cat nutritional requirements than about human needs. The perfect pet diet, they say, is already in supermarkets. And a recent canine-human dog food tasting session indicated that, however awful it looks, most commercial dog food is no worse than bad hamburger.

The only trouble with most dogs' diets is what people feel compelled to put in them. Animal scientists seem to agree that all would be well if normally healthy dogs were simply given unlimited access to nothing but commercial dry food and water and nothing else. Table scraps and "all-meat" canned products are not necessary and, all by themselves, won't make a complete diet.

"A dog need never ever see a chunk of meat in a lifetime," said Bernard Wasserman, D.V.M., a prominent local veterinarian who has raised many dogs on dry food alone.

Dr. Albert Jonas, director of the Animal Care Division of the Yale School of Medicine, concurs. His laboratories maintain anywhere from 100 to 200 dogs at any given time on dry food.

But at home, Dr. Jonas admitted his Cairn terrier often chomps into a plate of leftovers ("It's a pet. You know, the children . . . "). Like many lay dog owners, Dr. Jonas has allowed his dog to taste the poorly balanced but more delicious (for dogs as well as people) delights of natural food.

There is no turning back from this. Once a dog has tried real meat from his master's table or meat from a can of dog food, he will probably never be satisfied with the nutritionally splendid boredom of that coarsely ground meal called kibble again.

And so, though he calls an all-leftover diet "bad news" and even turns up his nose at the very popular (with dogs and masters) all-meat dog foods such as Alpo, Dr. Wasserman recommends a compromise diet of dry food supplemented with meat to promote canine appetite and soothe human guilt.

Mrs. Pat O'Keefe, a spokesman for the industry-sponsored Pet Food Institute in Chicago, said she does not think this enthusiasm for dry food was well-founded. She was quick to point to more palatable semimoist and canned foods that are also complete and balanced foods, according to the guidelines laid down by the National Research Council publication, "Nutrient Requirements of the Dog."

Neither Dr. Jonas nor Dr. Wasserman was dogmatically opposed to nondry foods. But they may be reacting to a powerful trend among dog-owners toward buying unbalanced but very palatable products such as 100 per cent horsemeat.

At any rate, much of the mystery of dog food buying for the layman is in the process of disappearing. Already stringent labeling rules are now compelling manufacturers to indicate in plain language which foods are complete and which are supplementary.

But there will always be the problem of taste and connoisseurship. Both dogs and masters will always play an important role in deciding what Fido gets for dinner.

In order, therefore, to survey at least part of the vast current market in dog foods, one 4-year-old Saluki bitch and one 31-year-old male food editor both sampled 11 kinds of dog food. Neither subject had eaten for 16 hours prior to the experiment; both had been previously corrupted by frequent exposure over long periods of time to a wide variety of meats and meat by-products.

The Saluki, known to her friends as Cleo, point-blank refused to touch dry food—either Gaines Meal or Purina Dog Chow—although she was served it first.

On the other hand, it was a matter of some peril to interrupt her ravenous feasting on the other nine varieties, which ran the gamut from raw ground beef chuck to chicken-flavored Prime to Milk-bone biscuit to Top Choice chopped burger to Alpo horsemeat and meat by-products to liver-flavored Daily All-Breed Dog Food.

Cleo ate all the nondry food (and the biscuit) with equal ardor and then took a brief nap. Meanwhile, the food editor tasted small amounts of the same foods, jotted down his reactions and attempted to rate their taste by assigning a theoretically possible four stars to dog food that could be compared to ordinary human food, and so on down to no stars for muck that would make you retch. The stars had nothing to do with nutrition.

His enthusiasm nowhere approached Cleo's, but he did approve the ground chuck and found the Milk-Bone tasty enough to consume two biscuits, the second spread with butter. The two foods were the only ones to earn as many as three of the four stars.

Just below these in his estimation came chicken-flavored Prime, which actually bore a surprising resemblance to sweet Passover cake.

There was no disagreement with Cleo about the two dry

foods. But Purina Dog Chow was somewhat more palatable than Gaines Meal.

Sometimes an appealing stew odor belied a lack of taste. This was the case with Recipe's beef and egg dinner with vegetables and with Laddie Boy's chunks made with lamb. And both had a texture nigh unto that of cold cream.

The foods with the most unpleasant taste were the Top Choice chopped burger and Alpo horsemeat. One that could not be rated was liver-flavor Daily, an inexpensive homogenized food, brown-green in color and similar in effect to ipecac. It was not rated because it was impossible to force the human subject to taste it. The dog, however, did like it.

☆☆☆ *Ground chuck*. Needs seasoning.

☆☆☆ *Milk-Bone Biscuit*. Could replace Ry-Krisp with a little salt and butter.

☆☆ *Prime, chicken-flavored*. No chicken taste; moist, sweet cubes like yellow cake.

☆☆ *Medallion, beef-flavored chunks*. Texture like cake, a strong meat flavor.

☆ *Purina Dog Chow*. Stale biscuit texture, but subtle meat flavor; not appreciably dry when moistened.

☆ *Recipe, beef and egg dinner*. Excellent odor, like chop suey; mushy texture and no seasoning.

☆ *Laddie Boy, lamb chunks*. Best odor of all moist foods, but no taste, gooey texture.

Top Choice, chopped burger. Tasteless, rubbery, drastically red color, pasty in mouth.

Gaines Meal. Like concretized sawdust.

Alpo Horsemeat Chunks. Awful-looking, smelled like stew, tasted foul.

UNRATED
Daily All-Breed, liver flavor. Strong, mysterious odor, couldn't get it down.

189

Eskimohounds

For the Love of a Man

Jack London

WHEN JOHN THORNTON froze his feet in the previous December, his partners had made him comfortable and left him to get well, going on themselves up the river to get out a raft of saw-logs for Dawson. He was still limping slightly at the time he rescued Buck, but with the continued warm weather even the slight limp left him. And here, lying by the river bank through the long spring days, watching the running water, listening lazily to the songs of birds and the hum of nature, Buck slowly won back his strength.

A rest comes very good after one has travelled three thousand miles, and it must be confessed that Buck waxed lazy as his wounds healed, his muscles swelled out, and the flash came back to cover his bones. For that matter, they were all loafing—Buck, John Thornton, and Skeet and Nig—waiting for the raft to come that was to carry them down to Dawson. Skeet was a little Irish setter who early made friends with Buck, who, in a dying condition, was unable to resent her first advances. She had the doctor trait which some dogs possess, and as a mother cat washes her kittens, so she washed and cleansed Buck's wounds. Regularly, each morning after he had finished his breakfast, she performed her self-appointed task, till he came to look for her ministrations as much as he did for Thornton's. Nig, equally friendly, though less demonstrative, was a huge black dog, half blood-

From *The Call of the Wild*, by Jack London.

hound and half deerhound, with eyes that laughed and a boundless good nature.

To Buck's surprise these dogs manifested no jealousy toward him. They seemed to share the kindliness and largeness of John Thornton. As Buck grew stronger they enticed him into all sorts of ridiculous games, in which Thornton himself could not forbear to join, and in this fashion Buck romped through his convalescence and into a new existence. Love, genuine passionate love, was his for the first time. This he had never experienced at Judge Miller's down in the sun-kissed Santa Clara Valley. With the Judge's sons, hunting and tramping, it had been a working partnership; with the Judge's grandsons, a sort of pompous guardianship; and with the Judge himself, a stately and dignified friendship. But love that was feverish and burning, that was adoration, that was madness, it had taken John Thornton to arouse.

This man had saved his life, which was something; but, further, he was the ideal master. Other men saw to the welfare of their dogs from a sense of duty and business expediency; he saw to the welfare of his as if they were his own children, because he could not help it. And he saw further. He never forgot a kindly greeting or a cheering word, and to sit down for a long talk with them ("gas" he called it) was as much his delight as theirs. He had a way of taking Buck's head roughly between his hands, and resting his own head upon Buck's, of shaking him back and forth, the while calling him ill names that to Buck were love names. Buck knew no greater joy than that rough embrace and the sound of murmured oaths, and at each jerk back and forth it seemed that his heart would be shaken out of his body so great was his ecstasy. And when, released, he sprang to his feet, his mouth laughing, his eyes eloquent, his throat vibrant with unuttered sound, and in that fashion remained without movement, John Thornton would reverently exclaim, "God! you can all but speak!"

191

Buck had a trick of love expression that was akin to hurt. He would often seize Thornton's hand in his mouth and close so fiercely that the flesh bore the impress of his teeth for some time afterward. And as Buck understood the oaths to be love words, so the man understood this feigned bite for a caress.

For the most part, however, Buck's love was expressed in adoration. While he went wild with happiness when Thornton touched him or spoke to him, he did not seek these tokens. Unlike Skeet, who was wont to shove her nose under Thornton's hand and nudge and nudge till petted, or Nig, who would stalk up and rest his great head on Thornton's knee, Buck was content to adore at a distance. He would lie by the hour, eager, alert, at Thornton's feet, looking up into his face, dwelling upon it, studying it, following with keenest interest each fleeting expression, every movement or change of feature. Or, as chance might have it, he would lie farther away, to the side or rear, watching the outlines of the man and the occasional movements of his body. And often, such was the communion in which they lived, the strength of Buck's gaze would draw John Thornton's head around, and he would return the gaze, without speech, his heart shining out of his eyes as Buck's heart shone out.

For a long time after his rescue, Buck did not like Thornton to get out of his sight. From the moment he left the tent to when he entered it again, Buck would follow at his heels. His transient masters since he had come into the Northland had bred in him a fear that no master could be permanent. He was afraid that Thornton would pass out of his life as Perrault and François and the Scotch half-breed had passed out. Even in the night, in his dreams, he was haunted by this fear. At such times he would shake off sleep and creep through the chill to the flap of the test, where he would stand and listen to the sound of his master's breathing.

But in spite of this great love he bore John Thornton,

which seemed to bespeak the soft civilizing influence, the strain of the primitive, which the Northland had aroused in him, remained alive and active. Faithfulness and devotion, things born of fire and roof, were his; yet he retained his wildness and wiliness. He was a thing of the wild, come in from the wild to sit by John Thornton's fire, rather than a dog of the soft Southland stamped with the marks of generations of civilization. Because of his very great love, he could not steal from this man, but from any other man, in any other camp, he did not hesitate an instant; while the cunning with which he stole enabled him to escape detection.

His face and body were scored by the teeth of many dogs, and he fought as fiercely as ever and more shrewdly. Skeet and Nig were too good-natured for quarrelling—besides, they belonged to John Thornton; but the strange dog, no matter what the breed or valor, swiftly acknowledged Buck's supremacy or found himself struggling for life with a terrible antagonist. And Buck was merciless. He had learned well the law of club and fang, and he never forewent an advantage or drew back from a foe he had started on the way to Death. He had lessoned from Spitz, and from the chief fighting dogs of the police and mail, and knew there was no middle course. He must master or be mastered; while to show mercy was a weakness. Mercy did not exist in the primordial life. It was misunderstood for fear, and such misunderstandings made for death. Kill or be killed, eat or be eaten, was the law; and this mandate, down out of the depths of Time, he obeyed.

He was older than the days he had seen and the breaths he had drawn. He linked the past with the present, and the eternity behind him throbbed through him in a mighty rhythm to which he swayed as the tides and seasons swayed. He sat by John Thornton's fire, a broad-breasted dog, white-fanged and long-furred; but behind him were the shades of all manner of dogs, half-wolves and wild wolves, urgent and

193

prompting, tasting the savor of the meat he ate, thirsting for
the water he drank, scenting the wind with him, listening
with him and telling him the sounds made by the wild life
in the forest, dictating his moods, directing his actions, lying
down to sleep with him when he lay down, and dreaming
with him and beyond him and becoming themselves the stuff
of his dreams.

So peremptorily did these shades beckon him that each
day mankind and the claims of mankind slipped farther from
him. Deep in the forest a call was sounding, and as often as
he heard this call, mysteriously thrilling and luring, he felt
compelled to turn his back upon the fire and the beaten earth
around it, and to plunge into the forest, and on and on, he
knew not where or why; nor did he wonder where or why,
the call sounding imperiously, deep in the forest. But as often
as he gained the soft unbroken earth and the green shade,
the love for John Thornton drew him back to the fire again.

Thornton alone held him. The rest of mankind was as
nothing. Chance travellers might praise or pet him; but he
was cold under it all, and from a too demonstrative man he
would get up and walk away. When Thornton's partners,
Hans and Pete, arrived on the long-expected raft, Buck refused to notice them till he learned they were close to Thornton; after that he tolerated them in a passive sort of way,
accepting favors from them as though he favored them by
accepting. They were of the same large type as Thornton,
living close to the earth, thinking simply and seeing clearly;
and ere they swung the raft into the big eddy by the saw-
mill at Dawson, they understood Buck and his ways, and
did not insist upon an intimacy such as obtained with Skeet
and Nig.

For Thornton, however, his love seemed to grow and
grow. He, alone among men, could put a pack upon Buck's
back in the summer travelling. Nothing was too great for
Buck to do, when Thornton commanded. One day (they had

grub-staked themselves from the proceeds of the raft and left Dawson for the head-waters of the Tanana) the men and dogs were sitting on the rest of a cliff which fell away, straight down, to naked bed-rock three hundred feet below. John Thornton was sitting near the edge, Buck at his shoulder. A thoughtless whim seized Thornton, and he drew the attention of Hans and Pete to the experiment he had in mind. "Jump, Buck!" he commanded, sweeping his arm out and over the chasm. The next instant he was grappling with Buck on the extreme edge, while Hans and Pete were dragging them back into safety.

"It's uncanny," Pete said, after it was over and they had caught their speech.

Thornton shook his head. "No, it is splendid, and it is

terrible, too. Do you know, it sometimes makes me afraid."

"I'm not hankering to be the man that lays hands on you while he's around," Pete announced conclusively, nodding his head toward Buck.

"Py jingo!" was Hans' contribution. "Not mineself either."

It was at Circle City, ere the year was out, that Pete's apprehensions were realized. "Black" Burton, a man evil-tempered and malicious, had been picking a quarrel with a tenderfoot at the bar, when Thornton stepped good-naturedly between. Buck, as was his custom, was lying in a corner, head on paws, watching his master's every action. Burton struck out, without warning, straight from the shoulder. Thornton was sent spinning, and saved himself from falling only by clutching the rail of the bar.

Those who were looking on heard what was neither bark nor yelp, but a something which is best described as a roar, and they saw Buck's body rise up in the air as he left the floor for Burton's throat. The man saved his life by instinctively throwing out his arm, but was hurled backward to the floor with Buck on top of him. Buck loosed his teeth from the flesh of the arm and drove in again for the throat. This time the man succeeded only in partly blocking, and his throat was torn open. Then the crowd was upon Buck, and he was driven off; but while a surgeon checked the bleeding, he prowled up and down, growling furiously, attempting to rush in, and being forced back by an array of hostile clubs. A "miners' meeting," called on the spot, decided that the dog had sufficient provocation, and Buck was discharged. But his reputation was made, and from that day his name spread through every camp in Alaska.

Later on, in the fall of the year, he saved John Thornton's life in quite another fashion. The three partners were lining a long and narrow poling-boat down a bad stretch of rapids on the Forty-Mile Creek. Hans and Pete moved along the bank, snubbing with a thin Manila rope from tree to tree, while Thornton remained in the boat, helping its descent by means of a pole, and shouting directions to the shore. Buck, on the bank, worried and anxious, kept abreast of the boat, his eyes never off his master.

At a particularly bad spot, where a ledge of barely submerged rocks jutted out into the river, Hans cast off the rope, and, while Thornton poled the boat out into the stream, ran down the bank with the end in his hand to snub the boat when it had cleared the ledge. This it did, and was flying down-stream in a current as swift as a mill-race, when Hans checked it with the rope and checked too suddenly. The boat flirted over and snubbed in to the bank bottom up, while Thornton, flung sheer out of it, was carried downstream toward the worst part of the rapids, a stretch of wild water in which no swimmer could live.

Buck had sprung in on the instant, and at the end of three hundred yards, amid a mad swirl of water, he overhauled Thornton. When he felt him grasp his tail, Buck headed for the bank, swimming with all his splendid strength. But the progress shoreward was slow; the progress down-stream amazingly rapid. From below came the fatal roaring where the wild current went wilder and was rent in shreds and spray by the rocks which thrust through like the teeth of an enormous comb. The suck of the water as it took the beginning of the last steep pitch was frightful, and Thornton knew that the shore was impossible. He scraped furiously over a rock, bruised across a second, and struck a third with crushing force. He clutched its slippery top with both hands, releasing Buck, and above the roar of the churning water shouted: "Go, Buck! Go!"

Buck could not hold his own, and swept on downstream, struggling desperately, but unable to win back. When he heard Thornton's command repeated, he partly reared out of the water, throwing his head high, as though for a last look, then turned obediently toward the bank. He swam powerfully and was dragged ashore by Pete and Hans at the very point where swimming ceased to be possible and destruction began.

They knew that the time a man could cling to a slippery rock in the face of that driving current was a matter of minutes, and they ran as fast as they could up the bank to a point far above where Thornton was hanging on. They attached the line with which they had been snubbing the boat to Buck's neck and shoulders, being careful that it should neither strangle him nor impede his swimming, and launched him into the stream. He struck out boldly, but not straight enough into the stream. He discovered the mistake too late, when Thornton was abreast of him and a bare half-dozen strokes away while he was being carried helplessly past.

Hans promptly snubbed with the rope, as though Buck were a boat. The rope thus tightening on him in the sweep of the current, he was jerked under the surface, and under the surface he remained till his body struck against the bank and he was hauled out. He was half drowned, and Hans and Pete threw themselves upon him, pounding the breath into him and the water out of him. He staggered to his feet and fell down. The faint sound of Thornton's voice came to them, and though they could not make out the words of it, they knew that he was in his extremity. His master's voice acted on Buck like an electric shock. He sprang to his feet and ran up the bank ahead of the men to the point of his previous departure.

Again the rope was attached and he was launched, and again he struck out, but this time straight into the stream. He had miscalculated once, but he would not be guilty of it a second time. Hans paid out the rope, permitting no slack, while Pete kept it clear of coils. Buck held on till he was on a line straight above Thornton; then he turned, and with the speed of an express train headed down upon him. Thornton saw him coming, and, as Buck struck him like a battering

ram, with the whole force of the current behind him, he
reached up and closed with both arms around the shaggy
neck. Hans snibbed the rope around the tree, and Buck and
Thornton were jerked under the water. Strangling, suffocat-
ing, sometimes one uppermost and sometimes the other,
dragging over the jagged bottom, smashing against rocks
and snags, they veered in to the bank.

Thornton came to, belly downward and being violently
propelled back and forth across a drift log by Hans and Pete.
His first glance was for Buck, over whose limp and apparently lifeless body Nig was setting up a howl, while Skeet
was licking the wet face and closed eyes. Thornton was himself bruised and battered, and he went carefully over Buck's
body, when he had been brought around, finding three
broken ribs.

"That settles it," he announced. "We camp right here."
And camp they did, till Buck's ribs knitted and he was able
to travel.

That winter, at Dawson, Buck performed another exploit,
not so heroic, perhaps, but one that put his name many
notches higher on the totem-pole of Alaskan fame. This
exploit was particularly gratifying to the three men; for
they stood in need of the outfit which it furnished, and were
enabled to make a long-desired trip into the virgin East,
where miners had not yet appeared. It was brought about by
a conversation in the Eldorado Saloon, in which men waxed
boastful of their favorite dogs. Buck, because of his record,
was the target for these men, and Thornton was driven
stoutly to defend him. At the end of half an hour one man
stated that his dog could start a sled with five hundred
pounds and walk off with it; a second bragged six hundred
for his dog; and a third seven hundred.

"Pooh! pooh!" said John Thornton. "Buck can start a
thousand pounds."

"And break it out? and walk off with it for a hundred

yards?" demanded Matthewson, a Bonanza King, he of the seven hundred vaunt.

"And break it out, and walk off with it for a hundred yards," John Thornton said coolly.

"Well," Matthewson said, slowly and deliberately, so that all could hear, "I've got a thousand dollars that says he can't. And there it is." So saying, he slammed a sack of gold dust of the size of a bologna sausage down upon the bar.

Nobody spoke. Thornton's bluff, if bluff it was, had been called. He could feel a flush of warm blood creeping up his face. His tongue had tricked him. He did not know whether Buck could start a thousand pounds. Half a ton! The enormousness of it appalled him. He had great faith in Buck's strength and had often thought him capable of starting such a load; but never, as now, had he faced the possibility of it, the eyes of a dozen men fixed upon him, silent and waiting. Further, he had no thousand dollars; nor had Hans or Pete.

"I've got a sled standing outside now, with twenty fifty-pound sacks of flour on it," Matthewson went on with brutal directness, "so don't let that hinder you."

Thornton did not reply. He did not know what to say. He glanced from face to face in the absent way of a man who has lost the power of thought and is seeking somewhere to find the thing that will start it going again. The face of Jim O'Brien, a Mastodon King and old-time comrade, caught his eyes. It was as a cue to him, seeming to rouse him to do what he would never have dreamed of doing.

"Can you lend me a thousand?" he asked, almost in a whisper.

"Sure," answered O'Brien, thumping down a plethoric sack by the side of Matthewson's. "Though it's little faith I'm having, John, that the beast can do the trick."

The Eldorado emptied its occupants into the street to see the test. The tables were deserted, and the dealers and game-keepers came forth to see the outcome of the wager and to lay odds. Several hundred men, furred and mittened, banked around the sled within easy distance. Matthewson's sled, loaded with a thousand pounds of flour, had been standing for a couple of hours, and in the intense cold (it was sixty below zero) the runners had frozen fast to the hard-packed snow. Men offered odds of two to one that Buck could not budge the sled. A quibble arose concerning the phrase "break out." O'Brien contended it was Thornton's privilege to knock the runners loose, leaving Buck to "break it out" from a dead standstill. Matthewson insisted that the phrase included breaking the runners from the frozen grip of the snow. A majority of the men who had witnessed the making of the bet decided in his favor, whereat the odds went up to three to one against Buck.

There were no takers. Not a man believed him capable of the feat. Thornton had been hurried into the wager, heavy with doubt; and now that he looked at the sled itself, the concrete fact, with the regular team of ten dogs curled up in the snow before it, the more impossible the task appeared. Matthewson waxed jubilant.

"Three to one!" he proclaimed. "I'll lay you another thousand at that figure, Thornton. What d'ye say?"

Thornton's doubt was strong in his face, but his fighting spirit was aroused—the fighting spirit that soars above odds, fails to recognize the impossible, and is deaf to all save the clamor for battle. He called Hans and Pete to him. Their sacks were slim, and with his own the three partners could rake together only two hundred dollars. In the ebb of their fortunes, this sum was their total capital; yet they laid it unhesitatingly against Matthewson's six hundred.

The team of ten dogs was unhitched, and Buck, with his own harness, was put into the sled. He had caught the contagion of the excitement, and he felt that in some way he must do a great thing for John Thornton. Murmurs of admiration at his splendid appearance went up. He was in

201

Eskimohounds

202

perfect condition, without an ounce of superfluous flesh, and the one hundred and fifty pounds that he weighed were so many pounds of grit and virility. His furry coat shone with the sheen of silk. Down the neck and across the shoulders, his mane, in repose as it was, half bristled and seemed to lift with every movement, as though excess of vigor made each particular hair alive and active. The great breast and heavy fore legs were no more than in proportion with the rest of the body, where the muscles showed in tight rolls underneath the skin. Men felt these muscles and proclaimed them hard as iron, and the odds went down to two to one.

"Gad, sir! Gad, sir!" stuttered a member of the latest dynasty, a king of the Skookum Benches. "I offer you eight hundred for him, sir, before the test, sir; eight hundred just as he stands."

Thornton shook his head and stepped to Buck's side.

"You must stand off from him," Matthewson protested. "Free play and plenty of room."

The crowd fell silent; only could be heard the voices of the gamblers vainly offering two to one. Everybody acknowledged Buck a magnificent animal, but twenty fifty-pound sacks of flour bulked too large in their eyes for them to loose their pouch-strings.

Thornton knelt down by Buck's side. He took his head in his two hands and rested cheek on cheek. He did not playfully shake him, as was his wont, or murmur soft love curses; but he whispered in his ear. "As you love me, Buck. As you love me," was what he whispered. Buck whined with suppressed eagerness.

The crowd was watching curiously. The affair was growing mysterious. It seemed like a conjuration. As Thornton got to his feet, Buck seized his mittened hand between his jaws, pressing in with his teeth and releasing slowly, half-reluctantly. It was the answer, in terms, not of speech, but of love. Thornton stepped well back.

"Now, Buck," he said.

Buck tightened the traces, then slacked them for a matter of several inches. It was the way he had learned.

"Gee!" Thornton's voice rang out, sharp in the tense silence.

Buck swung to the right, ending the movement in a plunge that took up the slack and with a sudden jerk arrested his one hundred and fifty pounds. The load quivered, and from under the runners arose a crisp crackling.

"Haw!" Thornton commanded.

Buck duplicated the manœuvre, this time to the left. The crackling turned into a snapping, the sled pivoting and the runners slipping and grating several inches to the side. The sled was broken out. Men were holding their breaths, intensely unconscious of the fact.

"Now, MUSH!"

Thornton's command cracked out like a pistol-shot. Buck threw himself forward, tightening the traces with a jarring lunge. His whole body was gathered compactly together in the tremendous effort, the muscles writhing and knotting like live things under the silky fur. His great chest was low to the ground, his head forward and down, while his feet were flying like mad, the claws scarring the hard-packed snow in parallel grooves. The sled swayed and trembled, half-started forward. One of his feet slipped, and one man groaned aloud. Then the sled lurched ahead in what appeared a rapid succession of jerks, though it never really came to a dead stop again . . . half an inch . . . an inch . . . two inches. . . . The jerks perceptibly diminished; as the sled gained momentum, he caught them up, till it was moving steadily along.

Men gasped and began to breathe again, unaware that for a moment they had ceased to breathe. Thornton was running behind, encouraging Buck with short, cheery words. The distance had been measured off, and as he neared the pile of firewood which marked the end of the hundred yards, a cheer began to grow and grow, which burst into a roar as he passed the firewood and halted at command. Every man was tearing himself loose, even Mathewson. Hats and mittens were flying in the air. Men were shaking hands, it did not matter with whom, and bubbling over in a general incoherent babel.

But Thornton fell on his knees beside Buck. Head was against head, and he was shaking him back and forth. Those who hurried up heard him cursing Buck, and he cursed him long and fervently, and softly and lovingly.

"Gad, sir! Gad, sir!" spluttered the Skookum Bench king. "I'll give you a thousand for him, sir, a thousand, sir—twelve hundred, sir."

Thornton rose to his feet. His eyes were wet. The tears were streaming frankly down his cheeks. "Sir," he said to the Skookum.Bench king, "no, sir. You can go to hell, sir. It's the best I can do for you, sir."

Buck seized Thornton's hand in his teeth. Thornton shook him back and forth. As though animated by a common impulse, the onlookers drew back to a respectful distance; nor were they again indiscreet enough to interrupt.

What Do You Know About Dogs?

Harold H. Hart

AT LEAST ONE out of every four persons in the country has a dog at home. Whether you own a pet or not, you've probably accumulated a number of pet beliefs about dogs. Here's an opportunity to test the validity of your notions.

Probably few people other than breeders, veterinarians, etc., will know the correct answers to all the following 25 questions. You can consider yourself quite canny in regard to things canine if you score correctly on 20.

Answers on page 460

1. A cold and wet nose marks a healthy dog.

    True...... *False*......

2. Most dogs will not, as a rule, exercise themselves; they must be exercised.

    True...... *False*......

3. A dog will prefer the person who feeds him, above all other persons.

    True...... *False*......

4. A block of sulphur placed in a dog's drinking water is a good water purifier.

    True...... *False*......

5. If a dog were allowed to choose his own diet, he would at no time eat a single common vegetable.

    True...... *False*......

6. Puppies can see nothing during the first eight days of their lives.

   True...... *False*......

7. Generally speaking, if a dog's coat is brushed daily, he need hardly ever be bathed.

   True...... *False*......

8. If there's any great amount of painting going on, the dog should be removed from the house, since he can be poisoned by merely breathing paint fumes.

   True...... *False*......

9. A dog's tail is usually docked for reasons of health.

   True...... *False*......

10. Kerosene mixed with milk makes an excellent remedy for fleas.

    True...... *False*......

11. The country dog generally outlives his city cousin.

    True...... *False*......

12. Practically all puppies have worms.

    True...... *False*......

13. The mongrel dog is generally healthier, smarter, and easier to get along with than the pure-bred dog.

    True...... *False*......

14. The weakest sense of most dogs is their eyesight.

    True...... *False*......

15. There is no known sure cure for distemper.

    True...... *False*......

16. It is not uncommon for the female dog to eat her own puppies.

    True...... *False*......

17. Generally, it's a good idea to clip the coat of a dog in the summer time.

    True...... *False*......

18. A dog who wolfs down his food, swallowing it without

chewing, is either underfed or has been underfed in the past.

True. . . . . . *False*. . . . . .

19. There is usually more danger in running away from a vicious dog than in standing still.

True. . . . . . *False*. . . . . .

20. There is no substitute for meat as a prime necessity in a dog's diet.

True. . . . . . *False*. . . . . .

21. A full, black-roofed mouth is the mark of a pure-bred dog.

True. . . . . . *False*. . . . . .

22. The female dog cannot and will not permit herself to be bred at any other time than during her seasonal periods.

True. . . . . . *False*. . . . . .

23. It is not unusual for dogs to get hysterically frightened before or during a thunderstorm.

True. . . . . . *False*. . . . . .

24. A dog's normal temperature runs between 101 and 102 degrees.

True. . . . . . *False*. . . . . .

25. Puppies should not be given small objects, such as nails, bottle caps, etc., to play with, because of their tendency to swallow such objects.

True. . . . . . *False*. . . . . .

A Lesson in Compassion

COUNTLESS STORIES have been told, written, acted and produced on the movie and TV screens regarding blind people around the world and how they are helped, to a large degree, in overcoming their handicap. Most notable and best known is that of Helen Keller's achievements and her help through a sighted companion, Anne Sullivan. Agencies such as the Seeing Eye, American Foundation for the Blind and The Lighthouse for the Blind, among many others, are synonymous with the work they perform for those with this dreaded handicap. However, when it comes to dog's best friend, it is not man, *but dog*, especially when a dog goes blind.

A seven-year-old Spaniel named "Minky" and her friend, a German Shepherd dog called "Simba," are the pets of Mr. Lsme Bidlake of Tunbridge Wells, Kent, England. Recently, their friendship became much closer when Minky's eyesight began to fail. The first to notice was Simba.

Proving the old saying, "A friend in need is a friend indeed," Simba watched Minky closely, making sure she could manage by herself and keeping her from harm. Minky finally became blind and it seemed that her days of running carefree across the fields with her friend were at an end.

Simba, however, had other ideas and was determined that this was not to be the case, if she could help it. Making

Reprinted by permission of *Dog Fancy* Magazine.

209

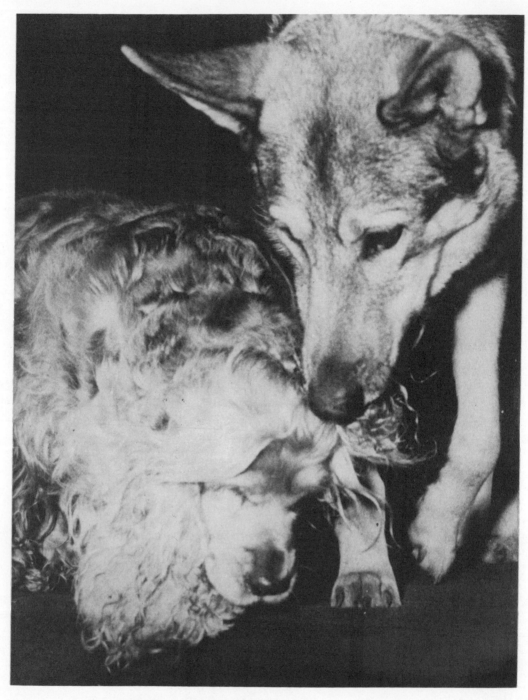

*Simba gently takes hold of Minky's ear in order
to guide the blind Cocker Spaniel*

up her mind to assist her companion, Simba would simply take hold of the Spaniel's ear and lead her around the house, up and down stairs, from one room to another. Eventually, with true canine instinct and trust in her friend, Minky went outdoors—with Simba taking care to cross the roads safely and they resumed their romps across the fields and through the forest.

Just another, if not rare, example of how dogs in their own way and by some finer instinct are truly a "friend" when the need arises to both man and their own.

Cocker

The Care and Training of a Dog

E. B. White

THERE IS A book out called *Dog Training Made Easy* and it was sent to me the other day by the publisher, who rightly guessed that it would catch my eye. I like to read books on dog training. Being the owner of dachshunds, to me a book on dog discipline becomes a volume of inspired humor. Every sentence is a riot. Some day, if I ever get a chance, I shall write a book, or warning, on the character and temperament of the dachshund and why he can't be trained and shouldn't be. I would rather train a striped zebra to balance an Indian club than induce a dachshund to heed my slightest command. For a number of years past I have been agreeably encumbered by a very large and dissolute dachshund named Fred. Of all the dogs whom I have served I've never known one who understood so much of what I say or held it in such deep contempt. When I address Fred I never have to raise either my voice or my hopes. He even disobeys me when I instruct him in something that he wants to do. And when I answer his peremptory scratch at the door and hold the door open for him to walk through, he stops in the middle· and lights a cigarette, just to hold me up.

"Shopping for a puppy presents a number of problems," writes Mr. Wm. Cary Duncan, author of *Dog Training Made Easy*. Well, shopping for a puppy has never presented many problems for me, as most of the puppies and dogs that have entered my life (and there have been scores of them) were not the result of a shopping trip but of an act of God. The first puppy I owned, when I was about nine years old, was not shopped for—it was born to the collie bitch of the postman of my older sister, who sent it to me by express from Washington, D.C., in a little crate containing, in addition to the puppy, a bar of Peters' chocolate and a ripe frankfurter. And the puppy I own now was not shopped for but was won in a raffle. Between these two extremes there have been many puppies, mostly unshopped for. It is not so much that I acquire dogs as it is that dogs acquire me. Maybe they even shop for me, I don't know. If they do I assume they have many problems, because they certainly always arrive with plenty, which they then turn over to me.

The possession of a dog to-day is a different thing from the possession of a dog at the turn of the century, when one's dog was fed on mashed potato and brown gravy and lived in a doghouse with an arched portal. To-day a dog is fed on scraped beef and Vitamin B_1 and lives in bed with you.

An awful lot of nonsense has been written about dogs by persons who don't know them very well, and the attempt to elevate the purebred to a position of national elegance has been, in the main, a success. Dogs used to mate with other dogs rather casually in my day, and the results were discouraging to the American Kennel Club but entirely satisfactory to small boys who liked puppies. In my suburban town, "respectable" people didn't keep she-dogs. One's washer-woman might keep a bitch, or one's lawn cutter, but not one's next-door neighbor.

The prejudice against females made a deep impression on me, and I grew up thinking that there was something indecent and unclean about she-things in general. The word bitch of course was never used in polite families. One day a little mutt followed me home from school, and after much talk I persuaded my parents to let me keep it—at least until the owner turned up or advertised for it. It dwelt among us only one night. Next morning my father took me aside and in a low voice said: "My son, I don't know whether you realize it, but that dog is a female. It'll have to go."

"But why does it have to?" I asked.

"They're a nuisance," he replied, embarrassed. "We'd have all the other dogs in the neighborhood around here all the time."

That sounded like an idyllic arrangement to me, but I could tell from my father's voice that the stray dog was doomed. We turned her out and she went off toward the more liberal section of town. This sort of incident must have been happening to thousands of American youngsters in those days, and we grew up to find that it had been permanently added to the record by Dorothy Parker in her short story "Mr. Durant."

On our block, in the days of my innocence, there were in addition to my collie, a pug dog, a dachshund named Bruno, a fox terrier named Sunny who spent many years studying one croquet ball, a red setter, and a St. Bernard who carried his mistress's handbag, shuffling along in a stately fashion with the drool running out both sides of his jaws. I was scared of this St. Bernard because of his size, and never passed his house without dread. The dachshund was old, surly, and disagreeable, and was endlessly burying bones in the flower border of the DeVries's yard. I should very much doubt if any of those animals ever had its temperature taken rectally, ever was fed raw meat or tomato juice, ever was given distemper inoculations, or ever saw the whites of a veterinary's eyes. They were brought up on chicken bones and gravy and left-over cereal, and were all fine dogs. Most of them never saw the inside of their owner's houses—they knew their place.

The "problem" of caring for a dog has been unnecessarily complicated. Take the matter of housebreaking. In the suburbia of those lovely post-Victorian days of which I write the question of housebreaking a puppy was met with the simple bold courage characteristic of our forefathers. You simply kept the house away from the puppy. This was not only the simplest way, it was the only practical way, just as it is to-day. Our parents were in possession of a vital secret— a secret which has been all but lost to the world: the knowledge that a puppy will live and thrive without ever crossing the threshold of a dwelling house, at least till he's big enough so he doesn't wet the rug.

Although our fathers and mothers very sensibly never permitted a puppy to come into the house, they made up for this indignity by always calling the puppy "Sir." In those days a dog didn't expect anything very elaborate in the way of food or medical care, but he did expect to be addressed civilly.

Mr. Duncan discusses housebreaking at some length and assumes, as do all writers of dog books, that the owner of a puppy has little else to do except own the puppy. It is Mr. Duncan's theory that puppies have a sense of modesty and don't like to be stared at when they are doing something. When you are walking the dog, he says, you must "appear utterly uninterested" as you approach some favorite spot. This, as any city dweller knows, is a big order. Anybody who has ever tried to synchronize a puppy's bowels with a rigid office schedule knows that one's interest in the small phenomena of early morning sometimes reaches fever pitch. A dog owner may feign disinterest, but his masque will not suffice. Nothing is more comical than the look on the face of a person at the upper end of a dog leash, pretending not to know what is going on at the lower.

A really companionable and indispensable dog is an accident of nature. You can't get it by breeding for it, and you can't buy it with money. It just happens along. Out of the vast sea of assorted dogs that I have had dealings with, by far the noblest, the best, and the most important was the first, the one my sister sent me in a crate. He was an old-style collie, beautifully marked, with a blunt nose, and great natural gentleness and intelligence. When I got him he was what I badly needed. I think probably all these other dogs of mine have been just a groping toward that old dream. I've never dared get another collie for fear the comparison would be too uncomfortable. I can still see my first dog in all the moods and situations that memory has filed him away in, but I think of him oftenest as he used to be right after breakfast on the back porch, listlessly eating up a dish of petrified oatmeal rather than hurt my feelings. For six years he met me at the same place after school and convoyed me home—a service he thought up himself. A boy doesn't forget that sort of association. It is a monstrous trick of fate that now, settled in the country and with sheep to take care of, I am obliged to do my shepherding with the grotesque and sometimes underhanded assistance of two dachshunds and a wire-haired fox terrier.

Dachshunds

Comments on Canines

A dog teaches a boy fidelity, perseverance, and to turn around three times before lying down.

Robert Benchley

Nothing is more comical than the look on the face of a person at the upper end of a dog leash, pretending not to know what is going on at the lower.

E. B. White

If a dog's prayers were answered, bones would rain from the sky.

Turkish proverb

If a dog will not come to you after he has looked you in the face, you ought to go home and examine your conscience.
Woodrow Wilson

To HIS DOG, every man is Napoleon, hence the popularity of dogs.

Anon.

Dogs would make much more satisfactory pets if, instead of whimpering when a thunderstorm breaks in the middle of the night, they would tiptoe in and close the windows.

Anon.

The great pleasure of a dog is that you may make a fool of yourself with him and not only will he not scold you, but he will make a fool of himself too.

Samuel Butler

The dog is a Yes-animal, very popular with people who can't afford to keep a Yes-man.

Robertson Davies

In the streets of New York between 7 and 9 in the morning you will see the slow procession of dog and owner proceeding from street to tree to hydrant to trash basket. They are apartment dogs. They are taken out twice a day and, while it is a cliche, it is truly amazing how owner and dog resemble each other. They grow to walk alike, have the same set of head.

John Steinbeck

The more I see of men, the better I like my dog.

Frederick the Great

I know that I have had friends who would never have vexed or betrayed me, if they had walked on all fours.

Horace Walpole

Comments on Canines

How odd that people of sense should find any pleasure in being accompanied by a beast who is always spoiling conversation.

Lord Macaulay

If dogs could talk, perhaps we could find it as hard to get along with them as we do with people.

Karel Capek

You ask of my companions. Hills, sir, and the sundown, and a dog as large as myself that my father bought me. They are better than beings, because they know, but do not tell.

Emily Dickinson

To be sure, the dog is loyal. But why, on that account, should we take him as an example? He is loyal to men, not to other dogs.

Karl Kraus

There is no doubt that every healthy, normal boy (if there is such a thing in these days of Child Study) should own a dog at some time in his life, preferably between the ages of 45 and 50.

Robert Benchley

In the whole history of the world there is but one thing that money cannot buy—to wit, the wag of a dog's tail.

Josh Billings

The dog commends himself to our favor by affording play to our propensity for mastery, and as he is also an item of expense, and commonly serves no industrial purpose, he holds a well-assured place in men's regard as a thing of good repute.

Thorstein Veblen

A dog, I will maintain, is a very tolerable judge of beauty, as appears from the fact that any liberally educated dog does, in a general way, prefer a woman to a man.

Francis Thompson

When a doting person gets down on all fours and plays with his dog's rubber mouse, it only confuses the puppy and gives him a sense of insecurity. He gets the impression that the world is unstable, and wonders whether he is supposed to walk on his hind legs and learn to smoke cigars.

Corey Ford

"Offhand, I'd say you're suffering from an inferiority complex."

Comments on Canines

The probable view of the fox terrier or dachshund which lies upon our hearthrug is that he is one of a pack, the other members of which are the human inhabitants of the house. . . . From the dog's point of view his master is an elongated and abnormally cunning dog.

Louise Robinson

At night my wife and I did fall out about the dog's being put down in the cellar, which I had a mind to have done because of his fouling the house, and I would have my will; and so we went to bed and lay all night in a quarrel.

Samuel Pepys

Newfoundland dogs are good to save children from drowning, but you must have a pond of water handy and a child, or else there will be no profit in boarding a Newfoundland.

Josh Billings

Who loves me will love my dog also.

St. Bernard of Clairvaux

The psychological and moral comfort of a presence at once humble and understanding—this is the greatest benefit that the dog has bestowed upon man.

Percy Bysshe Shelley

If you pick up a starving dog and make him prosperous, he will not bite you. This is the principal difference between a dog and a man.

Mark Twain

He cannot be a gentleman that loveth not a dog.

Proverb

I like a bit of a mongrel myself, whether it's a man or a dog; they're the best for every day.

George Bernard Shaw

Oh, the saddest of sights in a world of sin
Is a little lost pup with his tail tucked in!

Arthur Guiterman

French Spaniels

222

Lo, Hear the Gentle Bloodhound!

James Thurber

IF BLOODHOUNDS COULD write—all that these wonderful dogs can really do, and it's plenty, is trail lost children and old ladies, and track down lawbreakers and lunatics—they would surely be able to set down more demonstrable truths about themselves than Man has discovered in several centuries of speculation and guesswork, lighted only here and there with genuine research. Books about the St. Bernard, storied angel of the mountain snows, and the German shepherd and other breeds famous for their work as army scouts, city cops, and seeing-eye dogs, sprawl all over the library, but the literature of the English bloodhound, an even greater benefactor of mankind, is meager and sketchy. Only one standard book is available, *Bloodhounds and How to Train Them*, by Dr. Leon F. Whitney of New Haven, first published in 1947. . . .

Man doesn't even know for sure how the bloodhound got his name. Dr. Whitney, veterinarian, geneticist, and researcher, and many other authorities, subscribe to the respectable theory that the "blood" is short for "blooded," meaning a patrician, an aristocrat, a thoroughbred. My own theory is that the "blood" got into the name because of the ancient English superstition that giants and other monsters, including the hound with the Gothic head and the miraculously acute nose, could smell the blood of their prey. The giant that roared, "I smell the blood of an Englishman!" had the obscene legendary power, in my opinion, to smell blood through clothing and flesh. Nobody knows to this day the source, nature, or chemistry of the aura that sets off each human being from all others in the sensitive nostrils of every type of scent-hound, but we will get around to that profound mystery further along on this trail. It seems to me, however, that legend and lore are more likely than early breeders and fanciers to have given the bloodhound his name. In any case, it has always had a fearsome sound to the ignorant ear, and one of the gentlest of all species, probably, indeed, the gentlest, has been more maligned through the centuries than any other great Englishman with the exception of King Richard the Third.

Dictionaries, encyclopedias, and other imposing reference volumes approach the bloodhound with an air of gingerly insecurity. Webster's International, touching lightly on the subject, observes, truly enough, that the bloodhound was originally used for hunting game, and adds "especially wounded game." This phrase may have grown out of the imperishable legend of blood scent, but it is also based on the fact that bloodhounds were ever slow and ponderous pursuers, more apt to catch up with a wounded stag or a stricken hart than one of unimpaired fleetness. The staid Encyclopedia Britannica gives our hero scant attention and alludes vaguely to an Italian type of the third century, a scent-hound, without doubt, but not a genuine bloodhound. There were scent-hounds, Dr. Whitney's researches prove, as far back as the age of Xenophon in Greece. Incidentally, the dogs that hunt by sight instead of smell, eminently the swift greyhound, originated, according to Webster, as long ago as 1300 B.C.

The sight-hounds have enjoyed, through the ages, a romantic tradition, for it is this type of canine hunter that has immemorially appeared in fairy tales, leading the mounted king and his three sons in swift pursuit of the fleet deer which turns out in the end to be an enchanted princess. But the scent-hounds of fiction have usually been terrifying creatures, and they have done their share in bringing libel to the fair name of the bloodhound. The terrible phosphorescent Hound of the Baskervilles, which terrorized the moors and bedeviled Sherlock Holmes and Dr. Watson, was a purebred Conan Doyle hound, but if you ask the average person to identify it, he will almost always say that it was a bloodhound, as savage as all the rest of the breed. Let us sniff a little further along the trail of reference volumes, before setting out on the ancient spoor of the bloodhound itself. The austere Oxford English Dictionary doesn't even attempt to account for the bloodhound's name, but with its famous bloodhound ability to track down sources, comes up with these variants of the name, used in England from 1350 through the eighteenth century: "blod-hounde, bloode hownde, blude hunde, blood hunde, bloud-hound, blod-honde." The name was spelled the way it is today by Oliver Goldsmith, Sir Walter Scott, John Keats ("The wakeful bloodhound rose, and shook his hide"), and Lord Byron, who once wrote "To have set the bloodhound mob on their patrician prey." Here the great hunter is no longer a patrician himself, but he hunts only patricians, as the Belvidere foxhounds, drawn years ago by D. T. Carlisle for *The Sportsman*, hunted only silver fox. The O.E.D., by the way, adds "stolen cattle" to the bloodhound's ancient quarry of wounded stags, wanted criminals, and wandering children. It could have brought the record up to date by putting lost dogs in the list, and at least one cat, which disappeared in an Eastern town not long ago and was found by a bloodhound that had sniffed its sandbox and followed the feline trail faithfully but with ponderous embarrassment, I feel sure.

The first scent-hound, or expert private nose, that

stands out clearly in the tapestry of time is the St. Hubert of France, in the eighth century. Some of these castle-and-monastery hounds, after 1066, were imported into England, and from them sprang three English types, the talbot, the staghound, and the bloodhound. Of these, only the bloodhound remains extant. The infamous libel that clings to his name, the legend that he is a dog of awful ferocity began, in this country, before the Civil War, when foxhounds and mongrels were used to hunt down escaped slaves and were trained to fierceness. There may have been a few purebred English bloodhounds in Virginia and other southern states a hundred years ago, but the dogs that pursued Eliza across the ice in *Uncle Tom's Cabin* were crossbred, bar-sinister hounds. It was such beasts that tracked down members of James Andrew's Northern Raiders after they had stolen the famous Iron Horse locomotive at Big Shanty, Georgia, and finally took to the woods of the Southern Confederacy. These inferior pursuers could be bought for five dollars a pair, but the purebred bloodhound then cost fifty dollars a pair. The reputation of the mongrels for ferocity was calculated to deter slaves from making a break for freedom, for if they did and were caught by the dogs, they were sometimes mangled or killed. The trail of a fugitive slave was usually fresh, and any nose-hound could follow it easily. This is also true of the trails of prisoners who escape from prison farms and penitentiaries today, and therefore the so-called "penitentiary hounds" do not need the educated nostrils of a thoroughbred. They are also trained to fierceness, since they must often deal with dangerous criminals.

However, the "blood" may have got into our hero's name, it has helped to stain him almost indelibly as a cruel and feral monster. The miraculous finder of lost boys and girls, the brilliant fingerman of thousands of sheriffs' posses, policemen, and private trailers, could be safely trusted not to harm a babe in arms. Dr. Whitney's bloodhounds once found a three-year-old Connecticut girl who had wandered away from her grandmother in a deep bramble of blackberry bushes. The dogs insisted on searching an almost impenetrable swampy region, but were deterred for hours by *Homo sapiens,* in uniform and out, who was positive the child could not have gone that far. When the human beings finally gave the dogs their own way, they dashed into the thicket. Half an hour later the hunting men came upon the little girl, sitting in a pool of water—she had taken off her playsuit to go for a swim. She was naked as a jay bird, but happy as a lark because of the two lovely wrinkled canine playmates she had just "found." Without the help of the hounds, she could never have been traced.

The Oxford Dictionary, with its characteristic erudition, reports that the bloodhound's Latin name is *canis sanguinarius,* a name the Romans never used. Now *sanguinarius* does not mean blooded, in the sense of purebred; it means of or pertaining to blood, and, figuratively, bloody, bloodthirsty, sanguinary. The gentle, good-tempered, well-balanced bloodhound is actually about as fierce as Little Eva, and you simply cannot discover one provable instance of a bloodhound's attacking a child or an adult, including a cornered criminal. Dr. Whitney says the hounds don't even seem to know that teeth were made for biting. It is true that one bloodhound I heard about became understandably vexed when his master pulled him off a hot trail, and showed his indignation by a thunderous growl. It is unwise to frustrate a bloodhound who has not come to the end of a trail he is following, and how could this one have known that the bandit he was after had been apprehended, according to a telephone call, fifteen miles ahead?

It has been nearly twenty years since I came upon a flagrant piece of calumny about my friend the bloodhound, in a four-volume set of books called *The Outline of Science, a Plain Story Simply Told,* but my indignation is still as strong as it was then. The anonymous "expert" assigned to write about canines in these books had this to say: "There are few dogs which do not inspire affection; many crave it. But there are some which seem to repel us, like the blood-hound. True, Man has made him what he is. Terrible to look at and terrible to encounter, Man has raised him up to hunt down his fellowman." Accompanying the article was a picture of a dignified and melancholy English bloodhound, about as terrible to look at as Abraham Lincoln, about as terrible to encounter as Jimmy Durante. It pleases me no end that this passage, in its careless use of English, accidentally indicts the human being: "Terrible to look at and terrible to encounter, Man. . . ." Even my beloved, though occasionally cockeyed, Lydekker's *New Natural History*, whose grizzly-bear expert pooh-poohs the idea that grizzly bears are dangerous (it seems they got the reputation of aggressiveness by rolling downhill toward the hunter after they were shot dead), knows better than to accuse the bloodhound of viciousness, or, at any rate, has the good sense to avoid the subject of his nature. Lydekker's blood-hound man contents himself with a detailed and fascinating physical description of the breed, which goes like this. "The most striking and characteristic feature of the bloodhound is its magnificent head, which is considerably larger and heavier in the male than in the female. While generally extremely massive, the head is remarkable for its narrowness between the ears, where it rises into a domelike prominence, terminating in a marked protuberance in the occipital region. The skin of the forehead, like that round the eyes, is thrown into a series of transverse puckers." The Lydekker dog man alludes, in conclusion, to what he calls "a foreign strain of the bloodhound, which is lower on its legs than the English breed."

This foreigner could not possibly be the hound I have been putting into drawings for twenty-five years, because I was only six when the first American edition of Lydekker's *History* was brought out. My dog *is* lower on its legs than a standard bloodhound, although I would scarcely put it that way myself. He got his short legs by accident. I drew him for the first time on the cramped pages of a small memo pad in order to plague a busy realtor friend of mine given to writing down names and numbers while you were trying to talk to him in his office. The hound I draw has a fairly accurate pendulous ear, but his dot of an eye is vastly over-simplified, he doesn't have enough transverse puckers, and he is all wrong in the occipital region. He may not be as keen as a genuine bloodhound, but his heart is just as gentle; he does not want to hurt anybody or anything; and he loves serenity and heavy dinners, and wishes they would go on forever, like the brook.

The late Hendrik Van Loon is the only man I have known well who owned a bloodhound, but he took his back to the kennel where he had bought it, after trying in vain to teach it something besides the fine art of pursuit. Whenever Mr. Van Loon called the dog, he once told me sorrowfully, it took its own good time finding him, although he might be no more than fifty feet away. This bloodhound never went directly to his master, but conscientiously followed his rambling trail. "He was not interested in me or where I was," said Mr. Van Loon. "All he cared about was how I had got there." Mr. Van Loon had made the mistake of assuming that a true bloodhound would fit as cozily into a real living room as my hound does in the drawings. It is a mistake to be sedulously avoided. "I would rather house-break a moose," the great man told me with a sigh.

The English bloodhound has never been one of the most popular housedogs in the world, but this is not owing solely to the dark slander that has blackened his reputation. He is a large, enormously evident creature, likely to make a housewife fear for her antiques and draperies, and he is

not given to frolic and parlor games. He is used to the outdoors. If you want a dog to chase a stick or a ball, or jump
through a hoop, don't look at him. "Bloodhounds ain't any
good unless you're lost," one little boy told me scornfully. It
must be admitted that the cumbersome, jowly tracer of lost
persons is somewhat blobbered and slubby (you have to
make up words for unique creatures like the bloodhound
and the bandersnatch). Compared to breeds whose members are numbered in multiple thousands, the bloodhound
is a rare variety, and there may not be more than 1,500
or 2,000 of them in America. An accurate census is discouraged by some bloodhound kennels, many of which are not
listed in the *American Kennel Gazette* for their own protection. Some years ago a Connecticut pack of twenty was
poisoned, presumably by a friend or relative of some law-
breaker that one or two of the hounds had tracked down.
The hounds are bred for two main purposes: to be exhibited
at dog shows around the country, and to be trained for
police work or private investigation. In 1954, at the annual
Eastern Dog Show in Boston, a five-year-old bloodhound
named Fancy Bombardier was selected as the best dog of
all the breeds assembled there, for the first time in the forty-
one-year history of the show. This was a rare distinction for
our friend, for it was one of the infrequent times a bloodhound in this country ever went Best of Show. Not many
judges are as familiar with the show points of a bloodhound
as they are with the simpler ones of other breeds. The won-
drous Englishman, with his voluminous excess wrinkled
flesh, his cathedral head and hooded, pink-hawed eyes,
deep-set in their sockets, might seem to some judges too
grotesque for prizes, but these are his marks of merit and
aristocracy.

Bloodhound-owners themselves disagree about bloodhound types and their comparative appeal, the orthodox
school vehemently contending that the purebred hound is

the favorite of dog-show galleries, the other school contending that the old patricians repel visitors and are frequently regarded as "hideous." Dr. Whitney, geneticist, eugenicist, and mammologist, among other things, is one of those who approve of the so-called American-type bloodhound, whose anatomy is less exaggerated. Its "streamlined" conformation is said to be a virtue in trailing, if not in the show ring. Some authorities believe that this American hound, if judiciously crossbred with the English type, would add a morganatic strain of sturdiness to the Grand Duke's descendants. The English dog, after centuries of pure breeding, does not have a powerful constitution and is subject to certain virus infections and a destructive stomach ailment called "bloat." . . .

The success of the dogs as trailers depends a great deal on what might be called the dogmanship of their trainers and handlers. Dr. Whitney, who has worked his own hounds with, and sometimes parallel to, the police of Connecticut, New York, and Rhode Island, has often found his man on cases in which official police dogs had failed. Expertness with a canine trailer is a knack, like a green thumb in the garden or a light hand in the kitchen, and some cops never get the hang of it. The training of a bloodhound may begin when the dog is a puppy, capable of toddling a trail only a few yards long, but a two-year-old beginner can sometimes be taught most of the tricks in six weeks; with others it may take six months. They may begin by watching a "runner" disappear from an automobile in which he has left his coat behind. The dog sniffs it carefully and sets out on the trail when the runner is lost to view. Youngsters are often used as runners, and they leave a blazed trail so that the handler can tell if the dogs get off the track. The handicap of time is slowly increased, and so is the number of runners. Eventually, five or more of them set out in single file and it is up to the bloodhound to follow the track of only one when the group scatters, the runner whose coat or cap or shoe the dog has examined with the sharpest nose in the world. He must learn to go up to a youngster whose shoe he has sniffed, paying no attention to another youngster, nearer at hand, who may be holding a piece of liver and smelling to high heaven of reward.

Bloodhounds have done more for humanity than all other canines and most men. Examples of their unique achievements would easily fill two sizable volumes, and I can only select a few at random. Let us begin with the late Madge, a bitch owned many years ago by Dr. C. Fosgate of Oxford, New York. Madge was once called upon to trace a lost boy in a town upstate. The trail was twenty-four hours old. Madge climbed fences, wandered through yards, went down alleys, and presently asked to be let into a grocery. Inside, she trotted to a crate of oranges, then crossed over and placed both front paws on the counter. The grocer then remembered that a little boy had come in the morning before, taken an orange from the crate, and paid for it at the counter. The end of the trail was tragic: Madge came to a pier end at a river and plunged unhesitatingly into the water. The boy had been drowned there.

For more than a quarter of a century, up to October 1954, to be exact, the record for following the coldest trail, 105 hours old, was held by a male named Nick Carter, generally considered to have been the greatest bloodhound that

ever lived. He was part of the most fabulous pack of bloodhounds in our history, one belonging to the late Captain
Volney G. Mullikin of Kentucky. An entire volume could be
devoted to the Mullikin hounds alone, and to their colorful
master. From about 1897 until 1932, the Mullikin hounds
brought about the capture of 2,500 criminals and wrong-
doers in Kentucky, Tennessee, West Virginia, and other
states. A hundred of them were wanted for murder, others
for rape, or burglary, or moonshining, or sabotage (Captain
Mullikin got $5,000 from a West Virginia coal company for
tracking down a gang of saboteurs), and almost every other
crime in the calendar, including arson. Nick Carter's old
cold trail of four days and nine hours brought to justice a
man who had burned down a hen house, but he closed a
total of six hundred cases, most of them major, during his
great career, and no other dog has ever come close to that
accomplishment. The Nick Carter case that I have encountered most often in my researches was one in which he
brought to justice a group of mischievous youngsters who,
for many weeks, had been in the habit of throwing rocks
through the windows of houses at night and easily avoiding
capture by the police. Nick was finally allowed to sniff one
of the rocks which had been pulled out from under a bed
with a cane and placed on a newspaper. Nick got the first
of the young miscreants in a matter of hours, and the other
boys were soon rounded up.

Captain Mullikin, whose photograph shows a lean,
rangy, keen-eyed man, was brave to the point of fool-hardi-
ness, and more than once stood off lynching mobs, protecting a prisoner whose guilt had not been proved. He and his
dogs were in the bloody midst of the Howard-Baker and
Hatfield-McCoy mountain feuds, and ran to earth a number
of assassins on both sides of each of these two family wars.
The captain's body showed scores of buckshot scars, most
of them on his legs. The fame of the Kentucky pack and its

valiant leader spread as far as Cuba, and the government of that island hired the Kentuckians, on a six-months' contract, to capture a notorious bandit. The hounds caught up with the man in a matter of days, but the Cuban government insisted on paying the full six-months' fee agreed upon.

When Captain Mullikin died, he left much of his blood-houndiana, including a mountain of newspaper clippings reciting the glorious feats of the captain and his dogs, to Dr. Whitney, to whose book I am indebted for these all too brief Mullikin facts. The doctor was also given the harness that had been worn by Nick Carter on his hundreds of cases. When a hound starts out on a trail, his leash is unfastened from his collar and snapped onto his harness, and this forms the go-ahead signal, along with some such invariable command as "Find him" or "Go get 'em." Incidentally, there are two kinds of working bloodhounds, known as open trailers—the ones that bay as they go—and mute trailers—the dogs that give no sign of their approach—and you can get into a rousing argument about comparative values in this field, too. Hounds of any kind hunting by themselves, alone or in pairs or packs, always bay on the trail of an animal quarry, but the leashed bloodhound can be taught either sound or silence in trailing a human being. No bloodhound ever gives tongue when he gets off the scent, which, it should be pointed out, is by no means the mere width of a footprint, but can sometimes be picked up by the dogs over an area of a hundred feet or more. . . .

A grown poodle poses with the professional grace of an actress, but a bloodhound resembles a Supreme Court Justice gravely submitting to the indignity of being photographed. Bloodhounds may look exactly alike to the layman, but they are not turned out of a rigid mold, like cast-iron lawn dogs. Bombardier's son, Essex Tommy, whose late grandfather had a fine trailing record with the Bethany State Police Barracks in Connecticut, is a wag, a gayheart, with the bloodhound habit of rearing up and planting his big friendly paws on your chest. This affable bloodhound mannerism has been known to frighten a common culprit, who does not realize his big pursuer merely wants to shake hands, like the American colonel that captured Hermann Goering at the end of the war. . . .

As puppies, bloodhounds are almost as playful as other dogs, but they soon become sedentary and are interested in no game except professional hide-and-seek. They are brought up outdoors, to thicken their coats and toughen them, but they have to be introduced to rough weather gradually. Once acclimatized, a sound dog may be able to sleep in the snow without chill or frostbite. They are neither climbers nor jumpers, and often have to be lifted over fences and other obstacles. Worn out after a long trail, they may have to be carried and fall asleep easily in their trainers' arms. Mr. Sheahan [a past president of the American Bloodhound Club] pulled down the lower eyelid of one patient bloodhound, to show its deep-set reddish eye, which seems to be slowly on its way to becoming vestigial. The stronger the nose, the weaker the eye, generally speaking, and bloodhounds sometimes bump into things on a trail. "You shouldn't be able to see a bloodhound's eye at a distance of thirty feet," Mr. Sheahan said. This is a show point in a true bloodhound's favor. Bloodhounds have a short vocabulary, and few changes of inflection or intonation. Fancy Bombardier kept saying "Who?" deepening the volume as his questioning went on. "*Who*?" he demanded. "Ralph!" I barked. "*Who*?" he roared. "Ralph, Ralph Rolf," I said, and so the stolid cross-examination continued. . . .

Most of the trails of lost children and adults fortunately end in the discovery of the persons alive and well. Some police authorities approve of perpetuating the libel that a bloodhound is a savage beast, accustomed to tearing his quarry to bits when he comes upon it. The purpose of this wrong-minded philosophy is to deter evil-doers, and make them think twice before committing a crime and seeking to escape. It is a badly thought-out reversion to the theory and practice of southern slaveowners a hundred years ago and, the point of morality aside, it is calculated to cause the parents of wandering children to fear the use of bloodhounds.

There is a widespread belief, among the uninitiated, that the bloodhound's usefulness in tracking down criminals came to an end with the era of the automobile and the advent of the getaway car. This is only partly true. It is common knowledge that our olfactory genius is interested in automobiles only for what they may contain in the way of human odors, and could not possibly tell a Buick from a Packard, or one tire from another. Everybody also knows that no hound, even if it were able to follow a tire trail, could trace an automobile over hundreds or thousands of miles. But these self-evident facts by no means completely hamstring or footcuff the relentless pursuers. Many fleeing criminals abandon their cars sooner or later, usually alongside a wooded area, thus becoming a setup for bloodhounds. The dogs will get into an abandoned car, inhale a long snoutful of evidence, and set out gleefully and confidently on the track into the woods. They can tell more about the driver or other occupants of an empty motorcar than the police experts in any laboratory. And, remarkable to say, bloodhounds have been known to follow the hot, short trail of a car by picking up, some yards off the road, the scent of the fugitive, if they have previously been able to sniff some personal belonging of his. One hound trotted in a ditch, parallel to the highway, for four miles, apparently detecting with ease the scent of his quarry, car or no car. This particular fugitive had made the mistake of turning into a driveway, four miles from his point of departure, and there was the car, and there was the man, and there, finally, was the hound, ready to shake hands and be congratulated.

Lo, Hear the Gentle Bloodhound!

This is probably the point at which I should dwell, briefly and in all bewilderment, upon just what it is that human scent consists of. All anybody seems to know is that the distinctive human smell the bloodhound selects from all others must have the infinite variability of fingerprints. Only the bloodhound comprehends this scent, which is so sharp to him and so mysterious to us, and all he has ever said about it is "Who?" Some bloodhound men think of the scent as a kind of effluvium, an invisible exudation that clings low to the earth, about the footprints of men. Whatever it may be, a few facts are definitely known about certain of its manifestations. Dampness, especially that of light rain or dew, often serves to bring out the scent, and it is further preserved by "cover," which, in the argot of the trailer, means underbrush, thicket, low-spreading plants and bushes, and the like. Bloodhounds are frequently handicapped by what is technically known as the "fouling" of a trail by sightseers and other careless humans. Wind also adds to the troubles of a hound, along with thoughtless trampling by men, in the case of a hunt over snow. . . .

The 105-hour record for cold trailing, so long held by the celebrated Nick Carter, was shattered in October 1954 by the well-nigh incredible achievement of three bloodhounds belonging to Norman W. Wilson of Los Gatos, California, a former navy pilot who dedicated himself to the training of bloodhounds after a friend of his had become lost in the Everglades and was found by some Florida hounds. On October 9, 1954, a man and his wife and their thirteen-year-old son went deer hunting in a heavily wooded region of Oregon, thick with second-growth fir and a dense undergrowth of ferns and brush. Just a week later their car was found parked near the woods. The sheriff of the county, aided by two hundred men, an airplane and a helicopter, searched the almost impenetrable area without avail for six days. Wilson and his dogs arrived by plane, and the dogs picked up the ancient scent near the car, using as a scent guide a pair of the wife's stockings. Their leashes were fastened to their harness and the command "Find them!" was given at 9:45 on the night of October 22, 322 hours after the family was thought to have left their car. The dogs "cast" in wide circles, trying to pick up the trail, until three o'clock the next morning, and resumed the search shortly after six o'clock. There had been rains on the night of October 10 and later, and the underbrush and ferns were wet. Fifteen hours after they had taken up the search, or 337 hours after the supposed entrance of the family into the woods, one of the hounds led its trailer to the body of the youngster. The parents were subsequently found, also dead. Mr. Wilson and the sheriff and other officials later submitted the story of the remarkable search, in affidavit form, to the Bloodhound Club, and it seems likely that the amazing new record will be officially accepted. The hounds had led the human searchers in a different direction from that which the sheriff and his two hundred men had taken, in their own dogless and fruitless search. Mr. Wilson, it should be said, receives no reward for his services and those of his hounds, beyond the expenses involved in a hunt. He had offered to help after reading about the missing persons in the newspapers. Nobody had thought to send for bloodhounds.

Curiously enough, no bloodhound man seems ever to have experimented to find out how many hours, or days, or perhaps even months or years, the scent of a man or a woman or a child might still cling to something that had once been worn. It is an obvious and interesting area of research, and I am sure the dogs would love it.

One of my favorite bloodhounds is Symbol of Kenwood, a two-year-old from one of the excellent kennels on the West Coast, and a member of the New Mexico Mounted Patrol. Last December Symbol traced two men, wanted for the murder of an Albuquerque policeman, down to the edge of the Rio Grande, promptly hit the water and swam across the river and pointed out his men. They had thought the broad expanse of water would frustrate any pursuing bloodhound. Symbol's feat made up for his impish delinquency of a few days earlier, when he had dug his way out of his kennel and wandered off. He was gone for forty-eight hours, and members of the Mounted Patrol looked for him in vain. He came home, finally, in excellent spirits, having presumably backtracked his own trail. He must have had a twinkle in his grave deep-set eyes as he rejoined the tired and baffled patrol, and I hope he wasn't punished too much. Everybody probably had his own theory as to where Symbol had gone, and everybody was wrong, as Man so often is in dealing with the bloodhound breed. These patient dogs have used, many a time and oft, their one monosyllabic interrogation in dialogue with men, who think their own wisdom is so superior. I wish I could be present some day to hear one of these man-and-dog conversations. Let us say that a parent, or a police officer, or a posse man is speaking first, like this:

"No child could possibly have got through that hedge, according to Sheriff Spencer and Police Chief MacGowan."

"Who?"

And here, gentle reader, let us leave our amazing hero, with the last, and only truly authoritative word.

Garm — a Hostage

Rudyard Kipling

ONE NIGHT, a very long time ago, I drove to an Indian military encampment called Mian Mir to see amateur theatricals. At the back of the Infantry barracks a soldier, his cap over one eye, rushed in front of the horses and shouted that he was a dangerous highway robber. As a matter of fact, he was a friend of mine, so I told him to go home before any one caught him; but he fell under the pole, and I heard voices of a military guard in search of some one.

The driver and I coaxed him into the carriage, drove home swiftly, undressed him and put him to bed, where he waked next morning with a sore headache, very much ashamed. When his uniform was cleaned and dried, and he had been shaved and washed and made neat, I drove him back to barracks with his arm in a fine white sling, and reported that I had accidentally run over him. I did not tell this story to my friend's sergeant, who was a hostile and unbelieving person, but to his lieutenant, who did not know us quite so well.

Three days later my friend came to call, and at his heels slobbered and fawned one of the finest bull-terriers—of the old-fashioned breed, two parts bull and one terrier—that I had ever set eyes on. He was pure white, with a fawn-colored saddle just behind his neck, and a fawn diamond at the root of his thin whippy tail. I had admired him distantly for

From *Actions and Reactions* by Rudyard Kipling.

241

THE DOG LOVER'S READER

more than a year; and Vixen, my own fox-terrier, knew him too, but did not approve.

" 'E's for you," said my friend; but he did not look as though he liked parting with him.

"Nonsense! That dog's worth more than most men, Stanley," I said.

" 'E's that and more. 'Tention!"

The dog rose on his hind legs, and stood upright for a full minute.

"Eyes right!"

He sat on his haunches and turned his head sharp to the right. At a sign he rose and barked twice. Then he shook hands with his right paw and bounded lightly to my shoulder. Here he made himself into a necktie, limp and lifeless, hanging down on either side of my neck. I was told to pick him up and throw him in the air. He fell with a howl and held up one leg.

"Part o' the trick," said his owner. "You're going to die now. Dig yourself your little grave an' shut your little eye."

Still limping, the dog hobbled to the garden edge, dug a hole and lay down in it. When told that he was cured, he jumped out, wagging his tail, and whining for applause. He was put through half a dozen other tricks, such as showing how he would hold a man safe (I was that man, and he sat down before me, his teeth bared, ready to spring), and how he would stop eating at the word of command. I had no more than finished praising him when my friend made a gesture that stopped the dog as though he had been shot, took a piece of blue-ruled canteen-paper from his helmet, handed it to me and ran away, while the dog looked after him and howled. I read:

Sir—I give you the dog because of what you got me out of. He is the best I know, for I made him myself, and he is as good as a man. Please do not give him too much to eat, and please do not give him back to me, for I'm not going to

242

take him, if you will keep him. So please do not try to give him back any more. I have kept his name back, so you can call him anything and he will answer, but please do not give him back. He can kill a man as easy as anything, but please do not give him too much meat. He knows more than a man.

Vixen sympathetically joined her shrill yap to the bull-terrier's despairing cry, and I was annoyed, for I knew that a man who cares for dogs is one thing, but a man who loves one dog is quite another. Dogs are at the best no more than verminous vagrants, self-scratchers, foul feeders, and unclean by the law of Moses and Mohammed; but a dog with whom one lives alone for a least six months in the year; a free thing, tied to you so strictly by love that without you he will not stir or exercise; a patient, temperate, humorous, wise soul, who knows your moods before you know them yourself, is not a dog under any ruling.

I had Vixen, who was all my dog to me; and I felt what my friend must have felt, at tearing out his heart in this style and leaving it in my garden.

However, the dog understood clearly enough that I was his master, and did not follow the soldier. As soon as he drew breath I made much of him, and Vixen, yelling with jealousy, flew at him. Had she been of his own sex, he might have cheered himself with a fight, but he only looked worriedly when she nipped his deep iron sides, laid his heavy head on my knee, and howled anew. I meant to dine at the Club that night, but as darkness drew in, and the dog snuffed through the empty house like a child trying to recover from a fit of sobbing, I felt that I could not leave him to suffer his first evening alone. So we fed at home, Vixen on one side, and the stranger-dog on the other; she watching his every mouthful, and saying explicitly what she thought of his table manners, which were better than hers.

There was one corner of a village near by, which we generally pass with caution, because all the yellow pariah-dogs of the place gathered about it. They were half-wild, starving beasts, and though utter cowards, yet where nine or ten of them get together they will mob and kill and eat an English dog. I kept a whip with a long lash for them. That morning they attacked Vixen, who, perhaps of design, had moved from beyond my horse's shadow.

The bull was ploughing along in the dust, fifty yards behind, rolling in his run, and smiling as bull terriers will. I heard Vixen squeal; half a dozen of the curs closed in on her; a white streak came up behind me; a cloud of dust rose near Vixen, and, when it cleared, I saw one tall pariah with his back broken, and the bull wrenching another to earth. Vixen retreated to the protection of my whip, and the bull padded back smiling more than ever, covered with the blood of his enemies. That decided me to call him "Garm of the Bloody Breast," who was a great person in his time, or "Garm" for short; so, leaning forward, I told him what his temporary name would be. He looked up while I repeated it, and then raced away. I shouted "Garm!" He stopped, raced back, and came up to ask my will.

But the long days in my office tried him sorely. We three would drive off in the morning at half-past eight and come home at six or later. Vixen, knowing the routine of it, went to sleep under my table; but the confinement ate into Garm's soul. He generally sat on the veranda looking out on the Mall; and well I knew what he expected.

Sometimes a company of soldiers would move along on their way to the Fort, and Garm rolled forth to inspect them; or an officer in uniform entered into the office, and it was pitiful to see poor Garm's welcome to the cloth—not the man. He would leap at him, and sniff and bark joyously, then run to the door and back again. One afternoon I heard him bay with a full throat—a thing I had never heard before—and he disappeared. When I drove into my garden at the end of the day a soldier in white uniform scrambled over the wall at the far end, and the Garm that met me was a joyous dog. This happened twice or thrice a week for a month.

I pretended not to notice, but Garm knew and Vixen knew. He would glide homewards from the office about four o'clock, as though he were only going to look at the scenery, and this he did so quietly that but for Vixen I should not have noticed him. The jealous little dog under the table would give a sniff and a snort, just loud enough to call my attention to the flight. Garm might go out forty times in the day and Vixen would never stir, but when he slunk off to see his true master in my garden she told me in her own tongue. That was the one sign she made to prove that Garm did not altogether belong to the family. They were the best of friends at all times, *but*, Vixen explained that I was never to forget Garm did not love me as she loved me.

I never expected it. The dog was not my dog—could never be my dog—and I knew he was as miserable as his master who tramped eight miles a day to see him. So it seemed to me that the sooner the two were reunited the better for all. One afternoon I sent Vixen home alone in the dog-cart

245

(Garm had gone before), and rode over to cantonments to find another friend of mine, who was an Irish soldier and a great friend of the dog's master.

I explained the whole case, and wound up with:

"And now Stanley's in my garden crying over his dog. Why doesn't he take him back? They're both unhappy."

"Unhappy! There's no sense in the little man any more. But 'tis his fit."

"What *is* his fit? He travels fifty miles a week to see the brute, and he pretends not to notice me when he sees me on the road; and I'm as unhappy as he is. Make him take the dog back."

"It's his penance he's set himself. I told him by way of a joke, afther you'd run over him so convenient that night, whin he was drunk—I said if he was a Catholic he'd do penance. Off he went wid that fit in his little head *an'* a dose of fever, an' nothin' would suit but givin' you the dog as a hostage."

"Hostage for what? I don't want hostages from Stanley."

"For his good behaviour. He's keepin' straight now, the way it's no pleasure to associate wid him."

"Has he taken the pledge?"

"If 'twas only that I need not care. Ye can take the pledge for three months on an' off. He sez he'll never see the dog again, an' *so* mark you, he'll keep straight for evermore. Ye know his fits? Well, this is wan of them. How's the dog takin' it?"

"Like a man. He's the best dog in India. Can't you make Stanley take him back?"

"I can do no more than I have done. But ye know his fits. He's just doin' his penance. What will he do when he goes to the Hills? The docthor's put him on the list."

It is the custom in India to send a certain number of invalids from each regiment up to stations in the Himalayas for the hot weather; and though the men ought to enjoy the cool and the comfort, they miss the society of the barracks down below, and do their best to come back or to avoid going. I felt that this move would bring matters to a head, so I left Terrence hopefully, though he called after me:

"He won't take the dog, sorr. You can lay your month's pay on that. Ye know his fits."

I never pretended to understand Private Ortheris, and so I did the next best thing—I left him alone.

That summer the invalids of the regiment to which my friend belonged were ordered off to the Hills early, because the doctors thought marching in the cool of the day would do them good. Their route lay south to a place called Umballa, a hundred and twenty miles or more. Then they would turn east and march up into the Hills to Kasauli or Dugshai or Subathoo. I dined with the officers the night before they left—they were marching at five in the morning. It was midnight when I drove into my garden, and surprised a white figure flying over the wall.

"That man," said my butler, "has been here since nine, making talk to that dog. He is quite mad. I did not tell him to go away because he has been here many times before, and because the dog-boy told me that if I told him to go away, that great dog would immediately slay me. He did not wish to speak to the Protector of the Poor, and he did not ask for anything to eat or drink."

"Kadir Buksh," said I, "that was well done, for the dog would surely have killed thee. But I do not think the white soldier will come any more."

Garm slept ill that night and whimpered in his dreams. Once he sprang up with a clear, ringing bark, and I heard him wag his tail till it waked him and the bark died out in a howl. He had dreamed he was with his master again, and I nearly cried. It was all Stanley's silly fault.

The first halt which the detachment of invalids made was some miles from their barracks, on the Amritsar road,

and ten miles distant from my house. By a mere chance one
of the officers drove back for another good dinner at the
Club (cooking on the line of march is always bad), and
there we met. He was a particular friend of mine, and I knew
that he knew how to love a dog properly. His pet was a big
retriever who was going up to the Hills for his health, and,
though it was still April, the round, brown brute puffed and
panted in the Club veranda as though he would burst.

"It's amazing," said the officer, "what excuses these invalids of mine make to get back to barracks. There's a man
in my company now asked me for leave to go back to cantonments to pay a debt he'd forgotten. I was so taken by the
idea I let him go, and he jingled off in an *ekka* as pleased as
Punch. Ten miles to pay a debt. Wonder what it was really?"

"If you'll drive me home I think I can show you," I said.

So he went over to my house in his dog-cart with the
retriever; and on the way I told him the story of Garm.

"I was wondering where that brute had gone to. He's
the best dog in the regiment," said my friend. "I offered the
little fellow twenty rupees for him a month ago. But he's a
hostage, you say, for Stanley's good conduct. Stanley's one
of the best men I have—when he chooses."

"That's the reason why," I said. "A second-rate man
wouldn't have taken things to heart as he has done."

We drove in quietly at the far end of the garden, and
crept round the house. There was a place close to the wall all
grown about with tamarisk trees, where I knew Garm kept
his bones. Even Vixen was not allowed to sit near it. In the
full Indian moonlight I could see a white uniform bending
over the dog.

"Good-bye, old man," we could not help hearing Stanley's voice. "For 'Eving's sake don't get bit and go mad by
any measley pi-dog. But you can look after yourself, old man.
You don't get drunk an' run about 'ittin' your friends. You

takes your bones an' eats your biscuit, an' kills your enemy like a gentleman. I'm goin' away—don't 'owl—I'm goin' off to Kasauli, where I won't see you no more."

I could hear him holding Garm's nose as the dog drew it up to the stars.

"You'll stay here an' be'ave, an'—an' I'll go away an' try to be'ave, an' I don't know 'ow to leave you. I don't think—"

"I think this is damn silly," said the officer, patting his foolish fubsy old retriever. He called to the private who leaped to his feet, marched forward, and saluted.

"You here?" said the officer, turning away his head.

"Yes, sir, but I'm just goin' back."

"I shall be leaving here at eleven in my cart. You come with me. I can't have sick men running about all over the place. Report yourself at eleven, *here*."

We did not say much when we went indoors, but the officer muttered and pulled his retriever's ears.

He was a disgraceful, overfed doormat of a dog; and when he waddled off to my cookhouse to be fed, I had a brilliant idea.

At eleven o'clock that officer's dog was nowhere to be found, and you never heard such a fuss as his owner made. He called and shouted and grew angry, and hunted through my garden for half an hour.

Then I said:

"He's sure to turn up in the morning. Send a man in by rail, and I'll find the beast and return him."

"Beast?" said the officer. "I value that dog considerably more than I value any man I know. It's all very fine for you to talk—your dog's here."

So she was—under my feet—and, had she been missing, food and wages would have stopped in my house till her return. But some people grow fond of dogs not worth a cut of the whip. My friend had to drive away at last with Stanley in the back seat; and then the dog-boy said to me:

"What kind of animal is Bullen Sahib's dog? Look at him!"

I went to the boy's hut, and the fat old reprobate was lying on a mat carefully chained up. He must have heard his master calling for twenty minutes, but had not even attempted to join him.

"He has no face," said the dog-boy scornfully. "He is a *punniarkooter* [a spaniel]. He never tried to get that cloth off his jaws when his master called. Now Vixen-baba would have jumped through the window, and that Great Dog would have slain me with his muzzled mouth. It is true that there are many kinds of dogs."

Next evening who should turn up but Stanley. The officer had sent him back fourteen miles by rail with a note begging me to return the retriever if I had found him, and, if I had not, to offer huge rewards. The last train to camp left at half-past ten, and Stanley stayed till ten talking to Garm. I argued and entreated, and even threatened to shoot the bull-terrier, but the little man was firm as a rock, though I gave him a good dinner and talked to him most severely. Garm knew as well as I that this was the last time he could hope to see his man, and followed Stanley like a shadow. The retriever said nothing, but licked his lips after his meal and waddled off without so much as saying "Thank you" to the disgusted dog-boy.

So that last meeting was over, and I felt as wretched as Garm, who moaned in his sleep all night. When we went to the office he found a place under the table close to Vixen, and dropped flat till it was time to go home. There was no more running out into the verandas, no slinking away for stolen talks with Stanley. As the weather grew warmer the dogs were forbidden to run beside the cart, but sat at my side on the seat. Vixen with her head under the crook of my left elbow, and Garm hugging the left handrail.

Garm—a Hostage

Once, and only once, did I see Garm at all contented with his surroundings. He had gone for an unauthorized walk with Vixen early one Sunday morning, and a very young and foolish artilleryman (his battery had just moved to that part of the world) tried to steal both. Vixen, of course, knew better than to take food from soldiers, and, besides, she had just finished her breakfast. So she trotted back with a large piece of the mutton that they issue to our troops, laid it down on my veranda, and looked up to see what I thought. I asked her where Garm was, and she ran in front of the house to show me the way.

About a mile up the road we came across our artilleryman sitting very stiffly on the edge of a culvert with a greasy handkerchief on his knees. Garm was in front of him, looking rather pleased. When the man moved leg or hand, Garm bared his teeth in silence. A broken string hung from his collar, and the other half of it lay, all warm, in the artilleryman's still hand. He explained to me, keeping his eye straight in front of him, that he had met this dog (he called him awful names) walking alone, and was going to take him to the Fort to be killed for a masterless pariah.

I said that Garm did not seem to me much of a pariah, but that he had better take him to the Fort if he thought best. He said he did not care to do so. I told him to go to the Fort alone. He said he did not want to go at that hour, but would follow my advice as soon as I had called off the dog. I instructed Garm to take him to the Fort, and Garm marched him solemnly up to the gate, one mile and a half under a hot sun, and I told the quarter-guard what had happened; but the young artilleryman was more angry than was at all necessary when they began to laugh. Several regiments, he was told, had tried to steal Garm in their time.

That month the hot weather shut down in earnest, and the dogs slept in the bathroom on the cool wet bricks where the bath is placed. Every morning, as soon as the man filled my bath, the two jumped in, and every morning the man filled the bath a second time. I said to him that he might as well fill a small tub especially for the dogs. "Nay," said he smiling, "it is not their custom. They would not understand. Besides, the big bath gives them more space."

Living with the dog as I did, I never noticed that he was more than ordinarily upset by the hot weather, till one day at the Club a man said: "That dog of yours will die in a week or two. He's a shadow." Then I dosed Garm with iron and quinine, which he hated; and I felt very anxious. He lost his appetite, and Vixen was allowed to eat his dinner under his eyes. Even that did not make him swallow, and we held a consultation on him, of the best man-doctor in the place; a lady-doctor, who had cured sick wives of kings; and the Deputy Inspector-General of the veterinary service of all India. They pronounced upon his symptoms, and I told them his story, and Garm lay on a sofa licking my hand.

"He's dying of a broken heart," said the lady-doctor suddenly.

" 'Pon my word," said the Deputy Inspector-General, "I believe Mrs. Macrae is perfectly right—as usual."

The best man-doctor in the place wrote a prescription, and the veterinary Deputy Inspector-General went over it afterwards to be sure that the drugs were in the proper dog-proportions; and that was the first time in his life that our doctor ever allowed his prescriptions to be edited. It was a strong tonic, and it put the dear boy on his feet for a week or two; then he lost flesh again. I asked a man I knew to take him up to the Hills with him when he went, and the man came to the door with his kit packed on the top of the carriage. Garm took in the situation at one red glance. The hair rose along his back; he sat down in front of me, and delivered the most awful growl I have ever heard in the jaws of a dog. I shouted to my friend to get away at once, and as soon as the carriage was out of the garden Garm laid his head on my

knee and whined. So I knew his answer, and devoted myself
to getting Stanley's address in the Hills.

My turn to go to the cool came late in August. We were
allowed thirty days' holiday in a year, if one fell sick, and
we took it as we could be spared. My chief and Bob the
Librarian had their holiday first, and when they were gone
I made a calendar, as I always did, and hung it up at the head
of my cot, tearing off one day at a time till they returned.
Vixen had gone up to the Hills with me five times before;
and she appreciated the cold and the damp and the beautiful wood fires there as much as I did.

"Garm," I said, "we are going back to Stanley at Kasauli.
Kasauli—Stanley; Stanley—Kasauli." And I repeated it twenty
times. It was not Kasauli really, but another place. Still I
remembered what Stanley had said in my garden on the last
night, and I dared not change the name. Then Garm began
to tremble; then he barked; and then he leaped up at me,
frisking and wagging his tail.

"Not now," I said, holding up my hand. "When I say
'Go,' we'll go, Garm." I pulled out the little blanket coat and
spiked collar that Vixen always wore up in the Hills to protect her against sudden chills and thieving leopards, and I
let the two smell them and talk it over. What they said of
course I do not know, but it made a new dog of Garm. His
eyes were bright; and he barked joyfully when I spoke to
him. He ate his food, and he killed his rats for the next three
weeks, and when he began to whine I had only to say "Stanley—Kasauli; Kasauli—Stanley," to wake him up. I wish I had
thought of it before.

My chief came back, all brown with living in the open
air, and very angry at finding it so hot in the Plains. That
same afternoon we three and Kadir Buksh began to pack for
our month's holiday, Vixen rolling in and out of the bullock-
trunk twenty times a minute, and Garm grinning all over and
thumping on the floor with his tail. Vixen knew the routine

of travelling as well as she knew my office-work. She went to the station, singing songs, on the front seat of the carriage, while Garm sat with me. She hurried into the railway carriage, saw Kadir Buksh make up my bed for the night, got her drink of water, and curled up with her black-patch eye on the tumult of the platform. Garm followed her (the crowd gave him a lane all to himself) and sat down on the pillows with his eyes blazing, and his tail a haze behind him.

We came to Umballa in the hot misty dawn, four or five men, who had been working hard for eleven months, shouting for our dâks—the two-horse travelling carriages that were to take us up to Kalka at the foot of the Hills. It was all new to Garm. He did not understand carriages where you lay at full length on your bedding, but Vixen knew and hopped into her place at once; Garm following. The Kalka road, before the railway was built, was about forty-seven miles long, and the horses were changed every eight miles. Most of them jibbed, and kicked, and plunged, but they had to go, and they went rather better than usual for Garm's deep bay in their rear.

After Kalka the road wound among the Hills, and we took a curricle with half-broken ponies, which were changed every six miles. Here, again, Vixen led Garm from one carriage to the other; jumped into the back seat and shouted. A cool breath from the snows met us about five miles out of Kalka, and she whined for her coat, wisely fearing a chill on the liver. I had had one made for Garm too, and, as we climbed to the fresh breezes, I put it on, and Garm chewed it uncomprehendingly, but I think he was grateful.

"Hi-yi-yi-yi!" sang Vixen as we shot around the curves; "Toot-toot-toot!" went the driver's bugle at the dangerous places, and "Yow! Yow! Yow! Yow!" bayed Garm. Kadir Buksh sat on the front seat and smiled. Even he was glad to get away from the heat of the Plains that stewed in the haze behind us. Now and then we would meet a man we knew going down to his work again, and he would say: "What's it like below?" and I would shout: "Hotter than cinders. What's it like above?" and he would shout back: "Just perfect!" and away we would go.

Suddenly Kadir Buksh said, over his shoulder: "Here is Solon;" and Garm snored where he lay with his head on my knee. Solon is an unpleasant little cantonment, but it has the advantage of being cool and healthy. It is all bare and windy, and one generally stops at a rest-house near by for something to eat. I got out and took both dogs with me, while Kadir Buksh made tea. A soldier told us we should find Stanley "out there," nodding his head towards a bare, bleak hill.

When we climbed to the top we spied that very Stanley, who had given me all this trouble, sitting on a rock with his face in his hands, and his overcoat hanging loose about him. I never saw anything so lonely and dejected in my life as this one little man crumpled up and thinking, on the great gray hillside.

Here Garm left me.

He departed without a word, and, so far as I could see, without moving his legs. He flew through the air bodily, and I heard the whack of him as he flung himself at Stanley, knocking the little man clean over. They rolled on the ground together, shouting, and yelping, and hugging. I could not see which was dog and which was man, till Stanley got up and whimpered.

He told me that he had been suffering from fever at intervals, and was very weak. He looked all he said, but even while I watched, both man and dog plumped out to their natural sizes, precisely as dried apples swell in water. Garm was on his shoulder, and his breast and feet all at the same time, so that Stanley spoke all through a cloud of Garm— gulping, sobbing, slavering Garm. He did not say anything that I could understand, except that he had fancied he was going to die, but that now he was quite well, and that he was not going to give up Garm any more to anybody under the rank of Beelzebub.

Then he said he felt hungry, and thirsty, and happy.

We went down to tea at the rest-house, where Stanley stuffed himself with sardines and raspberry jam, and beer, and cold mutton and pickles, when Garm wasn't climbing over him; and then Vixen and I went on.

Garm saw how it was at once. He said good-bye to me three times, giving me both paws one after another, and leaping on to my shoulder. He further escorted us, singing Hosannas at the top of his voice, a mile down the road. Then he raced back to his own master.

Vixen never opened her mouth, but when the cold twilight came, and we could see the lights of Simla across the hills, she snuffled with her nose at the breast of my ulster. I unbuttoned it, and tucked her inside. Then she gave a contented little sniff, and fell fast asleep, her head on my breast, till we bundled out of Simla, two of the four happiest people in all the world that night.

Water Spaniel

Dictionary

Dog LOVERS may pride themselves on their familiarity with all things canine, but if someone were to speak of a parti-colored dog slightly down in pastern, or a bird dog with a tendency to babble, blink, and potter, he might leave many dog owners in the dark. Like devotees of any sport or hobby, aficionados of dog shows and hunting have a jargon all their own.

When you consult American Kennel Club standards to see how your dog stacks up against the best of his breed, or attempt to follow dog show and field trial reports, you may find much of the terminology unintelligible. This dictionary provides definitions of some of the most commonly used dog terms.

ABBREVIATIONS

AKC	American Kennel Club
B.	Bitch
B. Am. B.	Best American Bred
BB.	Best of Breed
BoS.	Best of Opposite Sex
BW.	Best of Winners
C. D.	Companion Dog
C. D. X.	Companion Dog Excellent
F. T. Ch.	Field Trial Champion

M. F. H.	Master of Foxhounds
P. H. A.	Professional Handlers' Association
RB.	Reserve Winners Bitch
RM.	Reserve Winners Male
S.	Specials
T. D.	Tracking Dog
U. D.	Utility Dog
U. D. T.	Utility Dog Tracker
WB.	Winners Bitch
WM.	Winners Male

A

account for   A fox-hunting term meaning to kill or run the fox into its den.

action   The manner in which a dog walks, trots, or runs.

albino   An animal lacking normal pigmentation. An albino dog is marked by blue or gray eyes, a flesh-colored nose, and a white coat.

all rounder   A dog show judge considered capable of judging dogs of several different breeds.

almond eye   A slit-shaped eye with the outer corner pointing toward the ear. Typical of the Bullterrier.

Alsatian   The British name for the German Shepherd.

alter   To geld a male or spay a female.

American Bred   A dog born in the United States from a mating which took place in the United States. Also, a dog show class for American Bred dogs only.

anal glands   A pair of small secretory organs found on either side of a dog's anal opening.

angulation   The angle formed by the meeting of the bones, usually the upper and lower thigh bones, or the angle between the shoulder blade and upper arm.

anticipation   The action of a dog that performs an exercise before the command is given by his handler.

apple-headed   Having a domed or rounded skull. Typical of certain toy dogs.

apron   The frill or long hair below the neck on long-coated dogs, such as the Collie.

articulation   The moveable joints between bones and cartilages.

ascob   Abbreviation for "any solid color other than black."

ataxia   An inability to coordinate voluntary muscular movements, symptomatic of a disorder of the nervous system.

B

babbling   Baying by a hound before picking up a scent.

backing   Assuming a pointing stance behind another dog that has pointed a prey.

back-yard breeder   A small-scale dog breeder who raises only one or two litters a year.

back-yard champion   A dog that performs perfectly at home but fails to perform well when in a dog show.

bad mover   A dog whose action is poor, whose gait lacks freedom and smoothness.

bandy-legged   Bow-legged, or having hind legs that are too wide apart at the hocks.

bat ears   Ears that are large, erect, and rounded at the tip and resemble those of a bat.

bawl   The bay of a hound characterized by an unusually prolonged and drawly note.

bay   The prolonged barking or voice of the hound when trailing game or when game has been brought to a stand.

beard   Profuse bushy whiskers; not the whiskers of a Terrier.

beefy   Having overdeveloped hind quarters.

belton   A blended, flecked, or finely mottled combination of any two colors, especially white and another color.

bench   A raised platform used to exhibit dogs at a dog show. The platform is divided into stalls for the individual dogs.

bench show   Specifically, a dog show where a bench is provided for each entrant. The term is commonly used to mean any dog show.

Best of Losers   Slang for the Best of Opposite Sex award given a dog that had been expected to win Best of Breed.

Best of Winners   The dog or bitch that is adjudged best when Winners Dog and Winners Bitch are brought together in competition.

bird dog   A hunting dog trained to locate or to retrieve birds for a hunter.

birdy   A dog skilled at finding birds, or having exceptional scenting powers, is said to be birdy.

biscuit   A pale fawn color.

bitch   The female dog.

bite   The relative position of the upper and lower teeth when the dog's mouth is closed.

blacktongue   A disease characterized by ulcers of the mouth, and severe nervous symptoms; caused by lack of Vitamin B.

blanket   The color of the coat on the back and sides from the withers to the base of the tail.

blinker   A bird dog that points a bird and then leaves it, or avoids making a definite point.

blocky   Having a square or cubelike formation of the head.

bloom   Glossiness of coat.

bobtail   A naturally tailless dog or a dog with a tail docked very short.

bolter   A bird dog given to sudden breaking away from control.

bossy   Having shoulder muscles that are overdeveloped.

brace   A pair of dogs, usually of the same breed.

Brace Class   A special class for two dogs of the same breed belonging to one owner.

bracelets   Tufts of long hair encircling the lower legs of Poodles.

Bred by Exhibitor Class   A class for all dogs (except champions) six months of age or older, that are owned by the person who was the breeder of record.

breeching   Profuse hair on the thighs; tan colored hair on the thighs of Manchester Terriers and Doberman Pinschers.

breed club   An organization composed of breeders, fanciers, and exhibitors of the same breed of dog.

breeder   The person who owned or leased the dog's dam at the time she was mated is said to be the breeder of her pups.

brindled   Having dark streaks or spots on a gray or tawny background, especially with the markings blurred and without sharp margins.

brisket   The part of the body in front of the chest and between the forelegs.

broken color   A self-colored dog with the main color broken by spots or strips of white.

broken-up face   A receding nose, together with a deep stop, wrinkles, and undershot jaw. Characteristic of the Bulldog and Pekingese.

brood bitch   A female kept for breeding purposes.

brush   A tail heavily covered with hair, such as that of the Collie.

burning scent   In hunting, a freshly made trail.

burr   The side of the ear.

butterfly nose   A spotted nose of two colors.

button ears   Ears that fold over in front, as those of the Fox and Irish Terriers.

C

call-name   Name by which a registered dog is known and called at home.

camel back   A back showing too much roach or hump.

Caniche   A Poodle midway in size between the Miniature and Standard varieties.

canine teeth   Conical pointed teeth just behind the incisors.

carp back   An arched back.

cast   Ranging over the field in search of a lost trail.

castration   Removal of a male dog's testicles to prevent mating.

cat foot   A short round compact foot, resembling a cat's foot.

catalogue   A book made available by a dog club that is holding a show, which lists the name, ownership, birthdate, pedigree, registration number, and breeder of each dog entered in the show, along with other pertinent information.

chamois ear   A soft, thin ear.

champion   A dog that has been recorded a champion by the AKC as a result of winning 15 points in dog show competition under AKC regulations. The 15 points must be made up of two wins of 3 or more points, awarded by two different judges, with the remainder to be awarded by at least one other judge.

Charlie Chaplin feet   Feet that turn out.

chaser   A hunting term for a dog that runs after flushed birds. A serious fault.

Check   A Boxer with white markings that are more extensive than considered correct for that breed. Also, a hunting term denoting the point at which a dog temporarily loses a trail.

cheeky   Having full, thick cheeks; common in Bulldogs.

chest   The portion of the dog's body behind the brisket and in front of the abdomen.

China eye   A light walleye.

chiseled   Having a clean-cut, delicately modeled head.

chokeboard nose   Hunting term used to describe a bird dog's exceptionally keen scenting powers.

chops   Jowls or pendulous flesh of the lips and jaw. Typical of the Bloodhound and Bulldog.

chorea   A nervous jerking caused by involuntary contraction of the muscles; frequently follows distemper.

circuit   A series of dog shows arranged on consecutive dates to give exhibitors the opportunity to compete at several shows within a short period of time.

class dog   A dog that has not yet won a championship and is competing to win points for that title.

cloddy   Low, thickset and comparatively heavy in conformation.

close-coupled   Comparatively short from withers to hip bones.

cobby   Having a deep strong short-coupled body and relatively short sturdy legs.

cold-blooded dog   A dog that appears to be purebred but has no pedigree.

color breeding   Mating of dogs to produce puppies of some particular color or combination of colors.

colostrum   A specialized secretion of the mammary glands produced during the first few days after parturition, high in protein and antibodies.

Companion Dog   Title awarded by the AKC to dogs that have made their qualifying scores in Novice A or Novice B classes at obedience trials.

Companion Dog Excellent   Title awarded by the AKC to dogs that have won three Companion Dog degrees and have made three qualifying scores in Open A or Open B classes at recognized obedience trials.

conditioning   General health, coat, and appearance.

corky   Compactly built and lively.

coupling   Portion of the body between the ribs and pelvis; the loin.

coursing   The sport of chasing the hare with greyhounds.

cow hocks   Hocks that turn inward like those of a cow so that the shanks of the hind legs are very close.

crank tail   A short tail curving down and resembling a crank in shape.

crest   The upper arch of the neck; particularly applied to sporting dogs.

cropping   The practice of cutting a dog's ears to make them stand erect and pointed.

crossbred or crossbreed   A mongrel whose sire and dam are both purebred, but of different breeds.

croup   The part of the back above the hind limbs.

cryptorchid   An adult male dog with no visible testicles.

cull   A puppy of substandard quality.

culotte   The feathery hair on the back of the forelegs of the Pomeranian, Pekingese, and Schipperke.

cushion   Fullness or thickness of upper lips.

D

dam   The female parent.

dapples   Mottled markings of different colors, no one predominating.

delegate   A dog club representative to the AKC.

derby   A bird dog not yet thirty months of age. Also, a field trial Beagle during the entire year following its year of birth.

derby stakes   Field trial competition for sporting dogs not yet thirty months of age.

derby year   Year for a bird dog between eighteen months and thirty months of age.

dewclaws   Vestigial digits not reaching to the ground.

dewlap   A pendulous fold of skin under the neck.

dingo   Wild dog of Australia.

dishface   A somewhat concave face.

disqualifying fault   A fault considered so serious to a dog's breed that it disqualifies a dog from bench-show competition.

distemper   A highly contagious virus disease marked by fever and skin eruptions, and often resulting in death.

distemper teeth   Teeth discolored or pitted as a result of distemper or other disease accompanied by high fever during the teething period.

docking   The practice of shortening the dog's tail by cutting.

dome   Evenly rounded upper skull, convex rather than flat.

double coat   An outer coat providing protection from weather, brush, and brambles, together with an undercoat of softer hair for warmth.

down and stay   An obedience test exercise requiring the dog to lie still for a definite length of time.

downfaced   Having a foreface or muzzle that inclines downward toward the tip of the nose.

down in pastern   Weak or faulty pastern set at a pronounced angle from the vertical of the foreleg.

drop ear   Soft, pendulous ear which hangs close to the side of the cheek.

Dropper   A bird dog cross between a Pointer and a Setter.

dual champion   A dog that has won championships in both bench show and field trial competitions.

Dudley nose   A flesh-colored nose.

E

eclampsia   Convulsions common in lactating bitches, caused by shortages of calcium. Often called "nursing fits" or "milk fever."

eczema   A skin ailment resulting in scaly itching flesh and loss of hair.

elbow   The joint at the top of the foreleg next to the body.

elephant action   Lumbering, shuffling action.

enter   Hunting term meaning to start a young Foxhound with the pack for the first time. Also, to enroll a dog in a competition.

even bite   A firm meeting of the front teeth with no overlap.

ewe neck   A thin sheeplike neck having an insufficient, faulty, or concave arch.

Exhibition Only   A special classification for dogs entered at a dog show without the privilege of competing in any classes.

expression   The general appearance of all features of the head, viewed in relation to the features considered ideal for the particular breed.

eye teeth   The upper canine teeth.

F

faddist   A dog judge with strong feelings about the relative importance of some particular point of a dog's anatomy.

faking Changing a dog's appearance by artificial means, such as surgery, drugs, or cosmetics; strictly against AKC rules.

fall The long hair overhanging the face of the Yorkshire and Skye Terrier.

fallow Pale yellow color.

fancier A person interested in and usually active in some aspect of the sport of purebred dogs.

fangs *See* canine teeth.

fawn Light golden tan color.

feathers The long hair fringe on the back of the legs of some breeds, especially the Irish Setter.

feist A small dog of uncertain ancestry; a mongrel.

felted coat A coat which has matted and formed into dense wads of hair.

fiddle head A long, pinched, wolfish face.

fiddle front A front with forelegs out at the elbows, pasterns close, and feet turned out.

field champion A dog that has defeated a specified number of dogs in a series of AKC-licensed field trials.

field dog A dog used for hunting, or in field trials.

field trial A competition for certain Hound or Sporting breeds in which the dogs are judged for their ability and style in hunting.

finish To win a championship.

flag Long-haired tail.

flanks The loin and upper thighs.

flat-sided With ribs insufficiently rounded.

flews Pendulous lateral parts of the upper lip.

flush   To drive game birds from cover, to force them to take wing.

fly ears   Drop ears or semi-prick ears that stand up.

flyer   A young show dog of unusual promise.

foreface   The part of the head in front of the eyes; the muzzle.

foundation stock   The bitches and dogs with which a kennel is begun.

Fowler's solution   An alkaline solution of potassium arsenic used in medicine, and by English breeders to condition a dog's coat.

frill   The hair under the neck and on the chest. Characteristic of the Collie.

frog face   A non-receding nose, as on a Boxer, Bulldog, or Boston Terrier.

full cry   The loud baying of hounds on a fresh trail.

fur-and-feather dog   A sporting dog that can be used both to hunt and point birds, and to trail furred game.

furrow   A slight indentation down the center of the skull extending from the occiput to the stop.

Futurity Stake   A class at dog shows for puppies entered at or before birth and judged when the dogs are one year or eighteen months of age.

G

gait   Manner in which a dog walks, trots, or runs.

gay tail   A tail which is carried straight up; proper on some breeds but faulty in others.

gazehound   Sighthound.

geld   *See* castrate.

giving tongue Hunting expression for baying when on the trail of game.

goose rump A sloping rump with tail set low.

ground color The background color of a parti-colored dog.

group One of the six divisions into which the AKC has classified all breeds for competition. The six groups are: Sporting, Hound, Working, Terrier, Toy, and Nonsporting.

grizzle Bluish-gray color.

gun-barrel front Perfectly straight front legs.

gun dog A dog trained to find live game; includes all the Setter breeds, Pointers, Retrievers, and Spaniels.

H

hackles Hair on neck and back raised in fright or anger.

hackney gait A high-stepping, lively action.

handler Person who takes a dog into the ring at a dog show, or manages a dog in a field trial or obedience test.

hardmouthed Hunting term applied to retrievers that clamp down on and damage game when picking it up.

harefoot A long, narrow, close-toed foot characteristic of some dogs, especially the American Foxhound.

harelip A lip congenitally cleft, usually in the center of the upper lip but sometimes cleft on both sides of the center.

harlequin Mottled or pied in color.

haunches The back portion of the thighs.

haw The red inner eyelid, often prominent in Bloodhounds and St. Bernards.

heel   A command to a dog to walk close to his handler.

hie on   Command to send a dog out to seek game.

hocks   The tarsus or joint of the hind leg between the second thigh and the pastern.

hot spots   Hairless, raw patches in a dog's coat which often appear during hot weather.

hound marked   A coloration composed of white, tan, and black, typical of Fox Terriers.

hucklebone   The top of the hip joints.

hup   Command for bird dogs, meaning "down." Also, command ordering a dog to jump.

I

inbreeding   The mating of two dogs that are closely related; e.g., bitch to litter brother.

interseason periods   The time between the "in-season" periods of a bitch.

in season   Ready for breeding.

J

judge   The arbiter in a dog show, field trial, or obedience test.

K

Kelpie   A breed of Australian sheepherding dog.

kennel   The building in which dogs are housed. Also, all the dogs belonging to one owner.

kennel name   A name registered with the AKC giving the owner of that name the sole right to its use in connection with the exhibition of dogs. Also, a short name by which a dog is known in the kennel or at home.

kink tail   Short, twisted tail, typical of the Bulldog and Boston Terrier.

kiss marks   Tan spots on the cheeks and over the eyes. Typical of several toy breeds.

knuckled over   Faulty in the structure of the front leg, with the legs bent forward at the knee joint.

L

lactation   Period during which a bitch can produce milk.

layback   The receding nose of a Bulldog, Pug, or Toy Spaniel.

leather   The skin of the external ear, typical of certain Hound breeds.

liam   A leash.

licensed show   A show held with AKC permission under AKC rules, which can award points toward a championship.

line   The trail made by game.

line breeding   Mating of related dogs of the same breed to a common ancestor; e.g., a dog to his granddam or a bitch to her grandsire.

linty coat   A cottonlike coat.

listing fee   A dog show fee charged for the entry of a dog not registered with the AKC.

litter   All the puppies born at one time to a bitch.

liver color   A reddish-brown color.

loaded shoulders   Heavy, undesirably thick shoulder blades.

loin   The portion on either side of the body between the last rib and the hind legs.

long down   An obedience test exercise requiring the dog to lie still by himself for a definite period of time.

low-set ears   Ears which are attached to the head more to the side than on top.

lumber   Superfluous flesh or bone.

lurcher   A mongrel dog, used for hunting; especially, a cross between a Greyhound and a Collie.

M

maiden bitch   A bitch which has not yet produced a litter of puppies.

major win   A show win awarding a dog three or more points toward a championship.

mane   Thick profuse hair on the neck.

mask   The dark muzzle of some breeds, commonly seen in Boxers, Afghan Hounds, and Great Danes.

match show   Usually an informal dog show at which no championship points are awarded.

matron   *See* brood bitch.

mats   Thick wads of hair in the coats of long-haired dogs, brought about through lack of combing.

member show   A dog show given by an AKC member club.

merle   Bluish-gray color marbled with black.

middle piece   The portion of the body between the shoulders and hind legs.

milk teeth   A puppy's first set of teeth.

Miscellaneous Class   A class offered at a dog show for breeds for which the show-giving club does not offer a regular classification.

mongrel   Dog whose parents are of a mixed breed.

monorchid   A dog with only one visible testicle.

mops   Profuse hair on the paws.

Moyen   A Poodle midway in size between a Miniature and a Standard.

mute   Silent while trailing game.

mutton shouldered   Having overly heavy shoulders.

muzzle   The portion of the head in front of the eyes; the foreface.

N

nasolabial line   The crease that runs from the side of the nose to the corner of the mouth on the same side.

noseband   A white band encircling the muzzle, as often seen in the St. Bernard.

Novice Class   A dog show class for dogs six months or over that have never won a first prize except in the puppy class, nor one or more points toward a championship.

Novice A   An obedience trial class for dogs that have not won the Companion Dog degree. Dogs entered in this class must be handled by the owner or a member of his immediate family.

Novice B   An obedience trial class for dogs that have not won the Companion Dog degree. Dogs in this class may be handled by either the owner or a professional handler.

O

obedience trials   Tests held under AKC regulations, wherein dogs are scored on their performance in various exercises.

occiput   A prominent knoblike bone at the top of the skull.

oestrum   The period during which a bitch will accept a male dog for mating.

Open A   An obedience trial class for purebred dogs six months or over that have won the Companion Dog degree in obedience Novice Classes. Dogs must be handled by their owner or a member of his immediate family.

Open B   An obedience trial class for purebred dogs six months or over that have won the Companion Dog degree in obedience Novice Classes. Dogs in this class may be handled by either the owner or a professional handler.

Open Class   A breed class at a dog show in which there are no restrictions on entrants. Any purebred dog that is over six months of age may compete.

otter tail   The thick, tapering tail characteristic of the Labrador Retriever.

outbreeding   The mating of two dogs of the same breed that are from entirely different families.

overshot   Term applied to a dog's upper jaw that extends beyond the lower jaw.

P

pack The portion of a Poodle's coat covering the rump and hindquarters, which usually is clipped for show to about an inch in length. Also, a group of hounds that regularly hunt together.

pad The sole of the foot.

paddler A dog that walks or trots with forefeet wide.

paper foot A flat foot with a thin pad.

pariah Mongrel scavenger dog of the Orient.

parti-color A variegated coat color of two or more distinct colors, in clearly defined markings.

pastern The section of the front leg below the knee, or the section of the hind leg below the hock.

pedigree A table of genealogy, recording the names of a dog's ancestors.

penciling Dark lines divided by tan streaks, typical of the feet of Manchester Terriers.

Professional Handlers' Association An organization of licensed handlers who encourage ethical conduct and competence among members.

pigeon-toed Having feet which point inward.

pig-eye An unusually small squinty eye.

pig-jaw *See* overshot.

pile The dense undercoat of double-coated breeds.

piley Containing both soft short hair and long hard hair, as in the Dandie Dinmont Terrier.

pincer bite A bite in which the upper and lower front teeth meet at the edges rather than overlapping.

plucking   Removing dead or superfluous hair from the coat of a dog, especially of a wiry Terrier.

plume   A feathery tail with long profuse hair, as found in the Pomeranian and Pekingese.

pointing breeds   Hunting breeds which "freeze" into position when game is spotted, their noses pointing at the game; e.g., the Brittany Spaniel, the Pointer, all the Setters, the Weimaraner, the Wire-Haired Pointing Griffon.

point rating   The schedule fixed by the AKC for the awarding of points toward a championship. The number of points is based on the number of dogs or bitches competing in that breed.

police dog   Any dog trained to do police work. Also incorrectly used to refer to a German Shepherd.

pompon   The tuft of hair at the end of a Poodle's tail.

posing   Placing a dog in his best standing position.

pottering   Hunting over the same ground again and again; a serious fault.

premium list   A list of the prizes offered at a dog show, obedience test, or field trial, with the names of the judges who are to officiate.

prick ears   Ears which stand erect.

professional handler   A person licensed by the AKC to show dogs for their owners, and to accept a fee for this service.

proven bitch   A bitch that has given birth to one or more litters of puppies.

proven stud   A male dog that has sired one or more litters of puppies.

puppy   A dog under twelve months of age.

puppy match   An informal, unbenched dog show which awards no championship points.

puppy stakes   Bird dog field trial class for dogs under eighteen months of age.

puppy teeth   The first set of teeth in a puppy, which drop out at around four months of age.

Q

qualifying score   An obedience test score of 170 points or better.

R

rabbit dog   Colloquial term for the Beagle.

racy   Slight in build with long legs; e.g., the Greyhound and the Whippet.

rangy   Having an elongated, muscular body.

ram's nose   *See* Roman nose.

rattail   A long, pointed tail with short thin hair, the tip devoid of hair.

reachy   The structure typical of the Greyhound in which the hind feet and forefeet are far apart.

recall   An obedience test exercise in which a dog seated at one end of a ring is called by his handler to the other end of the ring.

registration   The listing of a dog's name, birthdate, ownership, and pedigree with an organization maintaining a recognized stud book, which certifies that dog as a purebred specimen of his breed.

Reserve Winner   A dog placed second in a Winners Class.

ribbed up   Showing desirable roundness in the rib area.

ringtail   A tail that is carried up and around in almost a complete circle.

roachback   A back arched convexly along the spine, as in the Greyhound.

Roman nose   A nose whose bridge forms a slight convex line from the forehead to the nose tip.

rose ear   An ear folding backwards and showing part of its inner surface, as in the Bulldog.

rounding   Cutting or trimming of the ends of the ear, as in the Foxhound.

ruff   Long profuse frill or apron on the neck and shoulders, as in the Chow Chow and Collie.

runner   A dog show employee who calls the competing dogs into the ring and acts as a liaison agent between the judges and the handlers' section.

S

sable   A lacing of black hairs over a brown or lighter ground color.

saddle   A rectangular black marking on the back and upper flanks. Also, the part of the Poodle's body directly behind the ruff.

scapula   The shoulder blade.

scissors bite   A bite in which the upper front teeth slightly overlap the lower front teeth.

scratch pack   A pack made up of hounds belonging to various owners.

screw tail   A short, kinky tail, as in the Bulldog.

scrotum   The pouch containing the testicles of the male.

second thigh   The portion of the hindquarters between the hock and the stifle; the lower thigh, corresponding to the human shin and calf.

seek back   Utility Class exercise requiring that a dog find and retrieve an object that his handler has dropped.

self-colored   Of all one color, or of one color with lighter shadings of the same hue.

self-hunt   A hunt by a bird dog undertaken for the dog's own amusement, without human supervision.

semi-prick ears   Ears carried erect with only the tips leaning forward.

septum   The bone between the nostrils.

set on   The juncture of the tail and the body.

shearing bite   *See* scissors bite.

shelly   Having a shallow, weedy body.

short coupled   Having a short body.

short sit   An obedience test exercise in which dogs are required to sit down by themselves for a definite length of time.

shot-breaking   The action of a bird dog which breaks away or chases birds when a shot is fired.

show lead   A thin, lightweight leash with a collar formed by a loop and sliding clasp at one end.

sickle tail   A tail with an upward curve, semicircular in shape.

sighthound   A dog which pursues game by sight rather than smell.

sire   The male parent.

sled dog   Dogs worked usually in teams to draw sleds, such as the Siberian Husky, Alaskan Malamute, Eskimo, or Samoyed.

Sleuth Hound   Old name for the Bloodhound.

sloping shoulder   A shoulder which is set obliquely or laid back.

snip   A pointed, shallow muzzle.

spay   To remove the reproductive organs of a female by surgery.

Specials Dog   A dog that has won a championship and is competing for Best of Breed or Best of Variety awards.

Specials Only   A dog show class in which only champions may be entered.

specialty club   *See* breed club.

specialty show   A show put on by a breed club offering generous prize money and trophies for the breed which the club sponsors.

spectacles   Shadings or markings over or around the eyes. Typical of the Keeshond.

splashed   Irregularly patched color on white background, or white on color.

splay feet   Feet that are abnormally flattened and spread out.

sport   A dog who does not resemble his parents or littermates.

spread   Width between the forelegs. Usually applied to Bulldogs.

spring of rib   Curvature of the ribs.

squirrel tail   A short tail carried up and curving more or less forward over the back.

standard An AKC-approved description of the ideal of each recognized breed which serves as a pattern by which dogs are judged at shows.

standoff coat A long or heavy double coat that stands away from the body. Typical of the Pomeranian, Collie, and Chow Chow.

steady A bird dog term for remaining in pointing position after the game has been flushed and a shot fired.

stern A tail, usually referring to a hound's tail.

steward An assistant to a judge at a dog show whose tasks include notifying judges when dogs are all in the proper class, awarding the ribbons and trophies, and informing the judges of absentees and other details.

stifle The thigh joint of the hind leg, equivalent to the knee in man.

stilted The stiff, choppy gait of a straight-hocked dog.

stop The depression at the juncture of the foreface and the forehead, pronounced in the Pug, Boxer, and Bulldog.

straight hocks Hocks that do not show a bend when viewed from the side.

straight shoulders Shoulder blades that are straight up and down, rather than sloping.

stud A male dog used for breeding purposes.

stud book A record of breeding particulars for dogs of a recognized breed.

stud fee A fee paid to the owner of a male dog for the services of that dog in mating a bitch.

superintendent A professional arranger and manager of dog shows.

sway-back   Concave curvature of the back, with a sagging between the withers and the base of the tail.

T

tallyho   A hunting cheer meaning "game in sight."

tracking dog   Title awarded to dogs that have passed tracking tests.

Team Class   A special class at a dog show for four dogs of the same breed belonging to one owner. The four dogs need not be of the same sex, but should be similar in size, color, and general type.

tendermouthed   An important attribute of retrievers that carry game without puncturing or ripping its skin.

terrier front   Forequarters characterized by straight pasterns and upright shoulders.

throaty   Having loose skin under the throat.

throwback   A dog that does not resemble his litter-mates. *See* sport.

thumbmarks   Small circular black marks on a lighter background, common on the forelegs of Manchester Terriers.

ticked coat   A coat with small isolated areas of a darker color against a white background.

tied-in elbows   Elbows that are excessively close to a dog's body, preventing freedom of movement.

timber   Bone, especially of the legs.

title   A field trial or bench show championship or degree awarded for three qualifying scores in obedience trials.

tongue   The voice of a hound when on scent.

topknot   A fluffy clump of hair on the top of the head, as in the Dandie Dinmont Terrier.

topline   The profile line running from the top of the skull to the base of the tail.

torn coat   A St. Bernard coat with white markings on a basic dark color.

toy dog   One of a group of dog breeds characterized by very small size.

trace   A dark stripe running down the back of a solid-colored dog, especially the Pug.

tracking dog   A dog that has passed an AKC-licensed tracking test.

training collar   A slip collar with a ring on each end, made so that it will tighten around the dog's neck if he lunges.

trousers   The heavy, shaggy hair on the hind legs of the Afghan Hound.

tucked-up   Characterized by shallow body depth, with a rise in the abdomen just behind the back of the ribs.

tulip ears   Ears which stand erect, curving forward slightly.

typey   Characterized by strict conformance to breed; exhibiting superior bodily conformations.

U

undershot   The lower teeth projecting beyond the upper teeth.

upper arm   The humerus, or the bone of the front leg between the forearm and the shoulder blade.

upsweep   The upturned portion of the lower jaw, common to Bulldogs and Pugs.

Utility Class   An obedience trial class for Companion Dog Excellent degree holders of any breed and of either sex. Dogs in this class may be exhibited by either the owner or a professional handler.

Utility Dog   A title given by the AKC to Companion Dog Excellent degree holders that have attained three qualifying scores in the Utility Class at recognized obedience trials.

Utility Dog Tracker   A dog that has won a Utility Dog degree and passed a tracking test as well; the highest title possible for a dog in obedience test trials.

V

varminty   A keen, piercing, very bright expression desirable in many Terrier breeds.

vent   Tan colored hair under the tail.

W

walleye   An eye with a light gray or bluish white iris.

waster   A weedy dog of sickly constitution.

weaving   The crossing of the front feet when in motion.

weedy   Scrawny, too lightly formed.

well let down   Having desirable angulation of hock and stifle joints.

well sprung   Well-formed, rounded ribs.

wet neck   A neck with a dewlap or other superfluous flesh.

wheaten   A pale yellowish, cream, or fawn color.

whelping   The act of giving birth to puppies.

whiptail   A long, slim tail carried stiffly. Typical of the Pointer.

whiskers   Longer, stiff hairs on the muzzle sides and jaws.

Winners   An award given at dog shows to the best dog (Winners Dog) and the best bitch (Winners Bitch) competing in the Winners Classes.

Winners Class   Class in which the first place winners of Puppy, Novice, Bred by Exhibitor, American Bred, and Open classes, dog and bitch, compete for championship points; awards are given for Winners Dog and Winners Bitch.

wire coat   An outer coat of coarse, crisp hair.

withers   The highest point of the shoulders, where the neck joins the body.

wolf color   An evenly distributed mixture of black, brown, and gray in coat coloration.

wrinkle   The loosely folded skin on the head and sides of the face.

wry mouth   A lower jaw that is tilted to one side and does not line up correctly with the upper jaw.

Y

yard work or yard training   The first steps in the training of a sporting dog, preliminary to the actual schooling on live game.

The Humanitarians

Josephine Z. Rine

THAT PERIOD in European history known as the Dark Ages, which began with the fall of Rome in 456 A.D., lasted until the fourteenth century when the Renaissance brought a revival in culture and the arts in gratifying contrast to the customs and morals of the medieval years. But for animals, the Dark Ages may be said to have continued from the time when animal worship began to wane until well into the nineteenth century, and in some parts of the globe even into the twentieth.

Less than one hundred years ago in Turkey, cruel indifference was still the order of the day. An observer tells of dogs lying in the streets of Constantinople half-starved and covered with horrible sores, hopelessly maimed and nonchalantly kicked by passers-by. In India much the same state of affairs has persisted, with diseased and vermin-infested dogs roaming the streets until they die of starvation. Cruelties of this kind are based upon a religious belief that no animal may be destroyed with impunity, however great its suffering. No such specious excuse underlies certain atrocities committed right here in America, where dog pit-fighting contests have lately been held.

The seventeenth and early eighteenth centuries are a shocking example of man's inhumanity to beasts. In England dogs were used as instruments for the people's amusement in so-called sports. It may appear contradictory to contend that man's relation to the animals was impersonal and at the same time to maintain that man was intensely proud of his dog. Yet in sports this was the case, since the dog's prowess as a fighter reflected glory upon the owner and put cash in his pocket as a result of his wagers. From the my-dog-is-better-than-your-dog attitude came sporting contests in which no thought was given to the dog's comfort or safety but solely to his courage and ability to withstand suffering.

Of all the sports in which the dog served as chief protagonist, bullbaiting was the favorite. As early as 1670 a voice was lifted against it as a "butcherly sport," but nobody heeded. Royalty did not choose to stop this "amusement of the lords and ladies," who took such sadistic delight in the public disembowelment of horses, cocks and dogs; in fact, they were in no position to place the blame for the popularity of bullbaiting upon the populace, for the kings themselves participated in it.

Bullbaiting with dogs in England grew out of bullbaiting with men and horses in Spain, a custom introduced into that country by the Moors. Or it may have been an inspiration consequent upon bull-running, in which Mastiffs were employed to help control unruly bulls in the market place. At any rate, in the twelfth century Mastiffs had been used to guard game and cattle. They were tied up during the day, loosed at night and turned into the forests as a deterrent to thieves. Mastiffs were fierce enough in those days, and each did a little poaching on his own account—he chased the King's deer. So the forest laws decreed that the dogs should be lamed and that "he who is found with a dog that hath not his claws cut off shall be amerced three shillings." The operation consisted of placing the forefeet upon a woodblock and with mallet and chisel chopping off three toes on each foot. This prompted the custom of laming Bulldogs to prove their pluck, the feet of female baiters being mutilated to see whether in

Bulldog of bullbaiting times

spite of the pain they would retain their hold as they attacked the bull. If they did, their puppies brought higher prices.

The Spanish baiter was the smooth-coated Mastiff-like dog referred to as the *metif,* the *alaunt,* the *alano* and the *butcher's dog.* He reached for the bull's ear first and pinned down the sensitive flap until the enraged animal roared. Early bullbaiting in England was done with these large ear-grabbing dogs until it was discovered that the Bulldog could do the job even better. The Bulldog had the advantage of the shorter foreface and undershot jaw to provide the necessary lock grip. Unlike the large ear-grabbers, the Bulldog seized the bull by the nose and, fastening his teeth in its nostrils, braced himself and held on so that the bull could not raise its head without pain. Sooner or later the bull did get its head up and frequently tossed the dog thirty feet in the air. At this point, men stood around with blankets stretched between them to catch the dog as he fell.

Interest in bullbaiting became so great that someone suggested it be organized as a sport. Lord Warren of Stamford was made promoter, and King John himself backed the enterprise. But with the bull running hither and yon, the spectators could not keep up with it. The women especially, with their voluminous petticoats, were often left far behind the finish line. Great ladies of high estate, be it noted, were as bloodthirsty as the men. So Lord Warren leased a big meadow and fastened the bull in the middle of it on a chain fifteen yards long.

So game did the Bulldog prove to be at holding fast, despite the rage of the bull, that the bloodthirsty middle-agers, encouraged by King John, discovered a sport admirably suited to their macabre tastes.

From the start the irritating voice of conscience must have troubled a few, who, with nice political flair, claimed that the flesh of bulls that had been baited was superior. Then, satisfied with a perverted rationalization of cruelty, they levied fines on the butchers who marketed the flesh of unbaited bulls. For a full seven hundred years flourished these so-called sports which involved the use of bears, lions, badgers and rats, all pitted against dogs.

It was not long before the lower classes, which enthusiastically joined royalty in the lust for organized killing, beat the kings at their own gory game by instituting the practice of pitting dog against dog for wagers ranging from $300 to $1000 a side. And, as commoners were more prolific than kings, they enlarged the scope of animal suffering and into it introduced a degree of rowdyism which soon taught the kings and their henchmen that their sowing of the wind resulted in the reaping of a terrific whirlwind.

Periodicals of the 1700s and early 1800s carried advance notices and detailed reports of dog fighting announced as "diversions." Articles of agreement were drawn up to ensure the appearance, on the date specified, of the dogs advertised.

Dogs were weighed in, washed in the same tub of water and then "tasted." Sometimes the official tasters, similar to referees, were responsible for this part of the program, while at other times the owners of the two contestants licked the hair of the opposing dog to guarantee that the coat had not been poisoned in such a manner as to blister the mouth of either dog and thus lessen his chances of holding the death grip. Fights frequently lasted for two hours amid the thunderous applause of the onlookers.

Another kind of contest was rat killing, in which rats were gathered in great numbers and placed in pits from which they could not escape. Wagers having been laid, the dog was let in, whereupon, to the accompaniment of rowdy yells, he nipped and shook his little foes until the count was taken and the record written down. One winner of many such matches is credited with killing sixty rats in less than three minutes.

Badger baiting was another of the diversions regularly practiced. (Hitler, by the way, outlawed badger baiting in Germany because it constituted cruelty to animals.) Huntsmen armed with spades, tongs and other paraphernalia first had to locate a likely earth, that is, an area of loose dirt strewn with moss, grass and rushes drawn out by the badger in the building of his tunnels.

The badger dog must on no account hunt silently; so, upon scenting a likely earth and finding the badger at home, the dog "speaks" until the badger comes out to accost him. Nagging the badger as he charges, backs and dodges, the dogs prevent his escape above-ground, while the huntsmen dig in behind with their spades to cut off his retreat into the earth. When the badger manages to get down again into his tunnels, the dog dives right after him and the fight takes place underground. If the huntsman errs in his digging he collapses the tunnels and smothers both the dog and the badger. With unbelievable strength, the badger cracks bones

291

*The vicious badger clawed the dog unmercifully
when attacked in its underground burrow.*

like peanuts, and if it manages to fasten on the dog, it rips
him to pieces with teeth and claws.

According to Blaine there were artificial badger digs also
wherein a trapped badger was placed in a box built to represent its burrow. The dog was thrown in and the lid held down
as the two proceeded to bite and claw each other unmercifully. At the psychological moment the handler reached in
and pulled the dog out by the tail, with the badger holding
on. The number of times the badger was "drawn" in this manner gave the dog a certain number of points for the match.

Dogs' bred for badger baiting were selected on a basis
of small size and low stature, Dachshunds and Sealyhams
being deemed best equipped for the job. These dogs weigh
approximately twenty pounds. The badger may attain a
weight of thirty pounds and a body length of twenty-five
inches. It has jaws of amazing strength, and claws almost
an inch long. Thus, the odds are all in the badger's favor.

In pursuit of the wild boar, too, innumerable dogs were
killed or painfully injured. As described by Gaston de Foix
in 1406, several dogs cooperated in the attack. The first to
reach the boar established the ear hold, another seized the
tender jowls, while a third bit into the hindquarters, which
were naturally vulnerable because of their thinner hide as

compared with the extra-thick shawl-skin of the animal's neck and forebody. The boar's tusks were his deadly weapon, which the dog avoided if he could by striking always from the side or back. If the dog on the jowl could not keep the victim's head from swaying, the boar lashed out to the side and with his tusks ripped to pieces whatever lay within reach.

The boar's scenting faculty, claimed by some as superior even to that of the dog, was his means of locating the animal foolish enough to travel alone. The wild boar and the peccary seldom hesitated to charge the single dog, but they ran from a pack rather than engage them in battle. The razorback, a somewhat less savage brother of the wild peccary, was at one time raised on open ranges in our South, where it was rounded up, caught and pinned to earth by means of the ear hold by dogs trained for the purpose.

Otter hunting was still another sport in which many a dog lost his life. For all his playful tactics, the otter is a dangerous adversary capable of inflicting terrible wounds and possessed of a nose remarkably strong for butting and striking. Fishermen claimed that the otter spoiled their sport by eating the fish, so they developed the Otterhound to help decimate the robbers.

The otter slept deep in the hollow of some old oak close beside a stream, the entrance to his holt being under water. At the first sign of disturbance the otter slipped into the stream with only a bubble chain to mark its trail. The dogs, which some maintain can detect the scent even in water, leaped in and swam around until the otter rose to the surface for occasional venting. The dogs grabbed it if they could, but the risk was great because the otter, a far more agile swimmer than the dog, sometimes grabbed first, pulled the dog down and held him under until he drowned.

The callousness of many old-time sportsmen was nothing new; an impersonal attitude toward dogs and other beasts had been ingrained in man for centuries. From the days of pagan Rome, man enjoyed pitting animals against each other. Lions battled elephants, and tigers pulled down giraffes as the people applauded. Wild animals were imported from Asia and Africa so that performers might kill them for the amusement of the spectators. In fact, the Circus Maximus was a hideous venue for man's inhumanity to beasts. In 600 B.C. the Circus Maximus was only a race track, but under subsequent rulers it was enlarged and embellished until it could accommodate 285,000 spectators. Here games, fights and chariot races were accompanied by the blare of trumpets and the music of flutes: here winning animals were honored and frequently sacrificed to celebrate successful wars.

Could it be that Dante had an inkling of things to come when in his *Inferno* he foresaw punishment for those who misused others? Less persuasive, indeed much heavier-handed against malefactors than his contemporary, Saint Francis of Assisi, he depicted Mastiffs which resembled wolves in behavior as they pursued and tore to bits the lost souls of hell. Or perchance he took a leaf from the Zend-Avesta, the sacred writings of the seventh-century Parsees, which ruled that "Whosoever shall smite a shepherd's dog, or a house dog, or a vagrant dog, or a hunting dog, his soul when sent to the other world shall fly amid louder howling and fiercer pursuing than does the sheep when the wolf rushes upon it." Truly, a slender but unmistakable thread of mercy was being woven into the fabric of life by the few who were endowed with compassion for the animals.

We must admit, however, that some of the cruelties of medieval years came to be exaggerated in the telling. One writer, for example, mentioned instances where the Bulldog held so tightly to the bull that it tore the dog's head from his body, and "yet the head clung to the bull." Ridiculous as such a statement appears, it did emphasize Bulldog tenacity. And this very tenacity, this steadfastness of purpose which marks the British character, was in later years responsible for the adoption of the Bulldog as Britain's national emblem. Another writer claimed that "the bull tossed the dog right up into the spectators' boxes." That dog, at least, had sense enough to let go. These are but small samples of fiction interlarded with fact as historians have become overenthusiastic in sharpening up their stories of the past. Nevertheless the dog's own "Dark Ages" were a grueling period in his life. Happily, they were not to continue forever.

We have learned that it is darkest before dawn, and that good can come out of evil. These familiar expressions have lived a long time because their truth has been established beyond dispute. If the cruelties meted out to the dog had been of a less serious nature they might have attracted little attention, but they were so sensational that they created a furor of protest among those who had the interest of animals at heart.

As early as 1723 a small but determined body of humanitarians began to protest the cruelties against animals perpetrated in the name of sport. Legislation was introduced into the English Parliament only to be thrown out again and again and its promulgators ridiculed. But the humanitarians finally won, and in 1823 bullbaiting was outlawed.

The eighteenth century was the turning point in the fortunes of the beasts for, beginning in 1723 with the writings of Bernard de Mandeville, it was evident that man was awakening from his long sleep of indifference to animal suffering. John Hildrop, Soame Jenyns, Humphrey Primatt, Jeremy Bentham, John Lawrence, George Nicholson and Thomas Young penned powerful indictments against the barbarisms of the times. Sir Richard Steele in his famous *Tatler* posed the unanswerable question regarding "the excuse for the death of so many innocent cocks, bulls, dogs and bears only to make us sport."

The writings of these men furnished the ammunition

prepared for Lord Erskine, who fought the first round when in 1809 he addressed Parliament on behalf of animals. Twice his proposed measure to punish cruelty failed. Then Richard Martin, member from Galway, Ireland, entered the ring. He proposed another bill to make cruelty to animals punishable by law. Martin had already proved his sympathy for animals. According to Papashvilys' *Dogs and People*, he erected shelters along the avenues of his great estate in Galway where farmers could feed and water their stock at his expense when on the long trek to market. Moreover, he widened the road and beside it provided grazing land for the animals as they passed along.

Like Erskine, Martin was ridiculed for his stand, but on he went in spite of it, and in 1822 he forced into law "An Act To Prevent the Cruel and Improper Treatment of Cattle." This was a milestone of no small significance. It left much to be desired, but it was enacted for the sole purpose of obtaining legislation of any type at all of a humanitarian character. It was 1833 before an amendment could be made to include specific protection for badgers, cocks and dogs. Then in 1835 came a real law, with teeth, providing punishment for "any persons who wantonly and cruelly beat, ill treat, abuse or torture domestic animals."

More important even than these laws was a meeting in 1824 of a group of men, led by Martin, who were deeply interested in animal welfare—a meeting which eventuated in the organization of The Society for the Prevention of Cruelty to Animals, the first permanent organization in the world designed to protect animals. Queen Victoria became its patron, giving her permission to attach the prefix "Royal" to its title.

Henry Bergh, here in America, was another of the world-famous knights who took up the battle on behalf of animals. Born in New York in 1823, he and Martin had much in common. Both were peppery individuals of wealth and leisure. Where Martin turned to politics, Bergh became a patron of the theater and the arts for the first half of his life. He traveled extensively abroad after 1863, when he was appointed secretary to the United States Legation in Russia. He saw, to his dismay, the cruelties perpetrated upon horses, cattle and other animals, and upon returning to this country he determined to devote himself to the alleviation of animal suffering.

That a man like Henry Bergh should lend himself to anything so trivial the people could not understand, and what they did not understand they ridiculed. And the press joined in the fun with many a biting cartoon. Even the staid old *Forest and Stream* published letters satirizing the novel idea of showing kindness to animals.

Despite the opposition of legislators at Albany, Bergh in 1866 obtained the charter for The American Society for the Prevention of Cruelty to Animals. He served as the society's first president, and continued as such until his death in 1888. Two rooms were rented in New York City as offices, and from that focal point he patrolled the streets as agent, as prosecutor and as chief executive, and he paid most of the bills!

From this modest beginning came a movement which has swept across the length and breadth of the land, with humane societies formed and functioning throughout the United States and Canada, in Hawaii, Panama and the Philippines. The work of each was necessarily local in character. Early in the history of the movement a need was seen for an organization of wider scope and authority. So in 1877 the American Humane Association was formed at Cleveland, Ohio, to serve as a clearinghouse for humane agencies throughout the country, and to assist in the handling of difficult problems. While the work of the AHA at the start concerned mainly livestock transportation, its scope was on enlarged. Eventually it became a federation of several undred societies.

The work of humane societies, wherever located, is much the same. They pick up lost, stray and abandoned animals off the streets, return them to their owners when claimed, or if unclaimed, they find new homes for them, and under certain circumstances they put them humanely to sleep. They teach proper care and feeding, conduct training classes where dog owners learn to school their pets in good behavior. They inspect pet shops, circuses and carnivals, stables and moving picture studios. In fact, they nose into every hole and corner where animals form the basis of sport, business and amusement of every conceivable sort. And they are ever on the alert regarding the need for legislation that will help to eliminate cruelty.

The American Society for the Prevention of Cruelty to Animals, oldest organization of its kind in the United States, has long maintained shelters both inside and outside New York City. These are staffed by veterinarians, technicians and attendants, day and night nurses, and office and management personnel. City clinics are open every day, with emergency service available Sundays, evenings and holidays. For those who cannot transport sick and injured animals to the shelters, ambulances stand by to bring them in.

During both World Wars an affiliate, the Red Star Animal Relief, furnished bandages and surgical instruments, ambulances, motorcycles and innumerable kinds of equipment to camps and to remount and embarkation centers. The expense was frightening, one sample being the $60,000 expended to furnish special ambulances for service on foreign battlefields.

One of the AHA's important projects was, and is, its Emergency Animal Relief, a series of units organized for immediate service anywhere in the nation in time of disaster. During one California holocaust, for instance, when innumerable homes were destroyed, hundreds of pets and farm animals were removed from the path of the fire. They were transported to animal shelters, and the injured were taken to veterinarians. Food was supplied as needed, and hay and grain was distributed to save the wildlife in areas where natural grasses had been burned off. And during several of our East Coast hurricanes all evacuated sections were patrolled by rescue squads to make sure that no animals had been left behind to suffer and perish.

In New York City, in addition to the usual services, the ASPCA has charge of dog licensing. Municipal licensing of this type is sometimes regarded as a catch-penny scheme from which the dog owner derives scant benefit. Actually, it has resulted in the safe return of lost dogs, whose ownership is traced by means of the license tag. With vacationers traveling so extensively by auto, it has lately become the custom to take the dog along. And in a strange city he is quite apt to escape and take in a little sight-seeing on his own when his people perforce go on without him. Eventually he is picked up and housed in the shelter. The ASPCA tells the story of a dog reunited with his owner 6000 miles away!

The custom of municipal licensing goes back more than 200 years. According to the English journal *Our Dogs,* it was instituted in 1735 with the specific purpose of reducing the number of stray dogs. Dogs, they said, "infested the roads in great numbers, barking and snapping at the horses' heels and causing many a rider to fall; that they poached the game, sucked the pheasants' eggs and resorted to all manner of shenanigans for which they should be taxed as a means of control." The proposal was ridiculed until it was realized that here was a method for raising much needed revenue. And so it did; but, it may be added, it has entailed considerable expense for its operation. For many a year it has been in vogue practically everywhere, conducted by either police departments or humane organizations.

Naturally, the changes wrought by time have increased

and diversified humanitarian services. The most recent of these is the ASPCA's Animalport, set up to care for the increasing number of live animals arriving at the Air Cargo Center of New York's International Airport. As opposed to inanimate cargo, delay in the pickup of live animals can be critical. So the Animalport furnishes experienced handlers who house, feed, water and exercise animals during stop-overs which may entail only a few hours but occasionally last several weeks.

The humanitarians have always been ready to institute and back legislation designed to protect animals. Scarcely a year passes without disclosing some new need, such as preventing dogs from running through the streets unattended. This type of legislation has served to reduce dog deaths and injuries on the highways as the auto becomes an ever growing menace. According to the National Dog Welfare Guild, sponsor of National Dog Week, two animal patrols working in the city of Memphis, Tennessee, picked up 213 dead small animals in one day. All too often a driver strikes a dog and, with a muttered "It's only a dog," speeds merrily on his way. One man whose dog lost his life in this manner was at least partially responsible for hit-and-run legislation in his state whereby anyone who strikes a dog must stop and report the accident or be liable to a fine.

Nor are dogs the only ones to suffer and die on the highways. The ASPCA reported a forty-car chain-reaction collision extending over three miles, in which eleven people were injured and $10,000 worth of property damage was done, all because a dog darted out into a busy street. It sometimes takes an accident of this magnitude to alert municipal authorities to the need for keeping dogs off the streets. They risk injury not only to themselves but to others, and in regions where rabies is present or suspected they can be a positive menace. Fortunately, most towns and cities today have ordinances forbidding dogs to run at large. And in "dog schools" the country over, instructors teach proper leash control as one of the fundamental responsibilities of dog ownership. In fact, this simple precaution is said to have done more than anything else to minimize the spread of rabies.

England solved the rabies problem a century ago by means of very strict licensing and muzzling laws and, in addition, by imposing a six-months' quarantine on all imported dogs. As a result, rabies has been wiped out of that country. In several other countries, too, quarantine restrictions involving various time limits have long been in vogue.

Except for dogs used as sheepherders or in connection with the handling of other animals, and dogs imported for breeding purposes, the United States has no quarantine applicable to dogs entering from other nations. They may be brought in duty-free if purebred and registered. However, in the presence of sporadic outbreaks of rabies, some states have imposed quarantine on incoming and outgoing dogs for whatever length of time is deemed expedient. Some states, too, as a regular practice, demand a certificate of inoculation, issued by a qualified veterinarian, for dogs crossing their borders. Since the incubation period can be as protracted as six months, the certificate guarantees that the dog is in good health and has been given anti-rabic immunization within that period of time.

On the whole, this country depends more upon inoculation than quarantine to remain rabies-free. Consequently, an ever increasing number of communities demand rabies vaccination as a prelude to municipal licensing. But neither quarantine nor inoculation can be entirely effective until the roving dog is eliminated. Rabies is not confined to dogs; it can and does affect farmstock and wildlife—foxes, coyotes, skunks and bats, among others. Since it is contracted only through the bite of a rabid animal, the leash-controlled dog runs little risk of infection. The free-running dog and the stray dog are the trouble-makers for, once bitten by a rabid animal, they are capable of spreading the deadly virus wherever they go.

The overproduction of dogs is another unfortunate problem being dealt with by humanitarians. That it is no myth is proved by the fact that within a period of thirty years or so our dog population increased 200 percent while the human population increased 50 percent. In the wild, overproduction would be a fact were it not for nature's own check—predators, food scarcity and disease—but, through artificial breeding, man so safeguards his stock that overproduction becomes serious.

The average humane society's practice of placing their strays in good homes can be a spurious act of kindness unless the females are spayed before being entrusted to unaccustomed hands. All too often abandoned females are allowed to return the favor of their rescue by producing puppies which in their turn are picked up off the streets and eventually foisted upon the very shelters from which their mothers came.

The sensible answer to overproduction is to spay and thus forestall the mating of stray females as well as the purebreds not kept specifically for breeding. Spaying does not harm the female. It does great good by preventing conception. A telling blow against overproduction is being dealt by such organizations as The Friends of Animals (11 W. 60th Street, New York, New York). These people practice as well as preach by underwriting the cost of spaying females whose owners cannot afford the entire cost of the operation.

There was a time when castration of the male was the method employed to forestall reproduction, but even this was looked upon with horror as "interrupting the ordained stages of life." At least that was the way the old-time people of India explained away the horde of misbegotten dogs that roamed their streets. They maintained that an animal has a soul, hence should not be destroyed. From that day to this, antipathy against interference with the dog's "right" to reproduce has persisted. In fact, it is only in this day and age that spaying has come to be recognized and accepted as the sole humane method of preventing overproduction.

Spaying is a type of conservation made necessary by the rapid changes in living conditions. Increase in the human population has been accompanied by the growth of urban housing centers where dogs are not allowed. Thus, owners who must move into such quarters, sometimes tearfully, sometimes with a sigh of relief, unload their pets upon already overcrowded shelters which have not enough room to accommodate them and not enough money to feed them.

Already concerted efforts to discourage indiscriminate dog breeding are bearing fruit, especially in the larger communities. In New York City, for example, there are 44,000 fewer dogs than there were fifteen years ago, as more dog-owning families move to less congested areas. However, the dog is not being received with open arms in the suburbs, as many apartments close their doors against him.

The no-dog rule current in most of the newer housing developments, as based upon the damage done to paths and shrubbery, is understandable; and in the long run it has served a good purpose in publicizing the owner's responsibility for making his dog behave. As a result, "Curb Your Dog" ordinances are quite usual. This means that, when exercising on leash, the dog must be guided to the curb or roadside to avoid soiling paths and sidewalks. This type of legislation was suggested back in 1936 by the Pennsylvania SPCA, but at the time was considered too drastic as well as too difficult to enforce. However, in New York City today it is rigidly enforced, with penalties up to fifty dollars imposed upon owners who disobey.

Naturally, rules of this type meet with opposition at the start. But gradually they are accepted in good spirit by the majority, who realize that the dog owner and the non-dog owner both have their rights; moreover, that such measures actually benefit the dog. As times goes on, the humanitarians and the dog fanciers, as well as those who may not like dogs at all, are working hand in hand as never before to give the dog his just due.

Young people too are being encouraged to participate. In large numbers they are being brought into the humane movement and the dog show sport combined under the offices of the 4-H Clubs of America. The AKC and its many affiliated clubs as well as humane societies the country over have long sought to interest boys and girls in their various activities and to learn the intricacies of dog care and management, in the main to awaken a sense of responsibility for animal welfare. The aims of the 4-H Clubs go a bit further; in fact, their primary object is to develop the potentialities of the younger generation.

Under the aegis of our Department of Agriculture and conducted by county agents and local leaders the country over, the 4-H Clubs of America is the largest organization of girls and boys in the free world, with a membership of over two million between the ages of ten and twenty-one years enrolled in its projects. For those who select dogs as their project, meetings are held in homes, schools and community centers where experts discuss with them problems of feeding, grooming and training.

Once the dog project is selected, the child agrees to see it through. He learns that the care of an animal like the dog involves regular day-to-day work. He learns to be systematic about it, too, for he must file a progress report from time to time indicating everything he does for and with his dog. On the form provided he describes his dog as a breed, age, sex, inoculations given, the number of hours spent in grooming, exercising and training. If he mates the female and sells the puppies, that also must be reported in detail. Did he attend obedience classes, and did his dog graduate? Did he take part in a dog show, a field trial or a stock demonstration?

To make it still more interesting, the enthusiastic 4-H'ers have a midsummer fair staged in their county, with cash prizes and ribbons awarded for the best exhibits. There are competitions for horses, sheep, goats, poultry and rabbits, and many more. For dog owners there is a dog show, unique of its kind, where the dogs are judged not on their form or feature but upon their condition, cleanliness, grooming, obedience and general health.

The fundamental purpose of 4-H dog club projects, as well as those having to do with other animals, is to develop in the younger generation the habits of good citizenship and the qualities needed for leadership. The youngsters learn to plan and carry out group activities, to conduct meetings according to parliamentary procedure, to stage demonstrations, to get up and talk before an audience, and to direct and take part in group discussions. Programs consist of systematic work interlarded with active sports, dancing, group singing and practically every type of useful recreation.

All this serves the good purpose of developing the youngster's personality and fitting him to take his place in a complex society. The dog projects especially create an awareness of the dog's needs and rights as well as of the owner's responsibility for his welfare. And who knows . . . maybe out of this crop of youthful citizens will come many who are ready and willing to undertake needed leadership in the cause of the animals!

There is still much to be done. In fact, there are two phases of dog care and management on which the various factions do not agree, namely, animal experimentation and the cropping of dogs' ears.

Ear cropping has been a "hot potato" since 1931, when the humanitarians first made a concerted effort to abolish what they termed a cruel and unnecessary practice, one that had been customary since bullbaiting days. In the bull pen both dog and bull had their ears cut short so that there would be less sensitive surface to mutilate. And when dogs emerged from the fighting pits with ears torn to ribbons, the flaps were trimmed close to the head to forestall further painful injury. Some terriers had their ears shortened so they would not be clawed when unearthing their quarry, and in late years hunting dogs had a portion of their ears "rounded," supposedly to minimize laceration when they worked their way through brush and briar.

All this was a universally accepted practice. Nobody thought much about it until, in 1877, a letter was published in the English *Our Dogs* urging its abolition. Fanciers were asked to express their views. In reply, King Edward VII, then Prince of Wales, wrote that "it would give him great pleasure to hear that owners of dogs agreed to abandon such an objectionable fashion." After considerable argument pro and con, it was ruled that no dog born after March 31, 1895, could, if cropped, win a prize at any show held under English Kennel Club rules. Cropping in England ceased then and there; since that time neither a dog cropped in that country nor any of his progeny may be exhibited.

In the United States that same year a proposal was made that no dog cropped after June 30, 1895, would be eligible to compete for prizes at shows held under American Kennel Club rules. A flurry of letters appeared for and against in the AKC *Gazette*. Spirited discussions raged at meetings for several months, but the measure was finally defeated.

In 1931 the humanitarians again tried to abolish cropping, but the hastily enacted legislation failed when the opposition of some of the fanciers made it too difficult and costly to enforce. The objectors could not defeat the laws, but they did succeed in having them so watered down that they could be circumvented. Certain of the measures they had amended to condone cropping if, for instance, it was done under complete anesthesia by qualified veterinarians, or if it was deemed necessary as a health measure when ears were injured in fights or accidents. The American Kennel Club, in support of state anticropping laws, has ruled that "Any dog whose ears have been cropped or cut in any way shall be ineligible to compete at any show in any state where the laws prohibit the same except subject to the provisions of such laws."

The following states have enacted anticropping laws: Massachusetts, New York, New Jersey, Pennsylvania, Connecticut, Michigan and Oklahoma. Prosecutions have been successfully made in Pennsylvania, Canada and England against persons who have cropped dogs' ears.

Cropping is still with us but to a lesser degree than ever before in the long history of dogs. Only eight breeds are customarily cropped today. Once upon a time deemed a necessity to minimize ear mutilation in bull pen and fighting pit, the practice became a fashion almost from the moment those so-called sports were outlawed by the humanitarians. Fashion, however, is proving a more implacable foe to cropping than legislation in this instance could ever be. In short, cropping is slowly but surely going out of style.

A Gathering of Antique Breeds

Rees's Encyclopedia, 1802

THE PEDIGREES of these dogs go way back, as attested in the preceding article. Indeed, in 1802 when these drawings appeared in Rees's Encyclopedia, a few of these breeds were on their way out. In several instances, those dogs which survive today look markedly different from their forebears.

Turnspit

Scotch Terrier

Bloodhound

Pug

Spaniel

English Toy Spaniels

Smooth Fox Terrier

310

Poodle

Small Barbet
or Poodle

Nakid, or Turkish Hound

311

Foxhound

Talbot, or Southern, Hound

English Rough Terrier

Water Spaniel

313

Iceland Dog and Siberian Dog

Boston Terrier

Pomeranian

How to Become a Dog Judge

Maxwell Riddle

THE AMERICAN Kennel Club doesn't publish a set of rules and procedures for people who want to become dog judges. Consequently interested people are always asking dog judges how they reached such a position. The truth is that many who apply make the grade, and as many more do not. Neither the successful nor the unsuccessful know exactly what happened. What follows is about all that can be known by anyone on the outside of the American Kennel Club.

The AKC sets up certain general procedures, which may be changed without notice. However, it can be assumed that what follows is, in AKC eyes, a well-tested system subject only to minor and relatively rare changes.

Ineligibles

Certain people are barred by their professions from being dog judges. A professional handler cannot be a judge, nor could the wife or husband of the handler. A handler who wishes to be a judge must resign as a handler and then must wait a year before he can apply for a judge's license. In the past, the American Kennel Club often granted certain professional handlers the right to judge at specialty shows held separately from all-breed events. During 1968, it passed a rule, effective January 1, 1970, withdrawing this privilege.

A judge can have a son or daughter who is a professional handler, but the handler is not allowed to live in his parents' household. And presumably the handler would be asked to show some discretion in the matter of showing dogs under his father or mother.

A judge cannot be engaged in the business of buying and selling dogs, since he could buy dogs for a low price and sell them for two or three times as much with the understanding that he would put them up at coming shows.

A breeder buys dogs. But as a rule he buys them for breeding purposes. Later, he may sell them when they fail to prove themselves in his breeding program, and he will sell puppies, both as show prospects and as pets. Such a breeder might also be a judge. His buying and selling is connected with his own breeding kennel, and he is not acting as a broker in the buying and selling of dogs. The rule prohibiting the latter probably came about because dog judges would go to England, buy a couple of dogs, sell them for big prices in the United States, and then put them up at shows.

A judge cannot solicit kennel advertising for a magazine or newspaper. It is felt that he might get lucrative advertisements in return for putting up the kennel's dogs.

A person who operates a professional grooming and boarding kennel is also ineligible to judge. In the past, a judge might groom and board the dogs of his clients, then put them up at shows where he judged. Now, the rule is strictly enforced.

When the American Kennel Club turns down an applicant for a judge's license it does so in the shortest possible, most specific terms, and it gives no reason for its action. Hundreds of disappointed applicants never learn why they were rejected, and they are embarrassed and hurt. The author does know of one person who kept at it until she did get an explanation. She was told that no one was being approved who had not bred and shown, or at least shown, two or more dogs to their championships.

Formal Application

The person who wishes to become a judge must write to the American Kennel Club for an application, which is in the form of an exhaustive questionnaire. Questions concern family background, occupation, experience in the dog game, and breeds owned and shown. A second questionnaire is designed to test the applicant's knowledge of the breed or breeds for which he is seeking a judge's license. He must describe his idea of an ideal dog of that breed, and he must list both the major qualities of the breed and what he considers to be the major faults.

Based on the number who ask about the procedure, the American Kennel Club must receive hundreds of applications from persons who have no more than a superficial knowledge of dogs and who know almost nothing about ring procedure.

People who have served steadily as ring stewards and who have judged at sanctioned match shows have had types of experience which is valuable to them. The questionnaires ask for details on such experience. Prospective judges should, therefore, apply to serve as stewards at as many licensed dog shows as possible. Where possible that stewardship should be under a judge who is judging the breeds in which his steward wishes to specialize.

Included in the questionnaire are half a dozen hypothetical situations which might come up in the ring. These are always highly technical, and they can sometimes send experienced judges to the superintendent for help in solving them. The applicant answers these to the best of his ability, perhaps using an AKC rule book to help him. In doing so, he learns a great deal about conducting a ring. He should secure a copy of the rule book and learn the rules thoroughly long before he applies for a license.

When he has completed the questionnaires the applicant has to swear that he has received no help from established judges in answering the questions. It can be presumed that those who cheat on this will not be particularly honorable judges.

The application goes to the American Kennel Club, and the exact course it takes there is not definitely known by those on the outside. Presumably, officers screen it. They may reject it or send it to the judges' committee. The personnel of this committee is a deeply guarded secret. When challenged by a rejected applicant, AKC officers will say only that they have taken no part in the committee's decision, and they will refuse to name any members of the committee.

The AKC files may contain information about an applicant. As a rule, this will be derogatory, since people seldom take the trouble to write in praise of other exhibitors to the American Kennel Club. It can be assumed, however, that AKC officials turn over any information they may have on the applicant to the committee.

Apprenticeship

If the applicant is given temporary approval by the committee, his name is then published in the official AKC magazine, *Purebred Dogs, The American Kennel Gazette.* ·Each month this magazine lists the names of applicants on the secretary's page. They are listed under the title "Apprentices," along with this wording:

"Applications for approval as judges have been received from the following persons who may only be approved to judge after they have served their apprenticeships. Letters in regard to the qualifications of these applicants should be mailed promptly and addressed to the attention of Secretary."

Perhaps here we should mention that a somewhat similar procedure must be followed by people applying for additional breeds. Under the title "Judging Applications," the names are given, together with the breeds for which application is made, and the request for letters by the secretary.

But we return now to the person applying to judge for the first time. He can expect that both his friends and enemies will write those letters. Probably more of his enemies than his friends will do so.

On first thought, one would guess that the chances of anyone's passing the letters test would be very poor. For if a person has bred and exhibited a number of champions, he is certain to have some bitter enemies. As one exhibitor said: "You're a great guy until you start to win. Then you become a progressively worse skunk until you produce a great champion. Then you haven't a friend left on earth."

But enough do get by this test so that one's faith either in humanity as a whole or the judges' committee is renewed. One must assume that the anonymous committee must have considerable experience and skill in recognizing the purely vicious letters that come in.

The AKC will notify the applicant that he has been approved to apprentice. The aspiring judge then begins his apprenticeship, which is carried out in the following way: The apprentice writes to a judge and asks to apprentice under him at a certain show. He also writes to the show-giving club for permission. This is usually granted.

Dog-show rules prohibit any person being in the ring other than the judge, one or two stewards who must be wearing official steward's ribbons, and the exhibitors in that class. When the apprentice appears in the ring, he or she is given a red apprentice steward's ribbon or badge, and a sign saying "Apprentice Judge in the Ring" is put up. In this way both the gallery and coming exhibitors understand the presence of the extra person.

It can be assumed that the apprentice knows the standard for his breed thoroughly. He is serving as an apprentice so that he can learn proper ring procedure. The judge can help him greatly in this. He should explain why he lines up the dogs as he does, how he places them so that the most people can see them, how he handles his judging book, how he marks absentees, and how he goes over the dogs. After he himself has examined a dog, the judge should say to the handler: "I have an apprentice judge with me. May he examine your dog?" The exhibitor can refuse to permit this, but very few do so. This is a courteous way to handle the matter, and it takes little of the judge's time, for the apprentice is only one dog behind in the examination. When the apprentice has completed examining the last dog, and both judge and apprentice have had a final survey of the class, the judge can make his placements.

The apprentice has to take his own notes and must write a critique, which is sent to the American Kennel Club for study. An apprentice must be in the ring at three shows at which at least a hundred dogs have been judged. It may be very difficult for him to find three shows with a hundred of his breed. In fact, he might have to apprentice at twenty shows to find that many. Therefore the American Kennel Club will permit the apprentice to be in the ring while a hundred dogs of somewhat similar type are being judged. For instance, the apprentice may be applying to judge Irish Terriers. He would then apprentice in rings in which terriers were being judged.

AKC Approval

After he has completed his apprenticeship and has sent in the three critiques, the AKC judging committee once more goes over the application. If all is in order, the apprentice is notified that his application has been approved, and that this fact will be published in a forthcoming issue of *Purebred Dogs, The American Kennel Gazette*. Only after publication can he accept judging assignments. He is not quite finished, however. At each of the three licensed shows which he first judges, he must write critiques which must be sent to the American Kennel Club.

It should be noted that judges in the United States are prohibited from soliciting assignments. The judge who does so is quickly suspended. So is a prospective judge who anticipates approval and accepts an invitation before final approval of his application.

Additional Breeds

A judge who has judged at three licensed shows is eligible to apply for additional breeds. The procedure to be followed is almost identical to that outlined for the beginner, but there is no apprenticeship. And after he has judged a certain number of times, the list of thorny situation questions to be answered will be dropped.

Canadians who wish to become American judges must follow the same procedure as Americans. This is at least the case for those having a license for one or more breeds in the United States. Presumably, the American Kennel Club would not license them at all if they were not already licensed for those breeds in Canada.

However, late in 1968, the AKC modified its rules for Canadians. It will now consider approving Canadians on a show-to-show basis for those breeds the Canadians are licensed to judge in their own country. Assuming the Canadian can pass all the requirements which American judges must, then the AKC could license him or her to judge a few, or all, of the breeds he or she can judge in Canada.

English, South African, Australian, and some European judges are extended the same privileges. Mexican and South American judges must still follow the system as used in licensing Americans. There is, however, some indication that the AKC may relax this rule in some cases.

Beth-Gêlert

William Robert Spencer

THE FOLLOWING ballad is one of the best-known English rhymed folk tales. The title was intended to give a clue to the nature of the dog it celebrates, for in old Saxon *Beth-Gêlert* means "brightest among the smartest."

The spearmen heard the bugle sound,
   And cheerily smiled the morn;
And many a brach, and many a hound
   Obeyed Llewellyn's horn.

And still he blew a louder blast,
   And gave a lustier cheer,
"Come, Gêlert, come, wert never last
   Llewellyn's horn to hear.

"O where does faithful Gêlert roam
   The flower of all his race;
So true, so brave—a lamb at home,
   A lion in the chase?"

In sooth, he was a peerless hound,
   The gift of royal John;
But now no Gêlert could be found,
   And all the chase rode on.

Beth-Gêlert

That day Llewellyn little loved
  The chase of hart and hare;
And scant and small the booty proved,
  For Gêlert was not there.

Unpleased, Llewellyn homeward hied,
  When, near the portal seat,
His truant Gêlert he espied
  Bounding his lord to greet.

But when he gained the castle-door,
  Aghast the chieftain stood;
The hound all o'er was smeared with gore;
  His lips, his fangs, ran blood.

Llewellyn gazed with fierce surprise;
  Unused such looks to meet,
His favorite checked his joyful guise,
  And crouched, and licked his feet.

Onward, in haste, Llewellyn passed,
  And on went Gêlert too;
And still, where'er his eyes he cast,
  Fresh blood-gouts shocked his view.

O'erturned his infant's bed he found,
  With blood-stained covert rent;
And all around the walls and ground
  With recent blood besprent.

He called his child—no voice replied—
  He searched with terror wild;
Blood, blood he found on every side,
  But nowhere found his child.

"Hell-hound! my child's by thee devoured,"
    The frantic father cried;
And to the hilt his vengeful sword
    He plunged in Gêlert's side.

Aroused by Gêlert's dying yell,
    Some slumberer wakened nigh;
What words the parent's joy could tell
    To hear his infant's cry!

Concealed beneath a tumbled heap
    His hurried search had missed,
All glowing from his rosy sleep
    The cherub boy he kissed.

Nor scathe had he, nor harm, nor dread,
    But, the same couch beneath,
Lay a gaunt wolf, all torn and dead,
    Tremendous still in death.

Ah, what was then Llewellyn's pain!
    For now the truth was clear;
His gallant hound the wolf had slain
    To save Llewellyn's heir.

The Most Celebrated Dog Case Ever Tried in Johnson County, Missouri—or the World

Gerald Carson

IT IS GENERALLY agreed that the dog was the first animal to be domesticated by man, probably because of the clear advantages of a mutual-assistance pact based upon cooperation in the search for food. The dog had the nose. The man had the eyes. The dog was faster, the man more cunning. At any rate, social relations developed between these two, and man found that he could not, or at least would not, get along without the dog. The Egyptians named the brightest star in the heavens the dog star, Sirius. Well-placed Romans kept a dog in the atrium and set in the walls of their dwellings a mosaic or drawing calling attention to the watchdog's fidelity in the words *cave canem*—"beware of the dog." A legal doctrine even developed in English jurisprudence to the effect that a dog's character was presumed to be good until the contrary was shown. But the greatest literary tribute extant to the qualities of man's ancient companion waited upon a court drama that was played out in a small, dingy courtroom in west central Missouri. The year was 1869, a time when the average rural American believed implicitly in his watch, the patent medicine of his choice, and his own, personal dog. The central figure in the Missouri case was "Old Drum," a black-and-tan foxhound, with perhaps a little bloodhound in him, who was executed as a supposed killer of sheep, five miles southwest of the hamlet of Kingsville in

Johnson County—near the Cass County line. Old Drum found his agony and apotheosis on a still October night and lives on today as a part of our national memory and in Missouri's dusty legal reports disguised as *Charles Burden, Respondent* v. *Leonidas Hornsby, Appellant.*

Game was still abundant in the post-Civil War years along the heavily timbered ridges of Johnson County, and Charles Burden, farmer, woodsman, and hunter—a character right out of James Fenimore Cooper—kept a pack of hounds for the chase. Old Drum was the leader and favorite, *primus inter pares*—"first among equals." Some dogs would follow false trails. But not Drum. Burden knew from his bugling music, sounding from the woodlots or tangled undergrowth, what kind of game Old Drum had flushed. In the vernacular of the hunter, the dog "never lied."

"He was good for varmints, wolves, and such like," Burden said, "and was as good a deer dog as I ever had. . . . Money wouldn't have bought him."

If you are familiar with the habits of the Missouri hound dog, you know that he lies around the place all day, sunning himself, snapping at flies, languidly scratching, apparently no

Beagle

good to himself or anyone else—a real hard-core welfare type. But about dusk he gets restless, yawns, stretches, and soon is ready to hit the trail. On the morning of October 28, Charles Burden, at peace with himself and the world, rode through the glories of the Missouri autumn past the house of his brother-in-law, "Lon" Hornsby, who raised sheep and cattle about a mile north of his own farm; and on to the post office and general store at Kingsville. He returned by the same road to be greeted as usual by Old Drum who leaped upon him, licking his hands and wagging an eager welcome. These were all little details that Burden recalled later. For that night Old Drum met his death and became the subject of legal battles that occupied the attention of four courts before the controversy ended.

It was after sundown. Burden and a neighbor were sitting in the dusk at the front of the house, smoking some of Burden's home-grown tobacco, listening to the baying of the pack. Joyous melody announced to their practiced ears that a fox was up and running across the open prairies, along a wooded creek, and into the hills; Old Drum was in the lead, as usual. Suddenly, at about eight o'clock, Burden heard a gun-shot. It came from the direction of Hornsby's farm. There was silence. Then the dogs were baying again. But Old Drum's voice was missing. Burden jumped to his feet, ran to get his hunting horn, and blew several blasts. All the dogs returned except one. Old Drum was not among them.

The next morning Burden saddled up and called on Lon Hornsby, a small, wiry man with flaming red hair and a quarrelsome disposition. During the summer and fall Hornsby had lost a number of sheep, killed by marauding dogs that had also raided his smokehouse. Hornsby had sworn that he would kill the first strange dog he found on his premises. He was making cider when Burden rode up.

"Lon, have you seen anything of my dog Drum around here?" When Hornsby said no, Burden persisted. "What dog was that you shot last night?" Hornsby acknowledged that he did have Dick Ferguson, his young nephew, shoot at a stray dog, "a black-looking dog," but the gun was only loaded with grains of corn, just to scare the rascal. Besides, everybody knew that Drum was not black, but had a black-and-tan coat.

Nevertheless, Old Drum was dead. Burden found him just above the ford on Big Creek below Haymaker's mill—about a mile from Hornsby's farm—lying with his head in the water. His body was filled with buckshot. There was mud on his underside, and there were sorrel hairs on the body, indicating that he had been transported and dragged some distance. Hornsby owned a sorrel mule. The evidence was circumstantial, but Burden brought suit for damages before a justice of the peace at Kingsville. One jury failed to come to an agreement, but in a second trial Burden won the verdict. A curious historical footnote to the trial is that one of Hornsby's attorneys was David Nation, later the husband of the muscular temperance fanatic and mystic Carrie Nation, who wielded her little hatchet so destructively in the hotel bars and saloons of Kansas.

Hornsby appealed to the Johnson County Court of Common Pleas at Warrensburg where in March, 1870, the earlier decision was upset. With Hornsby now ahead, it was neighbor against neighbor throughout the community. Threats were made on both sides. One Hornsby witness was warned he would be horsewhipped if he persisted in his testimony, and he prudently disappeared. Refusing to give up, Burden hired the Sedalia, Missouri, law firm of John F. Phillips and George Graham Vest, then the leading lawyers in that part of the state. The former later became a federal judge, the latter, a United States senator.

A new trial was obtained on the ground of new evidence. Once again the whole countryside gathered for court day in the old courthouse on North Main Street in Warrensburg. Everybody was on tenterhooks to know what a jury of farmers and fox hunters would do about convicting or exonerating Old Drum. Hornsby was also represented by able counsel, Thomas T. Crittenden, who later became governor of the state and broke up the Jesse James gang of outlaws, and Francis Marion Cockrell, who later served along with his adversary, Vest, in the United States Senate. Together, these men were known as the "Big Four" of the Missouri bar.

The most colorful figure in the courtroom was Vest, the Kentucky-born descendant of Scotch-Irish Presbyterians from Virginia. He was a graduate of Center College in Danville, Kentucky, and had read law in the office of James Harlan, lawyer, legislator, and attorney general of Kentucky, and father of John Marshall Harlan, who became an associate justice of the U.S. Supreme Court. In 1852, Vest graduated from the law department of Transylvania University. He settled in Missouri in 1859, entered into political affairs and was a Democratic Presidential elector on the Douglas ticket. When the Civil War came, Vest enlisted in the Confederate Army and, toward the end of the war, sat in the Senate of the Confederate States. A few years after the Old Drum case, Vest was elected to the U.S. Senate, thus acquiring the distinction of having sat in the highest legislative body of two nations.

At the time of the litigation over Old Drum, Vest was forty years old, one of the coming men of the state, an accomplished stump speaker—witty and emotional by turns— at his best in pleading before a jury, where he demonstrated a mastery of the forensic style then greatly admired. The trial was held on a rainy night in the dim light of kerosine lamps. Many witnesses were heard, including Hornsby's nephew, Dick Ferguson, who ingenuously declared on the witness stand, "My stars! I haven't seen Old Drum since I shot him." During this trial, according to the *Kansas City Star,* in a retelling of the story, "more oratory was turned loose than was ever heard in the most celebrated murder case ever tried in a Missouri court."

All of the arguments have long been forgotten, except Vest's closing appeal. A man of medium height and slender build, with a large head, drooping mustache, magnetic eyes, and great charm of mannner, Vest had up to this time taken only a minor part in the proceedings. But now it fell to him to sum up the case against Hornsby. Gravely addressing the presiding judge in the traditional words, "May it please the Court," Vest began to speak quietly and earnestly. He ignored the testimony. For about an hour he ranged through history, poetry, legend, and classical literature calling attention to sagacious and faithful dogs whom men have loved, quoting from the Biblical account of the dogs who came to lick the sores of the beggar Lazarus; citing Byron's line in Don Juan, " 'Tis sweet to hear the honest watchdog's bark' "; and the graphic description in John Lothrop Motley's *The Rise of the Dutch Republic* of how a dog had prevented the capture of William of Orange by the cruel Duke of Alva.

After pointing out the weaknesses in the arguments of opposing counsel and drawing attention to the law applicable to the case, Vest appeared ready to conclude. But then he moved closer to the jury box. He looked—someone remembered afterward—taller than his actual five feet six inches, and began in a quiet voice to deliver an extemporaneous peroration. It was quite brief, less than four hundred words.

"Gentlemen of the jury," Vest said, "the best friend a man has in the world may turn against him and become his worst enemy. His son or daughter that he has reared with loving care may prove ungrateful. Those who are nearest and dearest to us, those whom we trust with our happiness and our good name, may become traitors to their faith. The money that a man has, he may lose. It flies away from him, perhaps when he needs it the most. A man's reputation may be sacrificed in a moment of ill-considered action. The people who are prone to fall on their knees to do us honor when success is with us may be the first to throw the stone of malice when failure settles its cloud upon our heads. The one absolutely unselfish friend that a man can have in this selfish world, the one that never deserts him and the one that never proves ungrateful or treacherous is his dog.

"Gentlemen of the jury, a man's dog stands by him in prosperity and in poverty, in health and in sickness. He will sleep on the cold ground, where the wintry winds blow and the snow drives fiercely, if only he may be near his master's side. He will kiss the hand that has no food to offer, he will lick the wounds and sores that come in encounters with the roughness of the world. He guards the sleep of his pauper master as if he were a prince. When all other friends desert he remains. When riches take wings and reputation falls to pieces, he is as constant in his love as the sun in its journey through the heavens. If fortune drives the master forth an outcast in the world, friendless and homeless, the faithful dog asks no higher privilege than that of accompanying him to guard against danger, to fight against his enemies, and when the last scene of all comes, and death takes the master in its embrace and his body is laid away in the cold ground, no matter if all other friends pursue their way, there by his graveside will the noble dog be found, his head between his paws, his eyes sad but open in alert watchfulness, faithful and true even to death."

When Vest had concluded, he bowed to the judge and sat down. The presiding justice was entranced. Great sobs shook the courtroom. Hounds of the Old Drum type were "folks," a part of the family, on the middle border a hundred years ago. For a magic moment the spectators were transported, uplifted by the loneliness and ultimate tragedy of all life that struck home to all who heard the appeal. Seeing themselves as in a mirror, the jury wept.

Crittenden, one of the adverse attorneys, leaned over to

his associate Cockrell, and whispered, as he recalled later
that the dog, though dead, had won. He added, "we had
better get out of the courthouse with our client, or all would
be hanged." Vest's closing words, in which he depicted the
"noble dog" at his master's grave, was not sheer hyperbole.
Such a dog actually existed at the time in Scotland. His name
was "Greyfriars Bobby" and he guarded the grave of his
owner from 1858 to his own death in 1872. As Greyfriars
Bobby's fame spread, the Lord Provost exempted him from
the dog tax and a fountain was raised in his honor at Edinburgh by Angela, Baroness Burdett-Coutts, noted philan-
thropist and close friend of Queen Victoria. Another instance
of the faithfulness of dog to man comes from nearer home.
Lucien B. Kerr, Colonel of the Eleventh Illinois Cavalry,
survived the Civil War but was fatally wounded in a hunting
accident. The Irish setter that had accompanied him was
inconsolable. While the Colonel lay near death at his home
in Peoria, the dog, according to one account, stationed himself on the veranda outside the sick room. When Kerr refused
amputation of his arm and died, the dog was allowed to
enter the room. He put his paws on the bed, licked the face
of his dead master, returned to his post on the porch, and
died within the hour. Perhaps, from the perspective of a
more skeptical age, this may be regarded as an instance of
the pathetic fallacy. Perhaps the dog had the distemper.
But it is a fact that on the northwest corner of Colonel Kerr's
lot in Peoria's Springdale Cemetery, there is a reclining dog
"true, even unto death," sculptured in sandstone.

The Old Drum jury took two minutes to return a verdict
in favor of Burden and assess damages of $50. For his tribute
to all dogdom, Vest received a fee of $10. Hornsby appealed
to the Missouri Supreme Court, but his heart was not really
in it, and when the decision of the lower court was affirmed,
the case ground to an end. Old Drum had been vindicated
and given a martyr's crown in what one law journal called

"the most celebrated dog case in Johnson County, Missouri, or for that matter, in the world."

No court stenographer was present when Senator Vest pronounced his eulogy, and his words are sometimes referred to as the "Lost Speech." But it has been carefully reconstructed from notes taken by Crittenden and has survived, not because it was written or printed but, as Professor William Lyon Phelps once pointed out, "in the same manner as ancient epics, folk songs, ballads, cowboy choruses, sea chanteys, and lullabies." Vest's gem of sentiment on an aspect of the human—animal relationship has completely overshadowed his long and important career in the United States Senate from 1879 to 1903, a period when he had, according to the *Chicago Journal*, "half the brains of the Democratic side of the Senate." Vest opposed the high protective measures of his day, the acquisition of territory after the Spanish-American War, and on one occasion, thwarted an attempt by private interests to commercialize Yellowstone Park.

The eulogy was quickly recognized as a classic statement and has never disappeared from view since it was delivered. Some two years after Senator Vest's death in 1904, the speech was revived as a funeral oration over the grave of a dog, Pero, killed by an automobile in Denver. It became almost axiomatic for any attorney representing the owner of a slain animal to talk about men and dogs and what they mean to each other, invoking, of course, the memory of Old Drum. But courtroom procedures have changed with the passing years, and Old Drum may be near the end of his century of service so far as the higher courts are concerned. The Missouri Supreme Court recently set aside the conviction of a man who had killed another man's dog. The ruling was made on the ground that the lawyer for the dog's owner had improperly injected Old Drum into the case for its emotional effect upon the jury.

Regardless of what the courts may say about the legal proprieties, Old Drum has not lost his hold on the affections of dog owners. A bronze tablet has been attached to the wall of the old court house in Warrensburg, now the home of the Johnson County Historical Society, marking the scene as a historic site. Another monument stands on the banks of Big Creek just above the deer crossing where Drum was found after he was shot. The memorial includes in its construction rocks sent from most of the American states, the Great Wall of China, the white cliffs of Dover, Germany, France, Guatemala, Mexico, Jamaica, South Africa, the Virgin Islands, Panama, and the West Indies. The base bears a granite stone on which is incised the representation of a dog treeing a coon. A deer is being chased in one corner, a fox in the other. The lettering reads "Old Drum—Killed 1869." A bronze statue, executed by Reno Gastaldi, the St. Louis sculptor, stands on the lawn of the present court house, the model created from a study of some of the best hound dogs in the Middle West. It was dedicated in 1953 by the attorney general of Missouri and Captain Will Judy of Chicago, editor of *Dog World*. The text of the Old Drum speech appears on the marble base.

Burden and Hornsby eventually recovered from the economic effects of their litigation, were reconciled, and died in obscurity. But the dog they fought over seems destined to be remembered as long as men shall enjoy the companionship of a canine friend.

Diarrhea

J. J. McCoy

DIARRHEA IS NOT a disease, but a symptom of a disease or infestation of parasites. It may also be caused by a malfunction of the intestinal tract, triggered by faulty diet or the swallowing of foreign matter. While functional diarrhea is more common in young puppies, older dogs are also affected. A soft bowel movement is not diarrhea; a watery or bloody, loose movement is diarrhea.

To clear up ordinary diarrhea, you will first have to determine the cause. Check the dog's diet. It's possible that his food is too laxative. Dog foods containing liver are apt to be on the laxative side. Eliminate them. Add cooked starchy foods to the diet. Boiled rice, macaroni or barley will help solidify bowel movements in ordinary functional diarrhea. If you feed the dog milk, boil it. The commercial diarrhea medicines, such as Peptobismol, will bring ordinary diarrhea under control. For a 7- to 10-week-old puppy, 1 teaspoonful every 4 hours will bring quick results. In the case of bloody diarrhea or when the condition persists for more than a day or two, take a specimen of the dog's bowel movement to the veterinarian. The dog may have worms or intestinal parasites.

Dandy

W. H. Hudson

HE WAS OF mixed breed, and was supposed to have a strain
of Dandy Dinmont blood which gave him his name. A big
ungainly animal with a rough shaggy coat of blue-gray hair
and white on his neck and clumsy paws. He looked like a
Sussex sheep dog with legs reduced to half their proper
length. He was, when I first knew him, getting old and increasingly deaf and dim of sight, otherwise in the best of
health and spirits, or at all events very good-tempered.

Until I knew Dandy I had always supposed that the
story of Ludlam's dog was pure invention, and I dare say
that is the general opinion about it; but Dandy made me
reconsider the subject, and eventually I came to believe that
Ludlam's dog did exist once upon a time, centuries ago perhaps, and that if he had been the laziest dog in the world
Dandy was not far behind him in that respect. It is true he
did not lean his head against a wall to bark; he exhibited his
laziness in other ways. He barked often, though never at
strangers; he welcomed every visitor, even the tax-collector,
with tail-waggings and a smile. He spent a good deal of his
time in the large kitchen, where he had a sofa to sleep on,
and when the two cats of the house wanted an hour's rest
they would coil themselves up on Dandy's broad shaggy

side, preferring that bed to cushion or rug. They were like a warm blanket over him, and it was a sort of mutual benefit society. After an hour's sleep Dandy would go out for a short constitutional as far as the neighboring thoroughfare, where he would blunder against people, wag his tail to everybody, and then come back. He had six or eight or more outings each day, and, owing to doors and gates being closed and to his lazy disposition, he had much trouble in getting out and in. First he would sit down in the hall and bark, bark, bark, until some one would come to open the door for him, where-upon he would slowly waddle down the garden path, and if he found the gate closed he would again sit down and start barking. And the bark, bark would go on until some one came to let him out. But if after he had barked about twenty or thirty times no one came, he would deliberately open the gate himself, which he could do perfectly well, and let him-self out. In twenty minutes or so he would be back at the gate and barking for admission once more, and finally, if no one paid any attention, letting himself in.

Dandy always had something to eat at meal-times, but he too liked a snack between meals once or twice a day. The dog-biscuits were kept in an open box on the lower dresser shelf, so that he could get one "whenever he felt so disposed," but he didn't like the trouble this arrangement gave him, so he would sit down and start barking, and as he had a bark which was both deep and loud, after it had been repeated a dozen times at intervals of five seconds, any person who happened to be in or near the kitchen was glad to give him his biscuit for the sake of peace and quietness. If no one gave it him, he would then take it out himself and eat it.

Now it came to pass that during the last year of the war dog-biscuits, like many other articles of food for man and beast, grew scarce, and were finally not to be had at all. At all events, that was what happened in Dandy's town of Penzance. He missed his biscuits greatly and often reminded us of it by barking; then, lest we should think he was barking about something else, he would go and sniff and paw at the empty box. He perhaps thought it was pure forgetfulness on the part of those of the house who went every morning to do the marketing and had fallen into the habit of returning without dog-biscuits in the basket. One day during that last winter of scarcity and anxiety I went to the kitchen and found the floor strewn all over with the fragments of Dandy's biscuit-box. Dandy himself had done it; he had dragged the box from its place out into the middle of the floor, and then deliberately set himself to bite and tear it into small pieces and scatter them about. He was caught at it just as he was finishing the job, and the kindly person who surprised him in the act suggested that the reason of his breaking up the box in that way was that he got something of the biscuit flavor by biting the pieces. My own theory was that as the box was there to hold biscuits and now held none, he had come to regard it as useless—as having lost its function, so to speak—also that its presence there was an insult to his intelligence, a constant temptation to make a fool of himself by visiting it half a dozen times a day only to find it empty as usual. Better, then, to get rid of it altogether, and no doubt when he did it he put a little temper into the business!

Dandy, from the time I first knew him, was strictly teetotal, but in former and distant days he had been rather fond of his glass. If a person held up a glass of beer before him, I was told, he wagged his tail in joyful anticipation, and a little beer was always given him at mealtime. Then he had an experience, which, after a little hesitation, I have thought it best to relate, as it is perhaps the most curious incident in Dandy's somewhat uneventful life.

One day Dandy, who after the manner of his kind, had attached himself to the person who was always willing to take him out for a stroll, followed his friend to a neighboring public-house, where the said friend had to discuss some business matter with the landlord. They went into the taproom, and Dandy, finding that the business was going to be a rather long affair, settled himself down to have a nap. Now it chanced that a barrel of beer which had just been broached had a leaky tap, and the landlord had set a basin on the floor to catch the waste. Dandy, waking from his nap and hearing the trickling sound, got up, and going to the basin quenched his thirst, after which he resumed his nap. By-and-by he woke again and had a second drink, and altogether he woke and had a drink five or six times; then, the business being concluded, they went out together, but no sooner were they out in the fresh air than Dandy began to exhibit signs of inebriation. He swerved from side to side, colliding with the passers-by, and finally fell off the pavement into the swift stream of water which at that point runs in the gutter at one side of the street. Getting out of the water, he started again, trying to keep close to the wall to save himself from another ducking. People looked curiously at him, and by-and-by they began to ask what the matter was. "Is your dog going to have a fit—or what is it?" they asked. Dandy's friend said he didn't know; something was the matter, no doubt, and he would take him home as quickly as possible and see to it.

When they finally got to the house Dandy staggered to the sofa, and succeeded in climbing on to it and, throwing himself on his cushion, went fast to sleep, and slept on without a.break until the following morning. Then he rose quite refreshed and appeared to have forgotten all about it; but that day when at dinner-time some one said "Dandy" and held up a glass of beer, instead of wagging his tail as usual he dropped it between his legs and turned away in evident disgust. And from that time onward he would never touch it with his tongue, and it was plain that when they tried to tempt him, setting beer before him and smilingly inviting him to drink, he knew they were mocking him, and before turning away he would emit a low growl and show his teeth.

It was the one thing that put him out and would make him angry with his friends and life companions.

I should not have related this incident if Dandy had been alive. But he is no longer with us. He was old—half-way between fifteen and sixteen: it seemed as though he had waited to see the end of the war, since no sooner was the armistice proclaimed than he began to decline rapidly. Gone deaf and blind, he still insisted on taking several constitutionals every day, and would bark as usual at the gate, and if no one came to let him out or admit him, he would open it for himself as before. This went on till January, 1919, when some of the boys he knew were coming back to Penzance and to the house. Then he established himself on his sofa, and we knew that his end was near, for there he would sleep all day and all night, declining food. It is customary in this country to chloroform a dog and give him a dose of strychnine to "put him out of his misery." But it was not necessary in this case, as he was not in misery; not a groan did he ever emit, walking or sleeping; and if you put a hand on him he would look up and wag his tail just to let you know that it was well with him. And in his sleep he passed away—a perfect case of euthanasia—and was buried in the large garden near the second apple-tree.

Superstitions About Dogs

Arthur Trayford, D. V. M.
Gladys Hall

"OUR DOG HOWLED like a hyena the night before Grandma died" is an oft-told tale, differing only in the person of the deceased whose passing the dog "foretold."

Ever since the dog came out of the wild state and took up residence with man, superstitious people have believed that "a howling dog is a sign of death." The truth is that a dog may feel the primal urge to howl at any hour of the day or night, in many different circumstances, and for any number of often quite prosaic reasons. Dogs will howl when they are bored or when the dog next door is howling. They'll howl at the moon. They'll howl when some sound, such as whistles blowing or a plane breaking the sound barrier, irritates their sensitive eardrums. They'll howl from sheer pleasure and satisfaction (as a cat purrs) when someone they love is making a fuss over them, and from loneliness and resentment when they feel neglected. They'll howl when they are hungry, or thirsty, or when they want to be let into or out of the house. What is more natural, therefore, than that they should howl their heads off when a death in the family is imminent, since, at such a time, they are usually shoved out of the way, ignored, and forgotten by members of the troubled household who are otherwise and wholly preoccupied. It is sensible to assume, in short, that self-pity prompts a dog to howl when death is imminent rather than an occult presentiment of the approaching demise.

When a dog howls and there is no event, impending or otherwise, with which to associate the howling, it is taken as a matter of course and forgotten. But when a dog howls, and shortly thereafter a member of the family dies, the howling is remembered and an eerie significance is attached to it.

Another occult power attributed to dogs by superstitious people is that of "seeing ghosts." When, for no apparent reason, the motions of an active dog are suddenly arrested and it sits with its head raised, ears twitching, eyes fixed and staring, it is "seeing spirits" that are not visible to human eyes, the believers in ESP maintain.

The fact is that when a dog sits and stares, as if transfixed, at "nothing," it is manifesting extrasensory perception of a sort in that, being farsighted, it is probably watching a tiny insect, too tiny and too far up in the air to be discernible to human eyes. Since the dog's sense of hearing is appreciably keener than his sense of sight, however, it is more likely that some sound of a higher frequency than the limit of human hearing (such as the fainter-than-a-whisper whir of an insect's wings) is holding him spellbound, rather than a disembodied spirit that, by means of clairvoyance, he is able to "see."

FALLACIES ABOUT DOGS

That "barking dogs never bite" is a fallacy, and a potentially dangerous one, for although dogs will sometimes bark good-humoredly, taking pleasure in the sound of their own voices, or from happiness, such as when they are welcoming a returning owner, or simply for the want of something better to do, there are other times when a dog's barking precedes and gives warning of attack. Since there is no way of determining just what a barking dog has in mind, the better part of common sense is not to make free with him.

There is also the completely erroneous idea that when a purebred female has been bred to a mongrel, or to a dog of another breed, she can never thereafter produce purebred puppies. The fact is that only the progeny of a mismating is affected. Telegony, or the supposed transmission of characteristics of one sire to offspring subsequently borne to other sires by the same female, is as biologically impossible in animals as it is in humans. Irrespective of one or more previous misalliances, a purebred female bred to a purebred male of her own breed can and does produce purebred puppies.

Another bit of dog lore that has no basis in fact concerns the vestigial digits, or "extra toes," known as dewclaws with which some puppies are born. They may appear on the hind legs, the forelegs, or both, and are a sign, many people believe, that the dog is not a purebred. This is so far from the truth that not only do dewclaws appear on many purebred dogs but a double dewclaw (or two on the same leg) is a requirement for Great Pyrenees to qualify for the show ring—actually, double dewclaws on hind legs, singles up front. In breeds where they are not a requirement for show purposes, dewclaws are usually snipped off a puppy's legs while they are in the rudimentary stage, not because they are indicative of crossbreeding or are unsightly, but because they are apt to catch in fabrics or in underbrush, which is a nuisance and can be painful to the animal.

That milk gives dogs worms and that, when ill, dogs eat grass are among the fallacies often stated as facts. The fact is, however, that milk of itself does not produce worms in dogs. In order for milk to transmit worms to an animal, it must be contaminated by feces or dirt containing worm eggs, and that this could happen under the present conditions of milk handling is, to say the least, unlikely.

In the early spring, dogs will eat grass because it is fresh, sweet-smelling, and tender, and it appeals to them. As for eating grass when they are ill, the fact (more remarkable than the fiction) is that they will eat grass as a preventive measure in order that they will not become ill. There are two types of grass, in particular, that serve to relieve dogs when they feel uncomfortable or as they are about to become ill. One type is a rough grass that acts as an emetic; the other is a smooth-textured grass that acts as a natural laxative. With unerring instinct, the dog that needs an emetic will eat the rough grass, while the dog that needs a cathartic for the relief of its particular discomfort will eat the smooth grass. By inducing vomiting or, as the case may be, evacuation, the dog's instinct tells him that he will be rid of the causative agent of his discomfort. Whether instinct further informs him that by so doing he has probably saved himself from a prolonged period of discomfort or illness is doubtful, but this, for all practical purposes, is what he has done.

That the cat and dog are hereditary or natural enemies is pretty generally taken for granted. Observably, it is not the usual thing for a cat and a dog to live together in peace and harmony. At sight of a dog, a cat will immediately take on a defensive attitude, arching its back, spitting, and, if the dog comes within reach, unsheathing its claws in readiness to scratch, whereupon the dog gives chase. Unless the cat is swifter than the dog or can escape up a tree, the chase is liable to end in a dead or badly mauled cat. Basically, the traditional enmity between cat and dog is fear—the fear common to all animals of a different species (and also to those of the same species) that one will outrun and outwit the other in the hunt for food; the related fear of two animals or a group of animals in which, because of a difference in size and strength, one is the natural prey of the other.

In the relationship between the cat and the dog, the cat is afraid of the dog. Because she is afraid, she assumes the defensive attitude, which arouses the dog's fighting instinct and prompts him to attack; or she turns tail and flees, whereupon, because movement incites the atavistic urge to pursue, the dog gives chase.

Despite the ancient feud between them, however, dogs and cats are not natural enemies, as evidenced by the fact that puppies and kittens of the same age or thereabouts do not recognize each other as a different—and inimical—species but merely, as anyone who has watched them frisk and tumble about together can testify, as playfellows. Nor do cats and dogs that have been raised together necessarily become enemies in later life. Providing they have been raised by owners who have taken care that each animal gets its full share of food and affection, many cats and dogs have been known to live sociably together all of their lives.

When a cat or a kitten is brought into a household where there is a grown dog, some problems are to be expected. By the use of a little strategy, however, most of them can be overcome. For example, it is advisable to keep

the animals apart (in separate rooms, if possible) for a few days after bringing the cat home, in order that each will become accustomed, before meeting at close range, to the smell of the other. Also, additional petting and attention should be given the dog in order to allay the pangs of jealousy he will be sure to suffer. If the dog can be given to understand that his status in the household is no wise changed by the presence of another animal, the probability is that he will come to take a protective or, at the least, a philosophical live-and-let-live attitude toward the new member of the family.

Many owners are mystified as to why a dog will invariably bury its bone—in many instances, moreover, a fresh, new juicy bone. Insofar as can be known, a dog will bury its bone for one or the other of two very practical reasons: In order to hide it from another dog, or because he doesn't feel hungry for a bone at the time it is given him and figures that by burying it he can, whenever he feels so disposed, dig it up and go to work on it.

When dogs dig up newly planted gardens as, in the spring of the year, many owners complain that they do, it is not because they have a taste for the corn kernels or zinnia seeds their owners have put in, but because they have a bone they want to bury or because they suspect a bone has been buried in the freshly turned earth. Dogs are seemingly convinced, in short, that the burial of bones is what freshly turned earth is for—a conviction that plays havoc with many a garden but has also saved many a life. During World War II, dogs were used for the purpose of nosing out land mines that had been buried by the enemy and so camouflaged that the men could not detect them. Dogs turned loose in the area would make a beeline for the small patches of ground that, however skillfully camouflaged, they sensed had been recently turned over, and, by signifying their interest in these areas, many mines were detected and removed in time, thereby saving innumerable lives.

A Dog Named Benjie

Justin F. Denzel

IN THE BIG kitchen of the McKenzie cattle ranch, Tony King bent over the sink scrubbing the big copper pots until they shone like new pennies. The last of the ranch hands and riders had finished breakfast and gone out to work

Over at the chopping block Charley Hank, the cook, swung a flashing meat cleaver, splitting veal chops for the noon meal. Without missing a stroke he looked up at Tony. "The boss wants to see you at the house. He says to bring Benjie with you."

Tony tried to guess what Mr. Gorman could possibly want with Benjie. Slowly a smile formed on his boyish lips. "Maybe he wants to use him for hunting," said Tony.

Charley Hank threw back his head in booming laughter. "That old bag of bones? He's blind as a bat. He wouldn't know a bear from a dead stump."

Tony looked down at the dog lying at his feet. Benjie was a bloodhound, dark brown with wrinkled skin. His eyes were useless. But he was Tony's friend, the only real one he had. Wherever Tony went, Benjie followed.

As Tony walked toward the big house, with Benjie at his heels, the warm March sun gave promise of an early spring. Tall Douglas firs cloaked the mountain ranges which planted their feet down at the very edge of the grazing land.

All his life Tony had lived in this Caribou country, the best cattle land in Canada. Orphaned at an early age, he

Reprinted by kind permission of Methodist Publishing House and Justin F. Denzel.

347

had been taken in and raised by old Pop McKenzie. Now Pop McKenzie was dead and things had changed. Mr. Gorman, the new owner, ruled with an iron hand. As Charley Hank said, "He cracks the whip all right, but he put this place back on a paying basis."

The big log house stood high on the hill under cottonwood trees. Nita, the Shuswap Indian girl, let Tony in the side door. She smiled down at him, her white teeth flashing. Tony had always liked Nita. She used to give him big stacks of buckwheat cakes and sausage for breakfast each morning. But all that seemed like a long time ago.

Shifting uneasily from one foot to the other, Tony waited in the large living room. All this was as familiar to Tony as his own name, for it had once been his home.

Through the big picture window he saw Mr. Gorman drive up in the jeep with his five-year-old son, David. The child was clutching a toy teddy bear tightly under one arm.

Mr. Gorman came in alone. He was a tall man, his face red from years of riding in the biting wind.

"I've called you up here, Tony, because I want to talk to you about Benjie."

Tony looked up, a puzzled expression on his face.

"Benjie's an old dog, Tony," Mr. Gorman continued. "He's blind and it is hard for him to get around. It isn't good for an animal to get that old. It isn't natural."

Tony swallowed hard. "He doesn't take much care, Mr. Gorman, just a few table scraps. He's not much bother."

"Tony, I'm a rancher; before that I was a veterinarian. I've worked with animals all my life. I know how you feel. But when an animal outlives its usefulness, it's only in the way. You've got to understand that."

Tony felt a knot of fear tighten in his stomach. "I'll keep him out of the way, I promise."

Mr. Gorman's words were firm. "What I'm trying to tell you, Tony, is that I think we ought to put Benjie away."

Tony shook his head in disbelief. "You mean for good?"

A Dog Named Benjie

Mr. Gorman nodded. "Yes, Tony, for good."

Tony could hardly believe his ears. Mr. Gorman wanted to kill Benjie.

Only a year ago Mr. Gorman had taken over the ranch, and Tony had to go up to the bunkhouse to live. Now he wanted to take away the only friend Tony had. It wasn't fair.

Tears came into Tony's eyes. He knelt down and put his arms around Benjie's neck. "Maybe he'll die soon anyway. Couldn't we just wait till then?"

A pained expression crossed Mr. Gorman's face, but his voice was firm. "I'm sorry, Tony. I want you and Benjie to come with me in the jeep. I've got some business to attend to. When I've finished, we'll stop down at the kennels."

Tony walked toward the door in silence, a lump of bitterness stuck in his throat.

As they drove along, Mr. Gorman tried to make conversation. "There's a litter of basset pups down at the kennels. While we're there you might pick one out for yourself. It will help you forget Benjie."

Tony heard the words, but they held no meaning for him. He didn't want to forget Benjie. He wanted to remember.

He thought of making a break for it, running away, taking Benjie with him. But what chance did he have? For almost two hours he was under the watchful eye of Mr. Gorman. After that it was too late.

They pulled up in front of the kennel and went inside. Mr. Gorman lifted Benjie onto a table. He looked at the dog's teeth and into his milk-white eyes. Shaking his head slowly he took a large hypodermic needle and filled it with a colorless fluid. Then he turned to Tony. "You'd better wait outside," he said. "This will only take a minute."

Sick at heart, Tony waited outside. He wanted to go back and plead for Benjie's life, but he knew it would do no good.

Suddenly through the mist of his tears he saw someone

coming down the hill. It was Nita, the Indian girl, her black braids flying as she ran. She rushed past Tony, out of breath and sobbing, calling for Mr. Gorman. "David's gone," she shouted. "David's gone. We can't find him anywhere."

Seconds later Mr. Gorman was running up the hill with Nita at his heels.

Tony walked back into the kennel expecting to find Benjie dead. But he was very much alive, wagging his tail and sniffing. The needle was lying on the table beside him, still unused.

Tony's heart beat fast. Here was the chance he had been waiting for. They'd be busy looking for the missing child. They'd never notice him.

Up in his room, over the mess hall, he hurriedly threw some clothes into a knapsack. He was almost ready to go when he heard a step behind him. He turned to see Charley Hank standing in the doorway, his big arms folded across his chest.

"Going some place?" he asked.

There was no time to try to fool anyone. "Yes, I'm getting out of here," said Tony.

Charley Hank rubbed the stubble on his chin. "Kind of a bad time to be running out, isn't it?"

"If you mean David," said Tony, "they'll find him."

"It's a big country. They might need help."

Tony shrugged his shoulders. "That's their business," he said, pushing his way out the door.

He started out along the edge of the woods, heading for the Caribou road. He saw no riders, no wandering ranch hands. He knew most of them were up in the hills searching.

He thought of David, frightened and alone, up in the mountains. The temperatures still fell below freezing at night. If they didn't find him before dark, the small boy wouldn't have much of a chance. He looked back over his shoulder to see Benjie following a few feet behind. The old dog had his nose close to the ground.

For the first time in all these years Tony saw that Benjie

followed him by smell alone. The dog was following a trail. If Benjie could track him that easily, why not somebody else? He tried to shake the thought from his mind, but it kept coming back to bother him. It was worth a try. Almost without thinking he turned and started back for the ranch.

David's small footprints were still in the damp earth next to the house. Tony led Benjie over the area, coaxing him, trying to get him to pick up the scent. But the old dog did not seem to understand.

Tony tried to think of what to do next. Suddenly he thought of Nita.

The Indian girl came to the door at his knock, her eyes red from crying. Tony explained what he wanted, and she disappeared into the house to return with a small stocking.

He held it close to the dog's nose. "Find him, Benjie. Find him."

Twice the dog started out, uncertain, only to make a wide circle and come back to where he started. Tony tried again, dragging the stocking across the tiny footprints. This time Benjie seemed to get the idea. He was trying to single out a trail.

He started across the fields, skirting along the edge of the foothills, occasionally doubling back. Then he turned left and started up into the mountains.

Tony was not at all certain that Benjie was following the right trail. Dozens of searchers had been over this very ground within the past hour. Benjie might easily become confused.

They continued up, climbing into the thick forests of Douglas fir. Thin sheets of ice still covered the quiet pools of water formed by the early thaws. Rocky ledges and steep ravines made the going difficult. As hours passed, Benjie's age began to tell.

In his blindness, Benjie trailed close to the ground, his nose and jowls scraped and swollen from the bare rough earth.

Darkness came and with it a biting chill. It went right

through Tony's heavy clothing and added a note of despair to his useless search. Tired and hungry he stumbled on in the dark. To Benjie it made little difference. In his world of darkness day and night were one.

Time after time Tony raised his voice, calling into the silence, but there was no answer. The temperature continued to drop. Dim moonlight shone through the branches, lending a ghostly glow to the mountain.

Tony lost all sense of time and direction. Now he had to follow Benjie or become lost himself.

He continued calling only to be answered by an echo. Another hour passed and he staggered on. It was no use. He gave up all hope. He tried to get Benjie to turn back, but the stubborn animal pulled away and continued his sniffing. He became excited, running in close circles, baying softly. At first Tony thought he was going crazy, but then he saw what was causing Benjie's actions. Lying in the underbrush, its glass eyes glowing in the dim moonlight, was a toy teddy bear.

Quickly Tony picked it up, calling to the dog. "Find him, Benjie, find him."

Benjie was wild now, crashing through the brush, the trail fresh in his nostrils.

A few hundred feet away they found the child. He was too weak to make a sound, but his eyes flickered and Tony knew he was alive.

Two hours later Tony staggered into the ranch bunkhouse, dead tired, the child sleeping in his arms.

Charley Hank looked up. The worried expression on his face turned into a wide, big-toothed grin.

He wrapped the youngster in a blanket. "There's coffee on the stove," he said. "I'll be back soon to warm up some stew."

Tony gulped the hot coffee and gave Benjie some cold stew. Then before Charley Hank returned he crept out the back door and into the night. He and Benjie walked along the Caribou road trying to fight off tiredness.

Benjie was the first to give in. Whining softly he stopped at the side of the road, licking the pads of his feet. Cold and tired, Tony lay down by the old dog.

He woke with a start, the early morning sun shining in his eyes. He and Benjie were covered with a heavy blanket, and a man's jacket was folded beneath his head. He looked up quickly and saw the jeep parked in the middle of the road. Sitting behind the wheel, quietly smoking his pipe, was Mr. Gorman. His eyes were tired from lack of sleep, but there was a smile on his lips. "Don't you think it's about time to come home?" he asked.

Tony got to his feet, eyeing Mr. Gorman. "I don't have a home," he said, "and I'm not going to leave Benjie."

"That's just what I wanted to talk to you about," said Mr. Gorman. "I was all wrong about Benjie. I guess I was wrong about a lot of things. If you'd change your mind, we'd like to have you come back and live with us up at the big house."

Tony could hardly believe his ears. "And Benjie, too?" he asked.

Mr. Gorman nodded. "And Benjie too."

353

A few minutes later they were bouncing along in the jeep, Tony's arm around Benjie's neck.

"I think we could do with a bit of breakfast," said Mr. Gorman. "What would you like?"

Tony's smile went from ear to ear. "Buckwheat cakes and sausage," he said.

Mr. Gorman winked. "Buckwheat cakes and sausage it is."

Setter

The Five Critical Stages
in a Puppy's Life

J. J. McCoy

Stage one: The first stage is from birth to about 13 days. At birth, the puppy is practically helpless. He's blind, deaf, toothless and is restricted in motion (he can crawl or slither on his stomach, with his paws making swimming motions). He experiences very little in the way of learning. He's strictly a creature of reflexes. His total behavior pattern is built around reflexes dealing with food, elimination and bodily contact with his mother and litter mates. When deprived of food or bodily contact, the pup will object by whimpering or whining. During this first stage, he lives in a half-world, aware only of his physical needs.

Stage two: This stage extends from the 13th day to the 19th, according to Dr. Scott. It begins on the 13th day when the puppy opens his eyes (13 days is an average; some pups open their eyes earlier, some later). For the next 7 days, the puppy moves very quickly through sensory, motor and psychological changes. At the end of the 7 days, the pup can see, hear and walk. His milk teeth appear and he can eat solid food. He can also form conditioned reflexes and adapt to a variety of situations. But he still shows no signs of any permanent learning ability.

Stage three: The third stage begins on the 19th or 20th day after birth and continues until the puppy is 7 to 10 weeks old. It is a crucial stage in the puppy's development, one that sets the pattern for future behavior. And it is the stage when socialization begins and the pup forms a relationship with human beings and other animals.

The third stage is ushered in by the pup's startled reaction to sounds. In stages one and two, the young puppies ignore sounds. But the puppy in stage three will really jump if you make a loud noise. He will also show an investigative curiosity about people and animals, and will tussle and scrap playfully with his litter mates. During this stage, the puppy's nervous system is still immature.

Neglect or faulty handling of the puppy during this third stage can result in serious damage to the behavior pattern. We've already learned what complete isolation can do to young puppies in this age group. Dr. Scott's group studied another effect of environment on the young puppy. Three-week-old pups were raised in individual cages, away from people and other dogs. They had no contact with the physical or social world beyond their cages. After three to four months in the cages, the puppies were taken out. They all seemed more or less physically sound, but they were woefully lacking in experience! These ivory-tower puppies couldn't adapt to the competitive life with other puppies their age, nor could they comprehend the world outside their cages.

In general, what happens to a pup during the third stage of his life will determine his future behavior.

Stage four: Stage four begins when the puppy is from 7 to 10 weeks of age. This is the usual age at which puppies are weaned from their mothers. The pup is not completely independent, but he now has some increased motor skills and his nervous system is similar to that of an adult dog. The 7- to 10-week age group is ideal for raising a puppy. It is the best age at which to establish a sound relationship between dogs and people. If the puppy has had a happy third stage, he's eager to form an attachment. And what's more, he's ready to learn.

Stage five: The fifth and final critical stage starts at about 12 weeks of age and lasts until the pup is 4 months old. Now the puppy starts to assert himself. He'll be bold, perky; testing you in all kinds of situations. It is time to teach him discipline.

An understanding of your dog's instincts and behavior is a must for intelligent dog ownership. It's true that dogs just grew up in the "old days." But don't compare the "old days" with today. Know your dog and know him well. He's an extraordinary animal!

Foxhound and pups

Superlatives

THE GREATEST racing dog in history was Mick the Miller, a greyhound owned by an Irish priest named Father Brophy. Mick flashed sensational speed on the English tracks, and the Father was offered $4,000 for the beast. He accepted on condition that he receive the Derby purse if the dog won the classic. The Miller came through, winning $50,000. In his three-year career on English soil, Mick never lost a race.

The dog who is reputed to have lived the longest was a black Labrador named "Adjutant," who died on November 30, 1963 at the age of 27 years and three months.

The smallest breed going is the Chihuahua. At maturity, this Mexican wonder generally weighs somewhere between two and four pounds, but some Chihuahuas tip the scales at no more than a pound.

The heaviest dog on record was a Wisconsin Saint Bernard who, at age five, weighed 295 pounds.

The largest litter ever thrown was 23, by a foxhound called Lena, on February 11, 1945.

Superlatives

The tallest dog extant is the Irish Wolfhound "Broadbridge Micheal." Owned by a woman in Kent, England, it measures 39½ inches at the shoulder.

The fastest dog in the world is either the saluki or the greyhound, depending on whom you talk to. The greyhound has been clocked at 41.7 miles per hour.

Greyhound

How Human Are Dogs?

Arthur Trayford, D. V. M.
Gladys Hall

A BOSTON TERRIER of our acquaintance once disappeared from its home on Long Island for a whole year. One morning it was found sitting at the front door of its owner's shop by which, during the day, it had been wont to spend its time. As mute evidence of the miles it had traveled, it was wearing a Midwestern dog license.

Due to underdeveloped taste buds, dogs do not have a keen sense of taste. They savor or reject their food according to the way it smells. For example, some dogs will not touch raw meat; they prefer cooked meat because of the more appetizing aroma. If the food has little or no smell, a dog must be very hungry (or very greedy) before it will eat. Most dogs, especially the gourmets (and there are gourmets among them), like seasoning because it accents the odor of food. The problem of an indifferent eater can often be overcome by sprinkling its food with garlic or onion salt or bits of cooked bacon.

Many dogs like fruits, including citrus fruits, for the same reason that they like candy: the sugar smell. On the other hand, they do not like peppermint or wintergreen or anything aromatic. And they definitely dislike the smell of alcohol. We have daily evidence of this at the hospital when we are preparing to give an injection. Prior to rubbing the skin with alcohol, a dog is usually quiet and well behaved; the instant it gets a whiff of the alcohol with which the swab is saturated, it will back away, bristling and growling. Nor do dogs take kindly to the overzealous attempts of an individual with alcohol on his breath to be affectionate. To nuzzle a dog after two or three cocktails is one sure way of asking for trouble.

Because anything that smells of malt appeals to dogs, they usually like beer, although they'll wait until it stops fizzing and becomes flat before sampling it. While it is fizzing, the bubbles hit them in the nose, and as the nose of the dog is extremely sensitive, they experience a prickling or stinging sensation from which they back away.

When dogs do become imbibers of anything stronger than beer (and some tall tales are told of those that do), it is the cocktail with the sweet smell that turns them from drys to wets.

Dogs panic at fire, and because the smell of smoke is associated with fire, they do not like the smell of a pipe, cigar, or cigarette. "But I am a chain smoker," owners will tell you, "and my dog doesn't complain." Perhaps not. Dogs are tolerant, particularly of those they love, but the degree of tolerance depends, it's well to remember, on the individual that is doing the tolerating. The fact remains that when a dog is in a room where there is a high concentration of smoke, it will almost invariably get up and leave. Dogs also dislike lighted matches. Strike a match near a dog and it will either stand still and bark or jump around until the match is extinguished. The owner of a German Shepherd had no difficulty at all in training the dog to extinguish lighted matches by trampling them underfoot. It is the fear of fire plus the keen sense of smell that makes dogs the alert and dependable fire alarms they are.

The dog that is basically a hunting dog, such as the

Pointer or the Springer Spaniel, can, on occasion, pick up the scent of birds from the air. When a female in the neighborhood is in season, males living as far as a mile away are able to pick up the scent.

But although the dog's scenting ability is one of its two keenest senses, it is also the one it loses most rapidly. For example, a dog that is left in a boarding kennel for a considerable period of time will usually not recognize its owner when he comes for it *until the owner speaks*. Dogs lose the sense of scent (allowing for individual differences) in about six weeks, whereas they seldom, if ever, forget the voice of a person with whom they have been closely associated.

Compared with human hearing, a dog's sense of hearing is so sensitive and acute as to be, in fact, extrasensory. Many sounds that are above or below the frequency range perceptible to human ears are heard clearly by dogs. The high-frequency overtones of sirens, whistles, and harmonicas are highly irritating and in some instances painful to a dog. The shrill screaming and shouting of children at play are also irritating to a dog's sensitive eardrums and to its nerves. For this reason it is advisable when children are playing noisily to keep a dog out of earshot or, if this is not possible, on leash.

Dogs know before we do when a hurricane is coming. The forerunning winds that whistle through tiny spaces such as cracks and window crevices, filling the house (especially an old house) with shrill, high-pitched sounds are inaudible to humans, but not to dogs. When a dog shakes its head continually as though its ears are in some way affected, it is invariably just before or during a windstorm or a thunderstorm.

Dogs also have a quite acute sense of touch. Their whiskers, having an antenna-type action, are tactile. And there are some tactile areas in the pads of the feet.

Compared with the strength and sensitivity of their

other senses, the eyesight of the dog leaves something to be desired. Generally speaking, dogs are farsighted. They see clearly at a distance, but close up, or within four to five feet of any given object, their vision is poor. Also, dogs are totally color-blind. They can distinguish only black and white, light and shadow.

We are often asked, "Can dogs see TV?" and before we can reply, the questioner (usually a woman) answers her own questions by tales of Loverboy barking excitedly when a dog appears on the screen and slinking away, tail between its legs, when the villain on foul murder bent makes his entrance.

When a dog of normal vision is four to five feet away from a television screen, it can see a clear-cut image. At a distance of less than four feet, the screen is a meaningless blur of light and shadow. Thus when a dog barks at the projected image of another dog on the screen, it is either because it is far enough away from the screen to see clearly, or, if close to the screen, because the televised dog makes its presence known by growling or barking. Similarly, a dog may appear to recognize the villain of the piece for what he is because, being extremely sensitive to intonation and inflection, it reacts to the menace in the voice.

Although dogs cannot think in the human connotation of the word and their sensory perceptions differ (most of them for the better) from ours, the physical organism of the dog and that of man are more closely related than that of any other member of the animal kingdom, including the ape. In experimental physiology, for example, many drugs are tried on dogs before they are given to man because the dog's reaction to drugs (the dosage being equal) is similar to that of a human. Certain surgical procedures are also carried out with dogs before they are used on man for the reason that, in surgery, the tissue or organic response is the same in the dog as it is in man.

In addition to the organic analogy between the human and the canine species, the dog has many qualities and characteristics, as well as emotions and emotional responses, so similar to ours as to give us a sense of kinship with all living creatures.

Love, for Instance: In addition to the love of man that the dog has evidenced ever since it emerged from the wild state, dogs can form canine attachments. In some instances, moreover, a male and a female can experience faithful or monogamous love, which is commonly regarded as a distinctively human prerogative.

As an example observed at first hand, a purebred Irish Setter female, long a patient of ours, now deceased, formed such an attachment when very young for a neighborhood male of extremely dubious lineage. In due course she had a litter by him, and although her owner tried time and time again to breed her to a purebred male Setter she would have none of him. She went back, in spite of all precautions, to her first love, and to the day she died would never mate with any other dog.

Friendship: Almost without exception, dogs like humans better than they like other dogs, but not altogether for the reasons commonly supposed: There is no food forthcoming from other dogs, or shelter provided. In terms of comfort and security, which they value, dogs can give each other nothing. Hence their preference, at least in part, for the companionship of man. (Some humans, it may be noted, like dogs better than other humans.)

But when dogs do make friends with other dogs they choose their friends, as we do, for reasons of congeniality. They will bypass the arrogant type, the lackadaisical do-nothing, the "Mama's boy" to run with the pooch that chases rabbits (and cars), the fellow that is outgoing and fun to be with. Nor do dogs show any particular preference for members of their own breed as friends. It appears to be strictly a matter of the individual. A hulking Great Dane and a miniature Dachshund can be better friends than two Great Danes. That there is communication between dogs seems highly probable, since they recognize barks—they can distinguish, that is, between the bark of a friend and that of a stranger.

Jealousy: The emotion of jealousy is very strong in the dog, as is apparent to any owner who has had a dog in the house before the arrival of a baby. When the baby comes and the attention is transferred from Fido to that little howling thing, Fido expresses his rage and resentment by "forgetting" that he was ever house trained, by becoming destructive as he had never been before, and by giving the family a generally sorry time of it. If another dog is brought into the house, Fido's reaction is the same—particularly if the newcomer is a male. In some instances, a male will accept a female amicably, and adult dogs of both sexes have been known to take a protective attitude toward a small puppy brought into a household. But for the most part, a dog that has been the one and only in the home doesn't want another pet or love object of any kind sharing its place in the home and in the affection of its owner.

Any dog worth its salt is possessive of the house in which it lives and of the family with which it lives. And any dog in possession of its faculties will get into the act, hair bristling, when its owner pets or pays attention to another dog. Jealousy such as this is normal and relatively harmless. It is when a dog develops an obsessively jealous attitude toward one particular member of the family that there is apt to be serious trouble.

We were once obliged to put to sleep a physically strong and healthy six-year-old German Shepherd female that was so insanely jealous of her mistress that when the woman's husband or children so much as touched her the dog, in a veritable lather, would have to be driven away with a whip. Let another dog approach her mistress and she would go in for the kill. When normal possessiveness becomes psychopathic jealousy you have an untenable situation· on your hands, such as that created by the German Shepherd. In such an extreme case, the dog has to go.

Vanity: "Vanity," it has been said, "is one of the most amiable of the large family of human frailties." It is also one of the most amiable—and amusing—of the large family of canine frailties. For example, show dogs are often referred to with pity because of the "unnatural life" they lead. According to their trainers, however, show dogs are no more to be pitied than show girls. Like their human counterparts, those who work with them maintain, show dogs enjoy the glamour treatment. With few exceptions, they bask in the attention focused on them while they are being clipped, trimmed, brushed, and pedicured. Their handlers pet them, talk to them, and the handling is a fondness. Family dogs or those in "private life" also enjoy the grooming process, providing they have been accustomed to a daily grooming from puppyhood (as they should be) and that they are handled, as show dogs are, with kindness.

Another evidence of canine vanity is the alacrity with which almost any average normal dog will learn to do tricks. You have only to observe the physical fitness of a troupe of trained dogs and the vim and vigor with which they go through the maneuvers of their act on stage or on television to realize that they are not in need of pity. Dogs that are non-pros also enjoy the spotlight that is focused on them when they perform. Owners often find that after teaching their dogs a few simple tricks, the dogs are appreciably more alert, responsive, spirited, and generally well behaved than they had ever been before. Generally speaking, dogs are show-offs at heart. To quote the long-time trainer of a circus dog act, "Applaud a dog, pet him, make much of him, and his ego swells before your eyes same as his stomach does after a fine full meal."

Modesty: A sense of modesty is often observed in dogs. For example, when the hair coat of a dog has been clipped too close to the skin, the dog, obviously ashamed of its scanty attire, will often hide under a bed or crawl under a bush outdoors. In some instances dogs that have been shaven and shorn will remain in hiding for days at a time, slinking out only when their stomachs call, until their coats grow out sufficiently to make them feel normal again.

Grief: Many dogs show a grief pattern following the death of a loved owner. They will refuse food, lose interest in everything, appear to be literally giving up the ghost. This reaction occurs most commonly, however, in dogs ten years of age and older, which indicates that the grief pattern is actually, at least in part, broken-habit pattern. Among younger dogs, a few will react to the loss of an owner in lachrymose fashion, but in most instances a young dog will soon transfer its affections to, and settle down with, anyone who takes over its care and feeding. It is the old dogs that grieve their hearts out and continue to grieve. Being creatures of habit, as all dogs are, old dogs are so set in their ways that no one can fill the place of the deceased, and so for them, too, it is some sort of an end.

Many tales are told of dogs that have been found crying at the gravesides of their departed owners. Grief or a sense of loss will often cause a dog to whine and howl. But when a dog's eyes well up and tears are shed, it is not from sorrow but because the lachrymal gland is obstructed or because there is faulty construction of the eye, which allows the lachrymal fluid to well up and spill over.

Memory: Dogs seem never to forget the voice of any person with whom they have once been closely associated. There is also reason to believe that they recall places in which they have lived at some previous time. Upon returning home after a long absence, for example, a dog will invariably make straight for its old familiar and favorite haunts—the corner of the kitchen where its feeding dish is kept, the good napping place under the back porch, the tree or bush under which it was wont to bury its bones.

It is recognition by means of the sensory perceptions, however, and not memory per se, that enables a dog to find places it has been and to recognize the voices of individuals it has known. Memory, as it serves humans, is a thought process, and dogs do not have a thought process.

Dreams: When a dog is sleeping and suddenly its legs begin to twitch, its body quivers, and strange guttural noises issue from its throat, it is dreaming—probably of chasing a rabbit, a squirrel, or another dog. It is generally presumed that dogs do not have nightmares. Judging by their bodily motions and the sounds they make while napping, their dreams are wish fulfillments of quarry chased—and caught.

Protective Instinct: In dogs with the best qualities of their kind, as in men who practice the humanities, the instinct to protect those they love (and their weaker brethren as well) is strong. There are many instances in which a dog has been known to stand guard over an injured master until help, in the person of someone the dog recognizes as a trusted friend, arrives and takes over. There are innumerable instances of dogs saving the lives of children by pulling them out of water over their heads, out of burning houses, and out of the way of oncoming cars. Dogs have also been known to protect their canine friends. In a neighborhood dog fight, for example, a dog will often go to the aid of the pooch that is getting the worst of it. There are also instances of a dog standing guard over an injured comrade. In exactly similar circumstances, however, a dog will occasionally reverse the procedure by killing the injured animal.

The Atavistic Reaction: When dogs are sick, they instinctively want to get away from humans and also from other dogs. The better to escape contact of any kind, they will usually seek out a cold, damp, dark place in which to get well, or to die.

In killing off a wounded comrade, as in obeying the instinct to hide when they are sick or wounded, dogs are experiencing an atavistic reaction to the habits of their remote ancestors when, traveling in packs, a weak or injured member was set upon and finished off by the others, lest their speed in pursuing game, or in being pursued by wild animals for which they themselves were game, would be retarded.

At any time in the life of a dog, this atavistic reaction can occur—a strong reminder that, although the dog, by virtue of domestication, is Man's Best Friend, it is still an animal and must be considered as such if the relationship between man and dog is to be a normal and mutually rewarding one.

Beware of the Dog

Albert Payson Terhune

I SUPPOSE EVERYONE has at some time had the wits scared out of him by a vicious dog. At any rate, the knack of getting along with dogs may come in decidedly handy for you, one day.

Twice during a recent morning's tramp I had to stop at farmhouses to ask my way. Both times, watchdogs came forward to meet me. The first cantered up to me, barking in thundrous challenge. I spoke to him in careless friendliness, all the time continuing my progress up the path. He gamboled along at my side, tail waving, nose gaily aloft. There was nothing to be afraid of.

Yet if I had taken to my heels there is a more than even chance that he would have nipped the first part of my anatomy he caught up with. Even a good-natured dog has an impulse to chase anyone or anything that runs in fear from him. The wild dog of old that did not dash forth thus to overhaul galloping prey went without food. The trait has endured. Hence his often fatal zest for chasing cars or trains.

The second watchdog was another matter. He advanced stiff-legged, head low, tail ramrod stiff. He was growling— not barking. A dog that growls in anger holds his head low, to protect his vulnerable throat in the impending scrimmage. This time I stood stock-still, my palms on my chest my feet close together. It was not a time for making friends, but for keeping unchewed.

The dog moved to me, still in battle formation, but increasingly puzzled. There was no salient part of me for him to bite. If I had tried to pet him, or turned to run, or kicked frantically at him, my hand or arm or leg would have been an ideal target for his teeth. But there I stood—what was the poor brute to do with me?

Nineteen times in twenty, a fierce dog will not hurl himself on a stranger who stands thus calm and motionless. My voice, speaking slowly and unconcernedly to him, increased his perplexity. For perhaps a minute, it was a deadlock. Then I took a step toward the house. Instantly he crouched for a spring. So I stood still again. The average fierce canine would have given ground at my advance, but this was one of the least amenable types of dangerous dog. The only move for me would be to back out of the yard, one step at a time and with long pauses between strides. Luckily the householder saw us and called off his cur.

In these two simple encounters lie the basic lessons in the art of getting along with dogs. Keep your head. Most dogs are not biters, if they are treated sanely and are let alone. To fondle a strange dog in the street or at a home you are visiting is like driving past a "stop" signal. Often you can get away unscathed, as many dogs are born mixers. But, when you meet a strange dog, don't bank on its being one of them.

Do not allow fear to master you when you are in the presence of an ill-tempered or vigilant dog. My reason for stressing this may sound fantastic, yet it is an established scientific fact. When you are frightened, nature pumps an undue amount of adrenalin through your system. This throws off an odor said to be like that of formic acid, which human nostrils fail to detect. Dogs, however, hate it. It rouses some of them to rage; in others it inspires only contempt. Many an

THE DOG LOVER'S READER

otherwise inoffensive dog will attack when that odor reaches
him. Here is an example:

Years ago, I used to visit a neighbor whose gigantic
cross-bred hound was a great pal of mine. I went away for
almost a year. On my return I called on this neighbor one
evening. His huge dog came bounding down the path. I
stooped over and rumpled his ears roughly between my
hands. Side by side we went to the house. He lay down on
the porch, while I went indoors. My host greeted me by saying he hoped his dog had been chained, as the brute was
murderously ugly to strangers.

While I was away his big cross-breed had died, and he
had bought another watchdog. This was the giant that had
greeted me. My host could hardly believe the dog had permitted such liberties. To prove it, I stepped out on the porch
where the new dog lay. By the light from the window I could
see what a man-killer he was. And I was scared. Yet I went
toward him with outward self-confidence, as if certain of a
friendly welcome. He launched himself at my throat with a
wild roar. I barely had time to catch him by the side of the
neck as he leaped. Now that he knew I feared him he attacked me. Yet I can swear no mere human would have
guessed I was afraid. His nostrils told him of my fright.

I think the total absence of fear-smell explains why so
many ill-tempered dogs are gentle with little children.

Some people "have a way with dogs" and can do almost
anything with most of them. Other people are invariably
disliked by dogs. If they don't like you, leave them alone. It
is no fault of yours. Don't be fooled by the old theory that
a man is to be trusted if dogs like him; and vice versa. That
is the most ridiculous of all the dog lies. Governors Baxter
of Maine and Pinchot of Pennsylvania sent a dog apiece to
state prisons to amuse the convicts. Eagerly the canines
made friends with the criminals. Surely in those two prisons
there must have been at least a few prisoners who were not

altogether saintly. But the dogs made no distinction among them. No, if dogs like you or dislike you, it is no criterion of your moral worth.

One or two more advisory tips: If your technique fails and you *are* bitten by a dog, remember this—not once in many thousand times is the dog rabid. Rabies exists, but it is very rare. Of the almost uncountable bites inflicted during a term of years on attendants in the New York City dog pounds, not one caused a case of rabies.

The bite of a healthy dog is only as dangerous as would be a similar wound inflicted by a piece of metal or bone—plus such possible food infection (*not* rabies) as may have been on the animal's teeth. If the bite is where your lips can reach it, suck it out thoroughly. Then bathe it in lukewarm (not hot) water and paint it with iodine. And don't worry. You are in no danger.

If you are afraid the biter had rabies—which he almost never has—use the same treatment but paint the wound with carbolic acid instead of iodine. The acid will burn for a short time, but you will be safe.

There are far more savage humans, in proportion, than savage dogs. You would not push past a military guard without the password. So why blame a watchdog for barring your way into the home he has been trained to defend? If you should walk over to even a fairly good-tempered man, in the street, and muss up his face with the palm of your hand or rumple his ears, the chances all are that you would find yourself on the receiving end of a punch in the jaw. You know that. And you don't incur such a silly risk. You leave the stranger alone. Therefore he leaves you alone. Do the same with dogs.

Obituary

E. B. White

DAISY ("Black Watch Debatable") died December 22, 1931, when she was hit by a Yellow Cab in University Place. At the moment of her death she was smelling the front of a florist's shop. It was a wet day, and the cab skidded up over the curb—just the sort of excitement that would have amused her, had she been at a safer distance. She is survived by her mother, Jeannie; a brother, Abner; her father, whom she never knew; and two sisters, whom she never liked. She was three years old.

Daisy was born at 65 West Eleventh Street in a clothes closet at two o'clock of a December morning in 1928. She came, as did her sisters and brothers, as an unqualified surprise to her mother, who had for several days previously looked with a low-grade suspicion on the box of bedding that had been set out for the delivery, and who had gone into the clothes closet merely because she had felt funny and wanted a dark, awkward place to feel funny in. Daisy was the smallest of the litter of seven, and the oddest.

Her life was full of incident but not of accomplishment. Persons who knew her only slightly regarded her as an opinionated little bitch, and said so; but she had a small circle of friends who saw through her, cost what it did. At Speyer Hospital, where she used to go when she was indisposed, she was known as "Whitey," because, the man told me, she was black. All her life she was subject to moods, and her feeling about horses laid her sanity open to question. Once she slipped her leash and chased a horse for three blocks through heavy traffic, in the carking belief that she was an effective agent against horses. Drivers of teams, seeing her only in the moments of her delirium, invariably leaned far out of their seats and gave tongue, mocking her; and thus made themselves even more ridiculous, for the moment, than Daisy.

She had a stoical nature, and spent the latter part of her life an invalid, owing to an injury to her right hind leg. Like many invalids, she developed a rather objectionable cheerfulness, as though to deny that she had cause for rancor. She also developed, without instruction or encouragement, a curious habit of holding people firmly by the ankle without actually biting them—a habit that gave her an immense personal advantage and won her many enemies. As far as I know, she never even broke the thread of a sock, so delicate was her grasp (like a retriever's), but her point of view was questionable, and her attitude was beyond explaining to the person whose ankle was at stake. For my own amusement, I often tried to diagnose this quirkish temper, and I think I understand it: she suffered from a chronic perplexity, and it relieved her to take hold of something.

She was arrested once, by Patrolman Porko. She enjoyed practically everything in life except motoring, an exigency to which she submitted silently, without joy, and without nausea. She never took pains to discover, conclusively, the things that might have diminished her curiosity and spoiled her taste. She died sniffing life, and enjoying it.

Foole and Gallant, Pioneer Dogs

Catherine C. Coblentz

Two MASTIFFS leaned over the side of the *Speedwell* as it came to anchor in Plymouth Harbor more than three hundred years ago. To one the trip had seemed long and unhappy; to the other it had been a joyful adventure.

The second dog had been made much of by the sailors, who called him Gallant. But the first was clumsy and always managed to be in everyone's way, so the sailors teased him and named him Foole.

Even as the dogs stood watching the land, Gallant from the corner of his eye saw a sailor approaching with a coil of rope in his hands. Dropping his forepaws from the railing, Gallant moved swiftly out of his way. But Foole was slower in seeing the man, and his leap was so ill-timed that rope, sailor, and dog sprawled on the floor together.

"Oh, Foole, what a nuisance you are!" came the angry words from the sailor as the dog's frantic efforts only succeeded in entangling them more thoroughly. "Why can't you be smart and careful like Gallant?" And the sailor kicked out ,at the animal. Just then Captain Martin Pring appeared.

"Foole is all right. He will show you what a fine dog he is, some of these days," declared the Captain, laughing at the efforts of dog and man to free themselves.

At the sound of Martin Pring's voice, Foole struggled more fiercely than ever. Finally with a great bound he left

From *Animal Pioneers*, © 1936 by Little, Brown & Co. Reprinted by permission of L. Huntley Cate, M.D.

the sailor alone among the rope coils, while he rushed to lick frantically at the Captain's hands.

"Yes, old boy, I know you're glad the journey is over. The sailors haven't been any too kind to your clumsiness," consoled the Captain. "And the name they have given you is a hard one to bear. But names can be lived down."

He patted Foole's head, and stopped with a caress for Gallant before setting about the business of seeing that the boat was properly unloaded and the men comfortably located on the New England shore.

For it was many years before the coming of the *Mayflower* that Captain Pring sailed into Plymouth Harbor with two ships to be loaded with sassafras roots. In those days an oil was made from these roots which was much in demand as a medicine in England.

The mastiffs were delighted to be on land. In and out of the cedar wood they rushed, and among the spruce and firs. Sometimes they chased a deer or a fox a little way, or leaped after the vanishing tail of a rabbit. At night they slept with the men behind a barricade. This barricade the sailors had built of logs and it was erected close to the shore.

Often in the evening the dogs saw a strange sight. When one of the boys who was with Martin Pring would bring out his zither and start playing it, Indians would slip softly out of the wood and up to the group of white men. Some evenings there might be only a few of them. At other times over a hundred would be there.

"Down, Gallant; down, Foole! Lie still," warned Captain Pring when he saw the Indians were afraid of the large dogs. So the two lay by the fire and watched the red men capering to the sound of the music.

The white men gave their visitors small pieces of bright cloth, or a few beads. In return, the Indians brought gifts of tobacco and tobacco pipes and skins.

At the end of a certain day one of the Englishmen did

377

not come in with the others. He was evidently lost in the woods about Plymouth, and Captain Pring called the two mastiffs.

"Go and find him," he said, holding out an old coat that belonged to the one who had strayed. The dogs smelled the coat and both bounded off, but after a little, Foole returned to the camp.

Seizing a short pole with a pointed iron at one end, he rushed over to Captain Pring with this held firmly in his mouth. As usual he expected to be patted, for carrying a half-pike in his mouth was his one and only trick.

This time Captain Pring looked at him in disgust and turned away without saying a word.

Foole crept under some bushes and lay there for a long time with his head between his paws, his eyes peering mournfully out at the world.

He saw Gallant march proudly back into camp with the lost man by his side.

"I never should have found my way if it hadn't been for Gallant," the one who had been lost declared. "I must have wandered at least six miles in the wrong direction."

Foole crept slowly out from under the bushes. Martin Pring was stroking Gallant. "Such a splendid dog! He is certainly living up to his name," said the Captain.

But when Foole thrust his cold nose into the Captain's other hand, the Englishman appeared not to notice.

After that Foole kept much to himself. All alone he watched from a little hill when the *Discoverer,* the first of the two ships to be loaded with roots, departed for England. Thirteen men and one boy sailed that day. So many less people to tease him!

On another hill the Indians watched the ship out of the harbor. There were but few white men left in their land, they thought. If they could get for themselves the shelter the strangers had built, they would have the piece of wood that made music. There would be much cloth, too, and many beads. Deep in the woods they gathered and made their plans.

At the barricade thirty white men and boys and the two mastiffs were left. Each day the dogs were sent with the men to the woods. One morning when the *Speedwell* was nearly loaded, Foole chanced upon his half-pike, which he had not carried since the day Gallant had won for himself so much praise.

But this morning he grabbed it with delight and insisted on taking it with him. It was so long it would catch between the trees and delay his progress.

"Such a fool!" said the men.

But Foole did not seem to hear, and, taking his station where he was told, carefully placed his half-pike at his feet. Somehow it seemed good company.

The weather was exceedingly warm, and when midday arrived the men ate their lunch and lay down in the shade for a short sleep. Gallant, too, closed his eyes, but Foole kept watching his half-pike as though he expected it to jump up and run away into the forest.

Suddenly the ship's cannon boomed through the stillness. Foole sprang up, his half-pike held in his mouth.

Gallant sleepily opened his eyes, but one of the men, who had been wakened, yawned and turned to his companions:—

"Guess the Captain is just seeing whether the cannon is in order before we sail."

Then Gallant followed the speaker's example and closed his eyes once more.

Everything seemed peaceful. There was only the occasional chirp of a bird, the humming of a bee, to break the stillness.

But Foole stood erect, listening. What if some danger threatened his Captain!

Across the hush broke the second shot of the cannon, sharp and menacing. Foole was off, his half-pike in his mouth.

Before Gallant was on his feet, or the sleepy men had struggled to their knees, Foole was at the edge of the forest and heading for the barricade. Once the pike's point caught against a tree trunk and wrenched his jaws cruelly. But he did not drop it. Somehow, by a quick turn of his head, he freed it, and across the clearing he rushed.

It did not matter to him that those log walls were surrounded by Indians armed with arrows and determined to capture the place. They had watched for such a moment when most of the men would be away, some of them in the woods and others with Captain Pring on the *Speedwell*, making ready for its sailing. The barricade was practically defenseless. All the food for the white men's journey was there, too.

The only thing that mattered to Foole was the find of his Captain. For somehow he understood that the second boom of the ship's cannon was Martin Pring's call for help.

Straight into the Indians' midst Foole rushed, and with wild yells the red men scattered as this huge dog armed with a shining weapon bounded fearlessly upon them. Even the dogs of these white men went armed!

And Martin Pring, leaving the *Speedwell,* from the deck of which he had seen the attack upon the barricade and the sudden appearance of Foole, was nearly knocked over by that mastiff. Martin Pring didn't seem to mind.

"Foole! Great, great Foole!" he cried. "I always said your day would come!"

It was six months from the time the mastiffs left England before they saw the shores of their homeland again— they were the first dogs of Englishmen to spend a summer in North America. And much was made of both of them—of Gallant, who had found the man who was lost, and of Foole,

who, with his half-pike, had broken up the attack of the
Indians on the Englishmen's barricade.

"The sailors who named the dog were the fools," declared Martin Pring.

Tibet Dogs

Shipping Your Dog by Public Carrier

J. J. McCoy

YOU MAY WANT to ship your dog by public carrier to another city, state or country. Trucking concerns, railroads, airlines and steamship lines will accept your dog for transportation, subject to certain rules. These carriers are considered to be semipublic agencies and are obliged to take your dog, *providing he is in good health and free from infectious disease*. You are required to produce a certificate stating the dog is in good health, free from infectious disease, and inoculated against rabies.

The carriers also have certain obligations. They must see to it that the dogs shipped on their conveyances are fed and watered. They must also take ordinary precautions against injury, suffocation, drowning, etc. But it is up to you to provide a strong crate or carrying box for the dog. The public carrier has the right to refuse to take a dog if he is not in an unbreakable and escape-proof crate or case. You cannot hold the carrier responsible if your dog gnaws his way out of the crate.

Rates for shipping animals interstate are customarily fixed by federal law. Transporting animals by public carriers within a state is regulated by a state agency. Since certain diseases are communicable from dogs to human beings and other animals, the various states and foreign countries control the movement of dogs into and out of their jurisdiction. If you plan to take your dog into another state or country, inquire in advance as to crating, inoculations, health certificates, etc. By doing this, you will save yourself disappointment. England, for example, has very strict rabies laws, especially against dogs coming from the United States. There is a six-month quarantine period in the British Isles. If you plan to visit the British Isles for two or three months, there would be no point in taking your dog, since he would be quarantined all the time you were there.

Reprinted by permission of Judy Publishing Co.

383

How to Choose a Veterinarian

Leon F. Whitney

THE FAILURE TO understand the simple processes of life, such as healing, bone knitting, and body functions, is to blame, I think, for those myriads of people who—possibly because of the habit acquired in taking their cars to a mechanic and ordering a new transmission or universal joint—take a dog to the veterinarian and say, "Kidneys out of order, Doc, fix her up." Or, "He's got kind of wobbly in the back end, sort of paralyzed. He's the only dog we have. We don't want anything to happen to him. Fix him up. When'll we call for him?"

A body just isn't like an automobile. You don't replace parts by taking something out and putting something else back. You remove causes and supply adequate nutrition; you may remove growths, but you must wait for the body itself to do the regenerating. Though it may disturb you to think of it, physiologically a dog is no different from Grandpa. You don't take *him* to the hospital and leave him with the admonition, "Fix him up, Doc. He's the only grandpa we have and we don't want anything to happen to him."

People are inclined to expect either too little or too much of their veterinarian. Perhaps they have been misled in part by seeing too many movies in which the "vet" is depicted as a dirty, mussed, careless drunk, with a large cigar in his mouth, spilling ashes over his patient. This old gent is perfectly content to sleep in the bedding beside a sick horse, and his boon companion is always Dickie, the stableboy.

Most people today know, I think, that veterinarians neither look nor act like this caricature. They are men who have spent a good many years of their lives in rigorous study in order to be able to help you and your pet. Their skills and their abilities are of the utmost importance to the welfare of your pet and to your own comfort and enjoyment. It is well worth spending some little time and thought in selecting the one who can best help you with your problems.

What is the most important factor in your choice of a veterinarian? What makes you select one man, and only one, to take care of the health of your pet? It is *confidence*.

Before you place your confidence in a veterinarian the main thing you want to decide is: How much does he know? In addition it is often wise to inquire into how he got that information, because what a person appears to know is not always the truth. When the veterinarian talks about a "slight cold in the kidneys" or a "cold in the intestine," when he advises cutting out chunks of a dog's skin in order to eradicate red mange or the surgical removal of the cecum to eradicate whipworms, an occasional client may be deeply impressed. Conscientious and up-to-date veterinarians are ashamed that members of their profession can be so ill-informed or unscrupulous.

When a client visits two veterinarians and is given two diametrically opposite diets for his pet, how is the client to know which man to trust? In the first place, he should try to decide which of the two is a conscientious student. That man is the one to trust. Why? Because much education is thirty years behind the times. What veterinarians were taught in college is sometimes almost the sum total of what they know about veterinary medicine today *unless they have studied dil-*

igently since they left school. What a man knows about the discoveries which have been made in recent years is the difference between a horse doctor of thirty years ago and a competent, modern veterinarian. Assuming that you know two men of equal educational background, one of whom has studied diligently since he finished his course while the other has not, you will have no difficulty in knowing where you can safely place your confidence.

There are certain indications which you will look for immediately in choosing a veterinarian. You cannot fail to notice the cleanliness and efficiency of his office or of his hospital. You will probably see on his walls his credentials, which must include study at an accredited college of veterinary medicine and a state license to practice.

But the pet owner is looking for something more. He wants to know that his doctor lives up to the ethics of his profession. He will consult the man who is guided by the code of ethics of the American Veterinary Medical Association. Here are my ideas of what that kind of veterinarian should be.

He should be completely honest. There are many opportunities to dodge around the truth. The ethical veterinarian will avoid them conscientiously. He will not give unnecessary injections at exorbitant prices, using five cents' worth of vitamin concentrates. He will not exaggerate the seriousness of an illness. He will try to effect a cure in a single visit. Not only does he do what he can for the patient in his office, but he respects the owner by instructing him in the care of the patient. If repeated visits to the office will give you added confidence, that is a matter for you to decide. The wise veterinarian, however, knows that the pet which costs the owner too much is a burden rather than a pleasure.

The ethical veterinarian charges moderate fees. There are, unfortunately, a few who callously feel that "it's not unethical to charge all the traffic will bear." It is. To be ethical, the veterinarian should consider all the factors involved. If a bill must be too large for the value of the animal, or if it is beyond the owner's ability to pay without hardship, that person should be advised that the very purpose of owning a pet—namely, to have something to enjoy—is gone. Veterinarians who overcharge do infinite damage to their profession by reducing the number of pet owners.

The ethical veterinarian is democratic. He does not exclude from his attention the laborer in work clothes, or the man with a dark skin. Yet there are doctors who do exclude the poor, the laboring man, and the colored man. They should be reminded that when a pet needs care, *it* is the patient, not the owner.

The ethical man thinks first of the service he may render. He does not ask to be paid before treating his patient. Prepayment is not only unethical, it is unprofessional as well. Money is not and cannot be the veterinarian's first consideration.

The modern veterinarian shares his discoveries freely with the members of his profession. Through the presentation of studies at association meetings and in the proper veterinary journals, he makes his observations available to others so that they can be used to relieve suffering.

Finally, the ethical veterinarian does not advertise. Neon signs are frowned upon as are blatant window advertisements. Claims of unusual ability to effect cures by secret methods are not used. The veterinarian does not allow his picture to be displayed in undignified ways. He does not issue circulars advertising his low fees. However, if he operates a hospital on a standard fee basis, he may upon request give you a card stating those fees.

The man in whom you can place your confidence may not wear all these qualifications like shining armor. They represent an ideal, but more and more the conscientious veterinarian is approaching this ideal. The veterinary profession today is distinguished by many truly magnificent characters—men who have the most unselfish attitudes, who sacrifice themselves for their patients just as willingly and unstintingly as ever the family physician gave of his strength and knowledge. That should not be surprising to anyone. A veterinarian must of necessity love animals, and the man who truly loves animals must also love his fellow men.

Newfoundland

388

Canine Sagacity

A CORRESPONDENT forwards to us the following anecdotes, illustrative of the remarkable reasoning powers of dogs.

The first case is one which occurred at a fashionable watering-place on the east coast of Ireland, some twenty years ago. This particular episode exhibits the remarkable sagacity displayed by a dog seeking a just revenge.

The jetty which stretched along the small harbor was at that time used as a promenade by the elite among the sojourners on the coast, where after the heat of the long summer days, the vacationers regaled themselves with the fresh evening breezes wafted in from the sea. Among the frequenters of this fashionable resort was a gentleman of some position who was the owner of a fine Newfoundland which inherited the time-honored possession of that noble breed—great power in swimming.

At the period of the evening when the jetty was most crowded with promenaders, his master delighted to put this animal through a series of aquatic performances for the entertainment of the assembled spectators. Amusement being at a premium on the coast, these nightly performances grew into something like an institution, and the brave *Captain*—for such was his name—speedily became a universal favorite on the jetty.

It happened, however, that among the new arrivals on

From *Chambers's Journal*, London.

the coast there came a certain major in Her Majesty's army, accompanied by two bulldogs of unusual size and strength. The value of a bulldog is generally inversely proportionate to its beauty, and so the appearance of the major and his dogs excited no very great pleasure amongst the strollers on the jetty. On the first night on which the major presented himself, nothing unusual occurred; *Captain* dived and swam as before. But on the second evening, the brave old favorite was walking quietly behind his master down the jetty, when as they were passing by the major and his dogs, one of the ugly brutes flew at *Captain,* and caught him by the neck in such a way as to render his great size utterly useless for his defense. A violent struggle ensued, but the bulldog came off the victor.

He stuck to his foe like a leech, and could only be forced to release his hold by the insertion of a bar of iron between his teeth. The indignation of the bystanders against the major was, of course, very great; and its fervor was not a little increased, when they saw poor *Captain* wending his way homeward, bleeding, and bearing all the marks of defeat.

Bulldog

Canine Sagacity

Some two or three evenings after this occurrence, when *Captain* again made his appearance on the jetty, he looked quite crestfallen, bore his tail between his legs, and stuck closely to the heels of his master.

That evening passed away quietly, and the next, and the next; and so on for about a week—*Captain* still bearing the aspect of mourning. But one evening about eight or ten days after the above encounter, as the major was marching in his usual pompous manner along the jetty accompanied by his dogs, something attracted his attention in the water, and walking to the very edge of the jetty, he stood for a moment looking down into the sea. Scarcely had the two bulldogs taken up their stand beside their master, when *Captain* seizing the opportunity for which he had so long looked, rushed at his former conqueror, and catching him by the back of the neck, jumped off the jetty with his foe in his mouth, down some twenty feet or more, into the sea.

Once in the water, the power of his enemy was crippled, while *Captain* was altogether in his element; and easily overcoming all effort at resistance, he succeeded in resolutely keeping the bulldog's head under water. The excitement on the shore was intense. The major shouted, and called out: "My dog! My beautiful dog! Will no one save him?" But no one seemed at all inclined to interfere, or to risk their lives for the ugly brute.

At length, the major called out: "I'll give fifty pounds to anyone who will save my dog;" and soon afterwards a boat which lay at some little distance pulled up to the rescue. Even then, however, it was only by striking *Captain* on his head with the oars that the Newfoundland could be forced to release his victim.

The bulldog was taken into the boat quite senseless from exhaustion and suffocation, and was with difficulty brought to itself again. *Captain*, on the other hand, swam in triumph to the shore, amid the plaudits of the spectators, who shared, in sympathy at least, his well-earned honors of revenge.

More remarkable than the sagacity displayed by the Newfoundland in the above case, is that which the following narrative illustrates. A gentleman of wealth and position in London had, some years ago, a country house and farm about sixty miles from the metropolis. At this country residence, he kept a number of dogs, and amongst them a very large mastiff and a Scotch terrier. At the close of one of his summer residences in the country, he resolved to bring this terrier with him to London for the winter season. There being no railway to that particular part of the country, the dog travelled with the servants in a post-carriage.

On his arrival at the town-house, the terrier was brought to the stable, where a large Newfoundland dog was kept as a watchdog. This individual looked with anything but pleasure on the arrival of the little intruder from the country. Consequently, the Scotch terrier had not been very long in his new home when this canine master of the stable attacked him, and in the language of human beings, gave him a sound thrashing. The little animal could, of course, never hope by himself to chastise his host for this inhospitable welcome, but he determined that by some agency chastisement should come.

Accordingly, he lay very quiet that night in a remote corner of the stable; but when morning had fully shone forth, the little animal was nowhere to be found. Search was made for him, high and low, but without success; and the conclusion reluctantly arrived at was that he had been stolen.

On the third morning after his disappearance, however, he again showed himself in London, but this time not alone; for to the amazement of everyone, he entered the stable attended by his old friend, the big mastiff from Kent. This great brute had no sooner arrived than he flew at the Newfoundland, who had so badly treated his little terrier friend.

A severe contest ensued, which the little terrier himself, seated at a short distance, viewed with the utmost dignity and satisfaction.

The result of the battle was that the mastiff came off the conqueror, having given his opponent a tremendous beating. When he had quite satisfied himself as to the result, this great avenger from out of town scarcely waited to receive the recognition of his master, who had been sent for immediately on the dog's arrival, but at once marched out of the stable, to the door of which the little terrier accompanied him, and was seen no more.

Some few days afterwards, however, the gentleman received a letter from his steward in the country informing him of the sudden appearance of the terrier there, and his as sudden disappearance along with the large mastiff; and stating that the latter had remained away three or four days, during which they had searched in vain for him, but that the big fellow had just then returned home again.

It then, of course, became quite clear that the little dog, finding himself unable to punish the town bully, and thought of his big friend in the country, had travelled over the sixty miles which separated them, in order to gain his assistance, and had recounted to him his grievance. It was plain also that the mastiff had consented to come and avenge his old friend, had travelled with him to London, and having fulfilled his promise, had returned home, leaving the little fellow free from annoyance for the future.

The following well-known story is a strong example of the great intelligence which may be developed in a dog by careful training. A fashionably dressed English gentleman was one day crossing one of the bridges over the Seine at Paris when he felt something knock against his legs. Looking down, he found that a small poodle dog had rubbed against him, and had covered his boots with mud. He was, of course, much annoyed; and he execrated the little brute pretty freely.

393

But when he got to the other side of the bridge, he had the boots cleaned at a stand for the purpose, and thought no more about the matter.

Some days after this occurence, however, he had occasion once again to cross that bridge, and the same little incident occurred. Thinking this somewhat odd, he resolved to watch where the little dog went to; and leaning against the side of the bridge, he followed with his eyes the movements of his dirty little friend. He saw him rub against the feet of one gentleman after another, till he had exhausted all the mud off his once white skin, then rush off down the bank of the river, and there roll himself in the mud collected at the side. Having thus got a new supply of dirt, the little animal ran up to the bridge again, and proceeded to transfer it to the boots of the passersby, as before. Having watched his movements for some time, the gentleman noticed that on one occasion, instead of running down to the river, he went off to the proprietor of the stand for cleaning boots, at the other end of the bridge, who received him very cordially.

Then for the first time the truth dawned on him; the little animal belonged to the man who cleaned the boots. He had been trained by the bootblack to perform these mischievous deeds for the purpose of bringing in custom.

Being very fond of dogs, the Englishman resolved to purchase this clever little fellow, and bring him back to England with him. When, however, he went to the dog's master, that person at first denied any connection with the dog, and only admitted the ownership when he was perfectly satisfied that his interrogator had no connection with the police. For some time, also, he refused to part with the little poodle, saying that no money could pay him for the loss of his dog, who really made his living for him. Tempted, however, by a very high price, he at last consented to sell the dog.

A few days afterwards, the gentleman brought the poodle over to England, travelling via Boulogne and Folkstone. His residence in England was some thirty or forty miles from Folkstone, and to this place he brought his little purchase. He had not been many days in his new home, however, when the little French poodle suddenly disappeared. Search was made for him everywhere, but to no effect. His new master offered a reward for him, but to no avail.

At last, the owner made up his mind that the little fellow had been either poisoned or stolen. One morning, about six weeks after his mysterious disappearance, the gentleman received a letter from a friend in Paris telling him that his dog was back again there, and at his old trade of soiling boots in the interest of his former master. The little fellow not liking the dullness of a country life, had resolved to return to his former home, and had made his way to Folkstone. There, as the gentleman afterwards ascertained, he had got on board a steamer going to Boulogne; and from Boulogne, he had found his way back to Paris.

A French merchant, having some money due from a correspondent, set out on horseback, accompanied by his Dog, on purpose to receive it. Having settled the business to his satisfaction, he tied the bag of money before him, and began to return home. His faithful Dog, as if he entered into his master's feelings, frisked round the horse, barked, and jumped, and seemed to participate his joy.

The merchant, after riding some miles, alighted to repose himself under an agreeable shade, and, taking the bag of money in his hand, laid it down by his side under a hedge, and, on remounting, forgot it. The Dog perceived his lapse of recollection, and wishing to rectify it, ran to fetch the bag, but it was too heavy for him to drag along. He then ran to his master, and, by crying, barking, and howling, seemed to remind him of his mistake. The merchant understood not his language; but the assiduous crea-

From *The General Character of the Dog*, by Joseph Taylor.

395

ture persevered in its efforts, and, after trying to stop the horse in vain, at last began to bite his heels.

The merchant, absorbed in some reverie, wholly overlooked the real object of his affectionate attendant's importunity, but waked to the alarming apprehension that he was gone mad. Full of this suspicion, in crossing a brook, he turned back to look if the Dog would drink. The animal was too intent on its master's business to think of itself; it continued to bark and bite with greater violence than before.

"Mercy!" cried the afflicted merchant, "it must be so, my poor Dog is certainly mad: what must I do? I must kill him, less some greater misfortune befall me; but with what regret! Oh, could I find any one to perform this cruel office for me! but there is no time to lose; I myself may become the victim if I spare him."

With these words, he drew a pistol from his pocket, and, with a trembling hand, took aim at his faithful servant. He turned away in agony as he fired, but his aim was too sure. The poor animal falls wounded; and weltering in his blood, still endeavours to crawl towards his master, as if to tax him with ingratitude. The merchant could not bear the fight; he spurred on his horse with a heart full of sorrow, and lamented he had taken a journey which had cost him so dear. Still, however, the money never entered his mind; he only thought of his poor Dog, and tried to console himself with the reflection, that he had prevented a greater evil, by dispatching a mad animal, than he had suffered a calamity by his loss. This opiate to his wounded spirit was ineffectual:—"I am most unfortunate," said he to himself, "I had almost rather have lost my money than my Dog." Saying this, he stretched out his hand to grasp his treasure. It was missing; no bag was to be found. In an instant, he opened his eyes to his rashness and folly.—"Wretch that I am! I alone am to blame! I could not comprehend the admonition which my innocent and most faithful friend gave me, and I have sacrificed him for his zeal. He only wished to inform me of my mistake, and he has paid for his fidelity with his life."

Instantly he turned his horse, and went off at full gallop to the place where he had stopped. He saw, with half averted eyes, the scene where the tragedy was acted; he perceived the traces of blood as he proceeded; he was oppressed and distracted; but in vain did he look for his Dog —he was not to be seen on the road. At last he arrived at the spot where he had alighted. But what were his sensations! His heart was ready to bleed; he cursed himself in the madness of despair. The poor Dog, unable to follow his dear, but cruel master, had determined to consecrate his last moments to his service. He had crawled, all bloody as he was, to the forgotten bag, and, in the agonies of death, he lay watching beside it. When he saw his master, he still testified his joy by the wagging of his tail—he could do no more—he tried to rise, but his strength was gone. The vital tide was ebbing fast; even the caresses of his master could not prolong his fate for a few moments. He stretched out his tongue, to lick the hand that was now fondling him in the agonies of regret, as if to seal forgiveness for the deed that had deprived him of life. He then cast a look of kindness on his master, and closed his eyes forever.

Some time since, discoursing with a lady on the sagacity of animals, she told me the following story, and as she is a person of the greatest veracity, I make not the least doubt of the truth of it:—Her husband was many years a worthy member of parliament; he kept a pack of hounds: among them was a favourite bitch, that he was very fond of, and which he permitted to be a parlour guest. This bitch had a litter of whelps, and the gentleman one day took them out of the kennel, when the bitch was absent, and drowned them: shortly after, she came to the kennel, and missing them, she sought for, and at last found them drowned in the pond: she brought them, one by one, and laid them at her master's feet in the parlour, and when she brought the last whelp, she looked up in her master's face, and laid herself down and died.

The servants of a gentleman, who had a house near the river's side, opposite to a little island in the river Thames (which is said from this circumstance to have been named the Isle of Dogs), observed that a Dog came constantly every day to them to be fed, and, as soon as his wants were satisfied, took to the water and swam away. On relating this to their master, the gentleman desired them to take a boat and follow the Dog, the next time he came. They did so— and the Dog at their landing expressed great pleasure, and made use of all the means in his power to invite them to follow him, which they continued to do, till he stopped, and scratched with his foot upon the ground; and from that spot he would not move.

Either that day, or the next, they dug up the earth in the place, and found the body of a man, but it was impossible to discover who it was, and after every requisite step had been taken to find out the murderer, the corpse was buried, and the Dog discontinued his visits to the island. The gentleman, pleased with a creature which had shewn such uncommon sagacity, and attachment to his former master, caressed him greatly, and made him the frequent companion of his walks.

When he had been in possession of the faithful animal some time, he was going to take boat at one of the stairs in London, when the Dog, which had never before been known to do such a thing, seized one of the watermen. The gentleman immediately thought that this fellow was the murderer of the Dog's master, and taxed him with it; and he directly confessed it, on which he was taken into custody, and soon after hanged for the crime.

There is a Dog, at present belonging to a grocer in Edinburgh, who has for some time amused and astonished the people in the neighborhood. A man, who goes through the streets ringing a bell and selling penny pies, happened one day to treat this Dog with a pie. The next time the Dog heard the pieman's bell, he ran to him with impetuosity, seized him by the coat, and would not suffer him to pass. The pieman, who understood what the animal wanted, shewed a penny, and pointed to his master, who stood at the street door, and saw what was going on. The dog immediately supplicated his master by many humble looks and gestures. The master then put a penny into the Dog's mouth, which he instantly delivered to the pieman, and received his pie in exchange. This traffic, between the pieman and the grocer's Dog, has been daily practiced for some months past, and still continues, to the great amusement of the neighbours.

Dr. Caius, in his curious treatise on British Dogs, tells us, that three mastiffs were reckoned a match for a bear, and four for a lion.

We have a curious account, recorded in Stow's Annals, of an engagement between three mastiffs and a lion, in the presence of King James the First. One of the dogs being put into the den was soon disabled by the lion, which took it up by the head and neck, and dragged it about: another Dog was then set loose, and served in the same manner:

but the third being put in, immediately seized the lion by the lip, and held him for a considerable time; till being severely torn by his claws, the Dog was obliged to quit his hold; and the lion, greatly exhausted in the conflict, refused to renew the engagement; but taking a sudden leap over the Dogs, fled into the interior part of his den. Two of the Dogs soon died of their wounds: the last survived, and was taken great care of by the king's son; who said, "he that had fought with the king of beasts should never after fight with any inferior creature."

The mastiffs of Great Britain were noted in the time of the Roman emperors, who appointed an officer, whose sole business it was to breed and send from hence such as would prove equal to the combats of the amphitheatre.

The following anecdote will shew, that the mastiff, conscious of its superior strength knows how to chastise the impertinence of an inferior: A large Dog of this kind belonging to the late M. Ridley, Esq. of Heaton, near Newcastle, being frequently molested by a mongrel, and teased by its continual barking, at last took it up in his mouth by the back, and with great composure dropped it over into the river, without doing any farther injury to an enemy so much his inferior.

A Canine Panorama

Here is another collection of 19th-century lithographs of familiar and unfamiliar dogs. Some of these drawings are of German origin, others of British; all are wonderful depictions of that noble creature, the canine.

Lurcher

Tibet Dog

Retriever

Landseer Newfoundland

Dachshunds

Siberian Wild Dogs

Spitzes

The Older Dog

Charles Leedham

FROM THE AGE of six years onward, most dogs can be considered as moving into the classification of "old." This age does not by any means indicate that the dog is infirm, or will be for several years to come. In American and foreign police departments which have dog squads, it is not unusual to find a dog eight, nine or even ten years old still putting in a full day of strenuous work on the beat with his handler. Guide dogs and sheepherding dogs often work to this age, and past it. Breeds and individuals vary widely in their reaction to age—even as there are vigorous and active humans in their eighties, and others who are elderly and fading by the age of sixty. The range is even wider in dogs, some of whom are genuinely old and feeble by the age of eight or nine, with others still playful and puppyish at twelve or thirteen.

The major implications of aging in the dog are strikingly similar to those in the human. Physically, there is a slow and inevitable loss of tone throughout the entire body—the muscles become weaker, the organs no longer function at peak efficiency, the body is less adaptable to change and stress, its resistance to disease, infection and injury slowly drops as age increases. There is often graying at the muzzle as a sign of age in many dogs, although dogs do not, fortunately, become bald as humans do.

Mentally, the old dog becomes more and more a crea-

405

ture of habit, depending on long-established patterns of behavior, familiar places and people, familiar foods. Even a very peaceable and accommodating dog may become irritable towards strangers, although the really old dog usually seems to realize his age-induced ineffectiveness and restricts himself to grumbling and complaining.

Old age, however, is no bar to pleasurable enjoyment of life for a dog, barring specific infirmities, up to the day his body simply gives up and stops running of its own accord. He will simply enjoy life at a slower pace, and if he is well cared for, may never feel any more pains of aging than the inevitably increasing stiffness and lack of energy that are age itself. To compensate for this physical deterioration, the old dog has the absolute security of his household and your increasing love and attention as you see him growing older— these mean a great deal to him.

In this light, if you get a new puppy as a hedge against the day the old dog dies, be very careful about the distribution of your affection. True, a new puppy needs love and care, but it is vitally important to the older dog that none be taken away from him. Much as you may realize this, it is easy to think that, oh well, the old boy is a member of the family after all, and he really doesn't need so much fuss made over him. He does, for after having enjoyed your exclusive attention and affection for so many years, he may bitterly resent the intrusion of a new puppy, and he may go into a mental decline which can actually result in his earlier death. So don't disturb his feeding, sleeping or exercise habits because of the pup, and above all, never let him think that he is any the less loved because of the new acquisition.

FEEDING

The major factor to remember in feeding is that the older dog will become increasingly disturbed by sudden or radical changes in his feeding and diet. Even as slight a change as a new feeding bowl may upset him to the point where he will refuse food for days—someone other than his master preparing and serving the food may also throw him off. And of course, any sudden changes in the food itself will disturb him.

If your dog has been getting an adequate diet for all his life, there will ordinarily be no reason to change it as he grows older. He will probably eat less, but this involves no change. The only reasons for specific dietary changes are obvious signs of infirmities, or drastic lessening of good bodily appearance—dry and shaggy coat, severe loss of weight. All older dogs begin to lose the sheen and smoothness of the coat, and may become thinner and more bony, but marked changes should not be written off as simply the effects of old age, but should be regarded as possible signs of problems. In such cases there may be specific internal degenerations or illnesses which require change or supplementation of the diet, and only your veterinarian can prescribe these for him to suit the individual case. If you do have to change the diet, or introduce new supplements, do it very slowly and gradually so he will adapt himself without upset.

Older dogs are usually considered poor risks by the operators of boarding kennels. The change of circumstances may upset the older dog so much that he will literally grieve himself to death, and the change of food will also upset him to the point where he may simply refuse to eat while in the kennel. Therefore, if it is absolutely essential that he be left in a kennel, make a particular effort in this case to supply his regular food to the kennel, and make arrangements that he be fed only that. Of course, if the old dog has been going to one kennel regularly during his life, he will accept it as a normal part of living, and will probably think nothing at all of going during your annual vacation or whenever.

Constipation can be a problem of the old dog, and if

this occurs, may be solved by changing his feeding schedule from once a day to two or even three smaller meals during the day. His digestive system is no longer able to handle the full load once a day as it used to, but will be able to handle the same daily amount if given in smaller meals. This recommendation does not violate the above advice about not changing his routines, for if it is done gradually he will come to accept it, and it is more important that the problem of constipation be solved.

If he has any tendency at all to become overweight, very definitely cut down his food to the point where he is simply maintaining himself at a good normal weight, not thin but without excess fat. Extra fat in the older body is one of the surest roads to early death. Here agin, make the adjustment gradually—don't just suddenly cut his food down to whatever level you think proper. It is no cruelty to even the oldest and most pampered dog to cut down his food to keep his weight in line for optimum health and longevity—it is in fact a kindness, for not only will he live longer, but he will feel better and be able to move around more easily on his weaker muscles with all that fat off him. If he has become accustomed during his life to tid-bits and snacks, there is no reason to stop them, unless they are contributing to an overweight problem.

You should have an abundant supply of fresh water always available—his consumption will very likely go up as his age increases. One of the most chronic infirmities of age is diminished kidney function, which requires a greater intake of fluid. To a certain point this is considered normal, but beyond this, drastically increased water intake and urination may indicate chronic nephritis, discussed later in this chapter.

EXERCISE AND REST

Although he will have slowed down considerably, there

is no reason to treat the older dog like an invalid. A certain amount of exercise is highly beneficial, for it will help maintain his muscle tone, stir his lagging appetite and help keep his excretory functions in order. On the other hand, don't urge him to excessive running or prolonged work. If he is very nearly prostrated after some activity, then it is dangerous for him and should not be continued at that intensity. Dogs in their infinite variety respond differently, some wanting nothing more than to loaf around as age advances on them. Some others, particularly those who have led active lives in, say, hunting with their masters, will be as eager as ever to go out and spend a day in the woods. With some such older dogs it seems almost a matter of pride to do as well as when they were younger, but in general they should be gently restrained, or allowed to work a little and believe they're doing as well as ever.

Be a little more careful about letting him take long walks in the cold and snow, and in the rain, and about letting him stay too long in the direct sun or in any heat. His bodily temperature regulating mechanisms have begun to lose their efficiency, too, and a snowy romp that would only have exhilarated him a few years ago may give him a severe chill now. Dry him off thoroughly when he comes in, and persuade him to sit quietly and rest awhile if he comes in from a walk in hot weather.

He will rest and sleep noticeably more as he gets older, and he may get grumpier about being disturbed by noises and people, but humor him. You'll get that way a little yourself before long.

GROOMING

It is more important now than ever that he be groomed regularly. The skin has lost some of its resiliency, and older dogs may have considerably lowered resistance to skin infections and parasites. An infestation of the major parasites that would only have caused minor annoyance and scratching in younger days may now cause severe reaction and inflammations. There is no need to bathe him less often or more often (except to control parasites) than when he was younger. Be only a little more careful about drying him after a bath, so that he doesn't get a chill.

The toenails can cause trouble, because now that he gets less exercise, they will tend to grow longer and perhaps require more frequent clipping. By this time, though, he will be a hardened veteran of such procedures, and may in fact welcome the extra attention that nail clipping brings him.

TEETH

Although dogs of all ages are relatively immune to cavities, the teeth do wear away through years of hard use, and almost all old dogs will begin to have tooth troubles. The biting surfaces of the teeth wear down, and if your dog has been chewing on bones, rocks or other hard items during his youth, they will be well worn. It is unusual for the wear to penetrate to the pulp of the tooth, and so there is rarely complication.

Calculus is very often a problem, particularly on the canine teeth and the premolars just behind them. Unless this is removed with some regularity, it will penetrate down to irritate the gums, and will result in chronic inflammation and possible infections.

Broken and loose teeth should of course be extracted by a vet, and it is a good idea to check the dog's mouth occasionally for such conditions. If several teeth have to come out, or have come out by themselves (this is not uncommon with short-nosed breeds, who may lose some of the front teeth spontaneously), it doesn't mean that the dog has to go on a liquid diet. He should, however, be restricted to relatively soft foods, which means that biscuits and unsoaked kibbles are out as dietary items. Otherwise, even a totally toothless old dog can live quite a happy and satisfactory life—he doesn't need his teeth for fighting any more, and if he doesn't have to chew his food, all will be well.

INFIRMITIES

Chronic or acute otitis is a common problem of older dogs—such infections of the ear are more common in those dogs with hanging ear flaps which tend to retain dirt and moisture within the ear itself. You may notice it first if your dog begins to stand or sit with his head leaning even slightly to one side—not cocked intelligently in the well-known "listening at attention" pose, but simply holding the head consistently at an angle. There is also evidence of pain and disturbance in one or both ears, as evidenced by continual rubbing or scratching which terminates in self-inflicted pain as the claws hit sensitive areas. On close inspection you may find that either ear is reddened towards the canal, and that there is grayish to yellowish material exuding from the canal in small quantities. If you find this sort of symptom, don't attempt to treat it yourself or clean out the canal, but take the dog to a vet—amateur attempts at treating otitis almost always cause more trouble than relief, both directly and due to the fact that they put off competent professional treatment.

With or without a history of otitis, hearing difficulties and final deafness or near-deafness often afflict dogs, particularly those over the age of ten. If a veterinarian's examination shows no treatable infection of the ear, or blockages by wax or other physical factors, there is, of course, nothing you can do about deafness and impaired hearing from the treatment angle. You can make life easier for your dog, however, if you keep his diminished hearing in mind and try not to startle him by coming up behind him. If you suddenly touch him

411

from the rear when he hasn't heard you approach, he may be really upset about it—it sometimes seems that the older dog is ashamed of not having heard you come. Additionally, remember that a deaf or near-deaf dog can no longer hear such sounds as may have been warning him of danger in the past—particularly automobiles, if he is accustomed to playing or lying in driveways, or crossing roads or streets.

Remember that a dog lives in an entirely different world. He has no way of communicating or receiving concepts, and if he is going deaf he cannot realize that it is something which is happening to him—he will believe simply that the sounds of the world are getting quieter. It is important, for dogs depend on their hearing a great deal, and when it goes they may still be depending subconsciously on it. If cars have always made a noise, there is no reason that they shouldn't still, as far as he is concerned. If you have ever swum in the surf, you will know how you develop an almost unconscious dependence on hearing big waves coming—if this were suddenly lost to you, you might be looking in another direction and really get swamped. Much the same can happen to a dog with automobiles or other dangers which ordinarily advertise themselves to him by noise.

Blindness or partial loss of sight is the most debilitating impairment of all, and is not at all uncommon in older dogs. If yours is a house pet, he may be almost completely blind before you notice it, for after a lifetime of getting used to the placement of the furniture, and his standard routes on the street when walking with you on leash, he may be able to get around quite well through habit plus hearing and smell. You may, in fact, first notice failing sight if you rearrange the furniture, and he bumps into a chair or other object placed in an unfamiliar spot. There is little constructive advice that can be given in such cases, other than what your own common sense would tell you, such as being careful about rearrangements of furniture until he has a chance to get used to the new situation, and increased caution about heights.

You may notice tiny growths from the edge of the eyelids, which cause irritation and eye-watering if in contact with the eye itself. If such growths do cause local irritations, your vet can usually take them off quite easily, and they should be removed.

Chronic nephritis, or kidney malfunction, has been estimated as occurring in as high as 80% of all dogs over eight years of age. There are two versions of nephritis. The one called non-uremic involves little more than allowing the dog access to as much water as he wants to drink, elimination of too salty and spicy foods from his diet, and more attention to his status as an old dog: avoidance of major surgery and anaesthesia, less exposure to extremes of cold and heat, prevention of constipation. Non-uremic nephritis is characterized by high thirst and the resultant larger amounts of urine, which tends to be pale yellow or even clear and watery.

The uremic version of nephritis is the dangerous one, and the symptoms of this type are apathy, depression, gradual loss of weight to the point of emaciation, arching of the back, stiff gait, and sometimes vomiting and a breath that smells either simply bad, or vaguely like ammonia. Such symptoms should lead you to an immediate visit to your vet, who can make a positive diagnosis, and attempt treatment. At best, at the present stage of knowledge of nephritis, treatment may swing the condition over to the non-uremic form, and the dog may live quite comfortably with the extra care needed for this lesser condition.

Incontinence, or gradual loss of control over retention of urine, may be a problem of some older dogs, either male or female. It is most often associated with chronic nephritis, for the increased drinking and resultant larger quantities of urine put a greater strain on the retentive muscles of the bladder, and these muscles are weakened by age. In such cases very little can be done about it except to give the older dog more frequent opportunities to go outside to relieve himself. It may reach the point where the old dog is forced to urinate during the night, no matter how well housebroken he was in younger days. If there is no way he can be allowed free access to the outside, such as a swinging panel in the door of a non-urban house, it might be well to set up a system of putting papers in a box in the kitchen for the old dog. He will hate to break his housetraining, but bladder pressures can overcome the strongest will and training, and if he is given papers in a box and allowed to use them in emergencies, it will make it easier for him, and of course for you.

Dribbling which occurs in spayed bitches as they get older is one of the few incontinent conditions which can be aided—sometimes this can be controlled or at least lessened by shots of hormones, and this possibility should be discussed with your vet.

Chronic severe constipation can often afflict the old dog, simply through impaired function of the intestines and abdominal muscles. If your dog has been unable to defecate, or does so only with straining and difficulty, resulting in very hard stools, try giving him a dose of Milk of Magnesia (about one teaspoonful per 10 pounds of dog.). If this does not bring relief within 12 to 18 hours, suspect internal disorders and have him examined. And *do not* dose him with laxatives or cathartics intended for humans! Some of them can kill him.

In the older male, even after only six years of age, constipation is often the result of enlargement of the prostate gland. This organ, enlarged, presses against the wall of the rectum and causes a physical barrier to passage of the feces. Continual straining in such cases can cause hernia—this is one of the reasons a severe case of constipation unrelieved after two doses of milk of magnesia should receive veterinary attention. The vet may be able to correct it by administration of hormones, or in extreme cases by castration, which causes the prostate to atrophy.

The most common problem of the older unspayed female is tumor or cyst of the mammary glands. Any lump or swelling in the bitch's breasts, particularly in the rear two pair, should be looked at by a veterinarian. He may be able to control the situation by hormone injections, but in severer cases he may have to remove the growth surgically. If at the time of surgical removal (or even hormone injections) he suggests spaying the bitch, don't be surprised. Spaying will often bring cysts and tumors under complete control, and the older bitch will be able to live out a healthy life. By this time there will certainly be no question of breeding her, or worries about unbalancing her hormonal system to her detriment.

DEATH AND EUTHANASIA

When the inevitable happens, through simple old age, as a result of heart failure or as the terminal phase of any disease or condition, it most frequently occurs at night, in sleep, when the body is at its lowest ebb. You will simply find your dog in the morning, dead without pain or suffering, his good life with you over. If it happens during the day when you are with him, you may be warned by several deep, gasping breaths at intervals of several seconds—this does not indicate that there is any pain, but is simply the failing body's last automatic attempts to keep air coming into the tired lungs. It is perfectly natural.

In such cases, grim though the precaution seems at a time like this, put some newspapers or preferably an old sheet or blanket under him as soon as possible after death, for when death occurs, the tone of all the muscles relaxes, and urine or feces that are contained at the moment of death will be released. If you use a sheet or blanket, put it not only under him but over him, for this precaution is not so much a sanitary one as preservation of his dignity in death. The sheet or blanket, too, will be there to carry the body in when you remove it for burial or other disposal.

Euthanasia is the most difficult subject of all. In the absence of any specific and painful infirmities, the old dog can be the best of all companions and may enjoy his life now even more than when he was a puppy. But if he is in constant pain from some chronic condition, or crippled, or so arthritic that he cannot even walk or walks only with difficulty, it is by far the kinder thing to have him put away humanely by your vet. It is well to realize at this point that because of his inability to communicate in abstract terms, the dog has no conception of the future, or of death. He cannot anticipate days to come, and thus cannot "miss" having lived longer.

The usually recommended method of euthanasia is by injection of an overdose of barbiturates into the bloodstream. With this method, the veterinarian simply injects about twice as much anaesthetic as would have been necessary to put the dog to sleep temporarily for an operation. The dog simply does that—goes to sleep without any pain or realization, and then dies in his sleep. Do not think the vet is heartless or cruel if he asks you to sign a statement that you have authorized the euthanasia—many vets will ask this as legal protection. You will probably want to be present when the anaesthetic is administered, and it is the rare vet indeed who will not allow it. It is the last thing you can do for your dog—to allow him to go into his final sleep in your arms or by your side.

There are occasional cases in which a dog is suffering from some chronic or recurrent serious disease which allows home nursing. When the case is one in which recovery is problematical, but in which you are trying to nurse him through, there may be episodes of such severe pain that you will want to have prior arrangement with your vet as to the administration of barbiturate pills yourself. Ask the vet to give or prescribe the necessary pills, and have a thorough understanding with him as to the circumstances which warrant their administration. He may only give you enough to assure unconsciousness, with instructions to bring the dog in as soon as possible for professional administration of euthanasia if it is warranted by examination. Go along with him on whatever he recommends.

The death of a beloved dog is a sad note on which to end this article, but this is the natural course and end of all affairs, of man or dog. This article has been written in the hope that your dog's life will have been full, active and healthy, and that at the end he will have left you with memories of good days only.

At the death of his own favorite dog in 1808, Lord Byron wrote one of the simplest and most moving tributes ever given, inscribed on a monument by the dog's grave:

> Near this spot are deposited the remains of one who possessed Beauty without Vanity, Strength without Insolence, Courage without Ferocity, and all the Virtues of Man, without his Vices. This Praise, which would be unmeaning Flattery if inscribed over human ashes, is but a just tribute to the Memory of Boatswain, a Dog.

Why Dawgs Are
Better Than Dogs

Bil Gilbert

ONE DAY LAST January I was walking on the Appalachian
Trail, along the northernmost extremity of the Blue Ridge,
from an old iron furnace at Pine Grove, Pennsylvania, to a
state highway twelve miles east, where I expected to get
a ride at five that afternoon. With me was a big red dog, a
collie-shepherd cross, Dain (aptly surnamed Ironfoot after
the Tolkien dwarf).

At noon it began to snow, a heavy fall. The snow, the
first significant storm of the winter, excited both of us; the
walking was easy along a flat plateau and so we moved along
faster than our normal two-and-a-half-mile-an-hour rate. At
three o'clock we came off the mountain and crossed a secondary road, only two miles from the highway where we
were to be met. Fortunately there was a tavern at this inter-
section of Trail and road.

Country bars and roadhouses are numerous in Pennsylvania and are among the overlooked glories of that state.
One can do very well in these unpretentious establishments
in terms of beer, food made out of pigs and eggs, and conversation. I hung my pack and poncho over a porch railing,
commanded by the barroom window, told Dain to stay with
the gear and went inside to kill the hour that our fast pace
across the Blue Ridge had given us. The dog, accustomed
to unscheduled stops, laid down on the snowy porch and

without panic or complaint prepared to wait. There were half-a-dozen patrons in front of the bar, and the owner and his wife behind it were setting up mostly boilermakers and eggs pickled in beet juice. In such places, entertainment is extemporaneous, do-it-yourself. Because of Dain, he in particular and dogs in general became the subject of conversation.

If I do say so he deserved the attention. He is a big, heavy-boned animal, at eighteen months weighing just shy of a hundred pounds. His coat is medium length, a solid red-gold, a shade lighter than red fox in prime pelt. His long muzzle is masked with·black, there is a blaze of white on his chest, a point of white on the tip of his tail, which he carries high, curled over his back. Outside the bar, waiting beside the pack, he gave the impression of being simultaneously alert and at ease. When a customer would enter or leave, Dain would give him a careful, pleasant look and, if spoken to, a polite thump of his thick tail. There was no cringing, yapping, growling of a dog hysterical with fear. Nor, when he was greeted, did Dain leap, slobber, fawn upon the greeter as dogs will who are so unsure of themselves and their place that they must seek reassurance from complete strangers.

419

"I had one of those big old red dogs like that," confided an orchard man at the bar who appeared to be about four beers and four shots into the snowy afternoon. "Fourteen years I had him and cried like a woman when we put him to sleep. Never had another like him. You want to sell? I'll put a hundred dollars down on this table this minute and take him with me.

"No, you don't, I don't blame you, you're lucky to get a good dog like that anymore. But I'll tell you what. If I could get ahold of a good bitch along his lines, we could breed him to her. Where do you live? Write it down. I want to know where I can find that red dog."

Now nobody has ever got rich, or seldom even made the price of drinks, wheeling and dealing in a country tavern on a Saturday afternoon. A good bit of the back-and-forth with the orchardist was intended and understood to be a sort of stylized way of making friendly conversation. It is impossible not to be chummy, trade beers, with a man who extravagantly praises your dog. Nevertheless I was pleased by the compliment, particularly since I had had so many dogs who, though they were occasionally given ribbons by a show judge, would never have won praise in the White Pine Tavern.

Since I was three, thirty-six years ago, I have never been without a dog and have often had them in multiple numbers. I have had dogs as pets, dogs by the kennel full; I have exhibited dogs, tutored them in obedience courses, given them behavior tests, dissected dogs. Of all these animals, Dain is the first mongrel I have owned and there is no question in my mind that for my purposes he is the best dog I have ever owned.

Dain is in a sense an antique animal. For some millennia, until fifty years or so ago, good dogs were dogs more or less like Dain, hardy, reliable, self-reliant, well-mannered, useful. But in this century, because of affluence, commercial promotion and snobbery, these values have become secondary. Now such an animal as Dain is worth perhaps $10 on the open, sober market (the situation in the White Pine Tavern being somewhat special). On the other hand, as I know from sad experience, a cringing Great Dane as delicate in mind and body as a Victorian poetess, but who, according to certain arbitrary standards, looks well in a show-ring will bring $500.

To fully appreciate this shift of opinion in regard to dogs and the resulting change in the kind of dogs we have to regard, it is necessary to consider how the domestic dog was made—and he was made as surely as the fantail goldfish or the electric toothbrush. The process probably began with packs of wild jackal-like canines who followed prehistoric hunters as scavengers. Sooner or later the hunters must have discovered that the jackals had their uses, flushing game, training, cornering, bringing it down, giving alarm at the approach of other predators. Archaeological evidence and logic indicate that the next steps were the deliberate feeding of the wild dogs, encouraging them to stay near the camp, raising wild puppies, and finally the intentional breeding of camp dogs. Thereafter, through selective breeding, out of necessity, by luck, during thousands of years a variety of breeds of dogs were developed to serve man in a variety of specialized ways. Sausage-shaped dogs were created for following rabbit runs, sprinters for the chase, burly dogs as guards, and so on. It was a continuing, tinkering process and the canine recipe was frequently changed to suit individual tastes. A man, for example, who had light, long-legged deerhounds and who wanted bear dogs would beef up his pack by introducing mastiff blood without feeling he was a contemptible miscegenist.

Man not only was a critical factor in the physiological evolution of the domestic dog, but also had a strong influence on the development of certain definite psychological traits

in the animals. Whereas in the physique, the aim of breeding was for diversity, creating dissimilar strains for specialized jobs, conformity was the apparent and logical goal when it came to behavior. Whether a dog was a herder, a hunter or a companion, one quality of temperament was useful above all others—responsiveness. An animal which would rest his head on a man's knee was more desirable for both practical and sentimental reasons than one that ran back to hide in the bushes. As men began to train dogs for relatively complicated work, the premium on responsiveness must have increased. Animals who possessed this hard-to-define but easy-to-observe trait to a marked degree were protected, prized, and the ones most likely to be used for breeding.

The results of this long-term, psychologically orientated breeding program have been extraordinary. No other species has much rapport with another as dogs do with man. A good, companion-type dog will understand thirty or forty commands and requests and will use half that many signals to express his own moods and desires. Dog specialists, used for herding, guarding, certain types of hunting, can master a considerably larger, more precise and complex vocabulary. And this is only the beginning, for overt signs play a less important part in man-dog understanding than a covert, almost extrasensory system of communication. In human terms and as the word is generally used, dogs are geniuses at recognizing and reacting to tiny outward indications of the inner feelings of men. They are better at this than any other animal, better than the more publicized, more intelligent apes and dolphins, often better at understanding men than other men are. Dogs sense and are strongly moved by human anger, elation, depression, pleasure, frustration, confidence, fear, zest, weariness, illness (even though these emotions are being tightly controlled).

On a dreadful day, January 1, 1966, to be precise, I walked seventeen miles across the mountains with three boys, Dain, and an excruciating hangover. For reasons of pride and moral example, I did not want the boys to know of my condition and was able, at some cost, to hide it from them, but not from the dog. Normally, Dain's trail position is twenty-five yards in the van, where working underbrush he puts up deer, birds, rodents for his amusement and my instruction. On the day of this death march, Dain stayed at my heels, acting much as I felt, thoroughly subdued, giving every indication of suffering from a sympathetic hangover.

It has been said in other context that to be truly loved is to be truly known by another, and that loving is truly caring to know another. If this is so, perhaps much of what superficially seems to be twaddle, dog as man's-best-friend-and-devoted-companion actually may represent an insight that is as meaningful as an aphorism by Sigmund Freud or Jean-Paul Sartre.

Along with the desire to get animals with various func-

423

tional physical features and of good temperament, there was a third, though usually minor factor, which influenced the creation of domestic dogs. This was aesthetics. Certain color-shape combinations inevitably seemed to certain men at certain times to be superior to other canine styles. The presumption is that beyond the pure pleasure of looking at one kind of dog, social considerations influenced this type of breeding. If, for example, Kublai Khan caried a Pekingese, then as sure as rice is rice, soon the Duke of Si-kiang and eventually all the Counts of Si-kiang were going to find intrinsic virtue and great beauty in the Peke. However, except for the nabobs who had time and means to indulge in biological fads, canine form, as a rule, followed function. It did until about the turn of this century when most of the traditional standards were overturned. Quite suddenly, in terms of the long dog-man association, how an animal looked became for many dog fanciers much more important than how a dog behaved. Spreading out from Great Britain (the first industrial, affluent society and the one where nostalgia for the squirearchy was strongest) the cult of the conformation pedigreed dog spread throughout what is loosely called the civilized world.

Today most of the selective, intentional, commercial breeding of dogs is influenced directly or indirectly by the requirements of the show-ring. These requirements are to produce animals which match as closely as possible certain standards of conformation established by governing dog bodies. Given this goal the results achieved in a half century or so have been good. A dozen Kerry Blue terriers, for example, in a show-ring now look as much alike as peas in a pod. (The Kerry Blue, originally a scrappy badger baiter, varmint hunter, pit fighter, was made by crossing wolfhounds, terriers, bulldogs, poodles and probably a few other strains. However, forty years ago or so Kerry Blues were "recognized" by the Kennel Clubs and the dog was genetically frozen.)

424

A casual show observer will be puzzled as to how, much less why, one dog will be designated as better than the others. The differences are there, but apparent only to an exhibitor, or hopefully to the ring judge. Conformation standards are numerous, exact and subtle.

Since function is now subordinate to form as a criterion for breeding, the modern "good" dog almost inevitably tends to be less robust than the old-fashioned good dog. For example, you will occasionally see a squatty, meaty Great Dane who looks capable of pulling a cart, one of the jobs his ancestors were bred to do. Such animals from an exhibitor's standpoint are undesirable atavistic sports, having about as much chance of winning in a show-ring against modern willowy dogs as a plump German farm girl has of making a career as a high-fashion model. This in itself is neither surprising nor wicked. Contemporary taste in many things from dames to Danes runs to slim. Furthermore, hardly anybody these days needs a dog to pull a cart. The difficulty is not that many "finely" bred dogs can no longer work (there is no real work left for them to do) but that they are so delicate in physique, so lacking in endurance and resistance to congenital and chronic diseases that they are not even hardy pets. (So far as I knew there is no canine health survey that supports this impression, but perhaps the phenomenal increase in small-animal vets, the sale of pills,

vitamins, tonics and other patent medicines for dogs bears
on the matter.)

Even more disturbing than physical deterioration resulting from modern form-over-function standards is a similar
and it seems to me equally inevitable degradation of canine
character. Frequently owners, exhibitors, connoisseurs of
standard breeds will describe their favorites as "high-spirited." What they would like to suggest with this phrase
is that dogs now, like folks now, are swingier, zingier than
they used to be. It may be true, but as far as I am concerned
"high-spirited" is a euphemism for neurotic. As the modern
dog is less able to work than the old dog (which is not so
important since few people need badgers pulled from holes
these days), so he is getting less able to handle social situations. (This is important. "Interpersonal" problems are mul-
tiplying, getting knottier for dogs as well as the rest of us.)

Take, for example, relationships between dogs. The
peace among both wild and domestic canines is traditionally
kept by an elaborate, effective hierarchal system. Each dog
has a definite rank (time and place may change his position
in relation to other dogs) and there is a vocabulary of visual,
aural, olfactory signs by which dogs make known their caste
situation. The key to the scheme is that a dog does not have
to gain or hold his place by fighting. All he has to do is make
his position known in the hierarchy. Normally male dogs will
not attack females. Adults will tolerate all sorts of impudence
from pups without retaliation. A large, strong, pugnacious
dog will back off from a smaller, weaker animal who is in
the sanctuary of his own territory. Even among peers, dogs
of the same age and sex meeting on neutral ground, there
are certain display signs which enable dogs in some mysterious way to determine without violence who ranks who.
An underdog seldom dares to attack his superior and the top
dog does not care or need to dirty his fangs on an inferior.

Left to themselves, dogs, even such supposedly ferocious creatures as wolves, seldom have serious fights.

There are signs that modern "high-spirited" dogs are having trouble maintaining this splendid social system. Since the time when pit fighting was popular there probably has not been such opportunity to watch dogfights as there is now in almost any suburban neighborhood, where nearly all the dogs, if not potential show champions, come from show-bred stock. In Shady Hills Acres, among the snarling, yapping beasts, all sorts of terrible breaches of traditional dog law and etiquette can be observed. (It is not all the fault of the animals or the new-style breeding. Too many dogs roam loose in two small an area. New dogs are constantly being introduced, old experienced dogs removed from the suburban packs. Like their owners, dogs need a sense of geographical place.)

A really dreadful example of this breakdown of the canine code was that of a four-month-old Shelty who was dragged off the front steps of his own house by a Boxer and, of all things, a Basset hound, and literally skinned alive. He most certainly would have been killed had not his owner intervened. Such behavior breaches two of the most important canine laws—the immunity of the young and the sanctuary of the home territory. In human terms it is the equivalent of a psychopath who takes a baby out of a crib and mutilates it for thrills. In some ways it is even worse. Through the centuries we have come to expect such violence from men, but we expect dogs to cure their barbaric impulses.

A traditional code has also governed relationships between men and dogs. Given half a chance a dog will regard his owner as a pack leader. Only under extreme provocation would a well-adjusted dog disobey, much less attack, such a superior creature. This veneration of rank is one of the reasons why dogs are, among the large carnivores, the easiest and safest to control. Other canine codicils have been adapted to man-dog affairs. A proper dog, for example, tolerates and protects children as he does puppies. His territorial writ follows the same boundaries as his owner. He takes pride in his own place, respects that of others.

But these restraints too seem to be weakening. A couple I know theoretically the "owners" of a physically magnificent but morally degenerate German shepherd, lived in real terror of this animal for two years. They moved slowly, spoke softly about the house, so as not to excite the dog into attacking them as he had on three previous occasions. Friends could not enter this house until the brute had been lured behind a closed door. On several occasions this dog escaped surveillance and roamed freely in the neighborhood. To put it frankly, he hunted children.

This behavior is extreme but not untypical these days. In the same neighborhoods where Boxers and Bassets are skinning Shelties there is a fair chance of watching or, worse, getting involved in man-dog donnybrooks. Snapping, yapping, unpredictable pets are becoming an increasingly serious obstacle to gracious living in Shady Lane Acres. Nipping is common, mauling not unexpected and every now and then it comes to killing. Recently, for example, Los Angeles newspapers reported three serious attacks on humans by dogs. A Great Dane and a German shepherd killed a twenty-month-old child, severely wounded a baby-sitter (the "owner" of the beast) who tried to save the infant; on the same day a collie savaged a convalescing Vietnam veteran. This new aggressiveness, the breaking of the old and honorable truce, is not a sign that dogs are getting fiercer, bolder, but rather that they are losing their self-confidence, becoming more timid. In nine cases out of ten, terror, not courage, is at the root of unprovoked attacks of dogs on men. A dog, unsure of where he belongs, to whom he belongs, what his rank is, is more easily frightened than an animal with a strong sense of place and person. Living in confusion, such dogs are understandably likely to view the world as threatening and to attack out of desperation.

Paradoxically some of the spectacularly "friendly" dogs, beasts who cringe before and fawn upon perfect strangers, are not displaying signs of overweening affection but of fearful hysteria. As a rule I am as wary of these sycophants as of the obvious canine thugs. It often takes very little to completely unhinge their addled minds—to turn them from slobberers into snappers.

It also seems that responsiveness, the ancient and basic canine virtue, is becoming rarer. In urban-suburban areas, now the natural niche of pedigreed dogs, an animal who responds dependably to what used to be the simplest, most elementary commands, sit, stay, heel, come, is regarded as something of a marvel. Innumerable dog-owning families put up with unruly, boorish, sometimes dangerous beasts because the animals are "too high-spirited" to learn good manners. Part of the failure may be laid to the fact that people are less adept now at making their wants known to their dogs. On the other hand one of the glories of the old-fashioned dog was that he could figure out what even a stupid owner wanted and would act accordingly.

Now obviously there were puny dogs, psychopathic dogs, dull dogs long before there was an American Kennel Club. (But in times past, no matter what an animal's appearance, he seldom survived or was used for breeding if he displayed obvious defects of character and lack of hardiness.) Furthermore, a half century of breeding pedigreed animals cannot completely change characteristics which were developed over thousands of years. (The change in dogs is far faster now because selective breeding techniques are more widely used and more effective than before.) Finally, breeders of show dogs do not intentionally try to produce and do not always produce namby-pamby neurotics. However the fact remains that in selecting pairs for mating the breeder is principally concerned with the appearance, since in a show-ring a dog only has to have enough hardiness, enough emotional control to stand relatively still for a half an hour. (It is well if the animal being judged does not bite the judge, but this is not essential. Some biters are show winners.) To get blue-ribbon dogs, exhibitors naturally try to introduce the best (in terms of conformation) bloodlines into their own stock. This means that when a bitch or stud wins consistently, they and their pups will be in great demand. As a result the genealogical charts of many show animals show descent from close common ancestors.

Among all animals, breeding of closely related pairs accentuates the characteristics of the parents in their offspring. Desirable conformation traits—say a certain length of leg or color of coat—can be quickly produced by breeding from a single bloodline in which these features are pronounced. However, breeding of near kin also exaggerates defects and seems to weaken the genetic resources of the line. (Congenital deafness in many purebred Dalmatians is a case in point.) The weaknesses are often such subtle ones as loss of phyical vigor and nervous stability.

Certainly it is no more immoral to breed, by the most effective means possible, dogs who meet arbitrary standards of appearance, than it is to raise blue tulips or midget cattle. The difficulty is, I think, that now many people who have no ambition to be exhibitors, potential dog owners who really need and want a good pet, have been convinced that the only way (or at least the only chic way) of getting one is to buy a registered dog whose breeding reflects the special standards of the show-ring.

Generally speaking, the citizen who shells out a hundred dollars or so for a registered dog does so because he believes or wants others to believe that he is buying a good dog, good according to conformation standards and good according to the old definition of a canine companion. He is likely to be disappointed. There are precious few potential show winners available at popular prices ($500 is a good starting figure for a competition dog). As far as character goes, the registered pet's "papers," of which new owners are often so inordinately proud, signify only that for some generations back his ancestors have been selectively bred for their appearance. Because considerations of form, not function, have controlled the animal's inheritance, the genetic odds are that he will be somewhat less stable, durable, responsive than a giveaway mongrel.

So what? Derivative taste, social one-upmanship, emulation of the gentry has led or leads us into far worse fixes than being saddled with an unfunctional dog. The so what, it seems to me, is not that people may be disillusioned with a pedigreed pet, but rather that they may be deprived of owning a good, antique dog. To be associated with such an animal is one of the genuine worthwhile pleasures possible in our condition. I could even be goaded into contending that for most of us, most of the time, the kind of dog we have is more important than the kind of finance minister Nigeria has. . . .

These Have Been
Reported As True

For a month, a mongrel pup maintained a lonely vigil above an old well near Rockford, Illinois. The townspeople, fearing that the dog's master had fallen down the 100-foot well, insisted that the water in it be drained. Thousands of curious onlookers watched as the 10-day, $1,000 pumping job was completed. At the bottom of the pit, the rescuers found only an ancient, five-inch bone.

The boy was delighted when, after months of prodding, his father agreed to let him keep a dog. When a fox terrier down the block had a litter, the father brought home one of the pups, but insisted that the new pet be kept in the basement at night.

The first night, not surprisingly, the puppy howled until dawn, keeping the entire neighborhood awake. The second night, he again disturbed the neighbors with his mournful cries.

The next morning, the boy's mother heard a pawing at the front door. She opened it to find the pup's mother standing on the porch. The terrier walked in, picked up her puppy by the scruff of the neck and, leaving the woman aghast, walked back out the door and returned home.

Postal authorities in Texas received a telephone call from a woman who complained about the substitute mailman on her route. "The regular carrier gets along fine with our dog," she explained irately, "but whenever the substitute makes the rounds, hc upsets the dog."

"Oh? Where is your dog now?" a postal official asked.

"He's out in the yard, under a tree," the woman replied.

"And where is the mail carrier?"

"He's up in the tree. He's upsetting my dog and making him bark."

A female mongrel was stretched out before the living-room fireplace as the woman of the house sat knitting nearby. The bored animal woke up, yawned, and looked around absently. Her eyes fell on a plate of chocolates in a dish on a low table.

The pet was very fond of sweets, but she had been taught never to help herself. Furtively, she sauntered over to the low table, picked up a piece of chocolate, and dropped down before the hearth with the candy between her paws.

There she nuzzled her prize for a while, avoiding the woman's eyes, then gave a long, sad sigh of resignation. As the woman watched, the dog took the chocolate in her mouth again, returned to the table, and dropped the candy back into the dish.

At the counter of an exclusive clothing shop, a woman with a toy poodle on a leash was standing next to a man who was also waiting to be served. The dog hovered around the man's legs, and the man continually drew back from the animal. Finally, the annoyed woman said, "For goodness sakes, my poodle won't bite you."

"Madam, I'm not afraid that your dog is going to bite me," replied the gentleman, "but as he keeps lifting his leg, I'm afraid he's going to kick me."

The great inventor, Thomas A. Edison, never a man to enjoy publicity, was once persuaded by his wife to attend a gala social function in New York. After trying for most of the evening to escape the well-wishers who surrounded him, the inventor at last managed to find a place to sit alone in a corner. But Edison continually glanced at his watch with a look of resignation on his face. When a friend edged near to him unnoticed, he heard the inventor sigh to himself: "If there were only a dog here!"

Little Ann arrived home one day with a mongrel bitch, but try as she might, she could not convince her mother that they should keep the dog.

About a week later, Ann arrived home from school and found the mongrel running about the yard, pursued by a pack of male dogs. Her eyes gleaming with pride, she burst into the house. "Mommy," she called out, "come to the window! My dog is just a natural-born leader!"

A man once went hunting with a pointer he had borrowed from a friend. While the friend was a crack shot, the man himself was a very poor shot, and each time he missed his target the pointer would look up at him in bewilderment.

After an unrewarding afternoon, the dog finally set a pheasant out in an open field, and glanced back at the hunter as if to say "You can't miss this one."

The man shot and missed. The pheasant rose and flew off, and again the man missed. The pointer sat down, raised his nose to the sky, and howled long and woefully. Then, without another look at the disappointed huntsman, he turned and trotted home.

These Have Been Reported As True

Pueblo, Colorado, is justly proud of its own version of "The Odd Couple." Charlie the Cat and Daisy the Dog set up joint residence in a doghouse owned by Jeff Anderson. Each critter has its own entrance to the house and, according to Mr. Anderson, both eat, sleep, and play in perfect harmony. What makes this story doubly amazing is that Charlie and Daisy did not grow up together; they are both strays.

Mrs. Arlene Higuera's pooch had had that hangdog look for a couple of days, and just wasn't the playful pet it had always been. So, naturally, Mrs. Higuera rushed her darling to the vet. After a simple operation to extract the 267 marbles in the dog's stomach, Fido was soon romping around the house with his accustomed panâche.

Rip was one of several dogs employed at major airports around the country to sniff out drugs that might be concealed in incoming cargo or luggage. Rip was the star of Miami International Airport's customs inspections team, but officials began to doubt Rip's sense of smell when he commenced to bark at some crates containing massive concrete pedestals for lawn statues.

But Rip's past record induced the officials to check out the cargo. Each pedestal was five feet tall and weighed 400 pounds. After drilling through 1½″ of steel-reinforced concrete on the first pedestal, the customs men discovered a sealed, galvanized steel container which held 80 pounds of marijuana! The other nine pedestals yielded the same trove. The street value of this haul was $160,000.

It will be a long time before anyone questions the super schnozzola of Canine Agent Rip.

How to Raise a Dog

Jack Alan

Dog owners, arise! Too long has the actual head of your family not even paid an income tax. Too long have you tried to conceal from your dog the fact that he really owns you. Too long have you searched in vain for the counsel you so sorely need when, panting and tongue hanging out, you fall back into the nearest chair and finally admit to yourself that the lively little fellow isn't going to sit up and beg, hasn't the slightest intention of leaving that frayed end of the tapestry alone, and is unshakeably convinced that the mathematical center of the living-room rug is the Comfort Station Supreme.

You can expect no help from dog books or dog doctors. In this all-important emergency, all they do is back away, muttering incoherent statements about Training and Psychology. And you are left holding the bag, one end of which has already been chewed away, like everything else you own.

I am no expert. I might as well tell you right now that I generally go to sleep with a large, greasy bone under my pillow because I have failed to sway my dog in his opinion that there isn't a better spot in town for bone hiding. My house is thoroughly dog-broken. But I do not intend to leave my fellow man with his dog having the upper paw in the household.

I believe my predicament to be an average one, a valuable case history. I will show you how I deal with my dog.

Maybe you will be able to discover where along the line something went terribly, terribly wrong.

Things started badly when I bought him. I didn't select him, he selected me. When I went to the kennel, I had decided definitely against buying four or five puppies, as I wanted to do. Phyllis claims that this is too many for a small apartment. Cunningly, however, I planned to get around this by getting as much dog as possible for my money—a Great Dane.

I looked critically at the batch of puppies, which, while only three months old, were the size of Airedales. Then one detached himself from the mob. He had a lot of filling out to do. He took, I noticed, several steps before his skin started moving along with him. He galloped over, sat down heavily on my feet, and looked me over carefully. I couldn't move, so I had to look at him, too. He was obviously admiring me. His next step was to take my trouser leg in his mouth and shake it, possibly to test the quality of the material. Then he gave several pleased body wiggles, attempted to climb up on me, and washed my hand thoroughly with a salmon-pink tongue. Then he sat down again on my feet and admired me some more.

I had been chosen.

Several months have passed, and we have learned much about each other. Neither of us regrets his choice, although my training methods seem to lack something.

I have found that the very first step must be to Gain His Confidence. To accomplish this, I sit on the floor next to him and say, "*Good* little dog!" This is a flat lie and he knows it, being well aware that he is neither little nor good. He backs away several feet, presses himself close to the floor, and turns up his eyes at me with a wary "You-are-up-to-something-tricky-and-I'm-not-going-to-like-it" expression.

I reach out reassuringly and pat his nearest paw. He withdraws the paw and licks it off fastidiously.

I attempt now to get his attention by cupping both hands and saying coyly: "Guess what I've got here?"

Showing signs of interest, he nuzzles into my hands. I am caught flat-footed with nothing in them. I run to get a dog biscuit to absolve myself. Meanwhile he stalks off bitterly to a corner of the room, tenses his forelegs, digs a hole in the carpet, and lies down in it.

I now change my approach, deciding to try the Great Big Playmate tactic. Crouching on all fours, I advance on him, barking several times with mock ferocity. He decides to humor me by pretending he thinks I'm a huge, dangerous dog. With a happy yelp, he flashes around a chair and dashes upon me from behind. Since he weighs roughly eighty-two pounds at the moment, I am now flat on the floor with him on top of me. He wants to pretend he is shaking me by the neck. This is too difficult unless he actually does shake me by the back of the neck. So he does.

I get up and brush myself off. I brush him off me, too, several times. I have now succeeded in gaining his confidence and showing him that I am a regular fellow who doesn't mind a good, clean romp, so I am through. But he isn't. He likes it too well to quit. He gets my tie in his teeth and hangs from it. It is some time before I get my breath.

He still refuses to stop. It is therefore time for me to Punish Him. I decide to lock him in the bathroom. This consists of the following steps:

1. He instantly senses my purpose and scrambles into the bedroom and under the bed.
2. I rush after him and say, "Come out from under there this minute!"
3. He doesn't.
4. I get down on the floor and look under the bed. We face each other. I blink, which gives him the round.
5. I mutter several dire threats. So does he.

6. I hold out my handkerchief, hoping he will grab it and pull, thereby enabling me to drag him out.

7. He grabs it and pulls.

8. We are now both under the bed.

9. I seize him firmly and wriggle out.

10. A head bumps severely against the box spring. It is not his.

11. I shove and pull him into the bathroom and back out, closing the door.

12. I stop closing the door to avoid catching his nose in it.

13. I shove him back and close the door, catching my hand in it.

14. We both howl simultaneously.

Returning to the living room, tired but victorious (look up Pyrrhic in any good encyclopedia), I now proceed to describe my dog to you. He is still a puppy, seven months old. He is a good dog to have for a case history because, although a thoroughbred, he has a character which is practically a cross section of that of America's dogs.

Although large and getting larger, it is his opinion that he is a lap dog and as such entitled to climb on my chair whether I am in it or not. When I can catch him to give him a bath, he emerges as a dull gold in color with a mouth fringed with black. This mouth is already large enough to contain my arm and, when I am giving him a bath, does. Like all his breed, he has a short coat, but he sheds it with the success of the collie. He has a way of searching out tidbits in his food which probably reveals that in spite of his pedigree he contains a trace of ant-eater. He has a beery sort of baritone. And he is very democratic in his ideas about love.

When I first got him I called him Gilbert, the name I still introduce him by. The only word he will always answer to, however, is Food, so I generally call him that.

Food, or Gilbert, is still in the bathroom, you will recall. This is my golden opportunity to get something to eat unbeknownst to him. Let me explain.

Since I have known Gilbert, I have had few square meals at home. This is because Gilbert is an adept at a quiet, effective sort of bullying. When I am eating, he is too wily to use strong-arm tactics, realizing that force will be answered with force. He therefore just looks at me tragically. He keeps looking at me. He meditates on man's inhumanity to dog. He sighs. Beginning to feel like a heartless gourmand, I transfer my little morsel of food to my mouth. His glance never wavers. He drools slowly.

As a result, I spend a large part of my time at my dinner table chewing things up a little for Gilbert. Then I give them to him, cursing.

But now that Gilbert is in the bathroom, I turn on the radio full blast and enter the kitchen singing loudly, hoping that both noises will distract him.

It is a losing game. Gilbert, who would sleep soundly through a collision with another planet, easily detects the noiseless opening of the electric icebox. No sooner do I reach a guilty hand to a roast-beef bone than Gilbert utters a series of agonized cries, giving the entire neighborhood the impression that I am murdering him by inches. In self-defense I rush to the bathroom to make him stop.

He is very happy as I open the door, particularly since a well-timed move enables him to snatch the beef bone from my hand and rush back to the bathroom.

I am about to follow him to get back my bone when the doorbell rings.

It is Mrs. Garble, a middle-aged woman I do not like. She is the president of Phyllis' club. She is also a cat lover. She expresses relief at being able to come in for once and not have that great brute of a dog jumping all over her. Looking nervously, she asks where he is. I tell her.

How to Raise a Dog

"What in the world is he doing in the bathroom?" she says.

"Well, really, Mrs. Garble," I reply primly, "he *said* he wanted to wash his hands."

This keeps her quiet for a moment. It then develops that she wants to see Phyllis, who isn't home. She looks at the carpet, which has no more than a normal amount of Gilbert's hair on it.

"Goodness gracious!" she says, clucking, "I don't see *how* you can keep a great Dane in a city apartment! Why, I'd just as soon keep a horse in one!"

I bristle and stifle a desire to say, "Oh, so you don't think I ought to keep my horse, either?"

Gilbert chooses this moment to enter. And not, to my surprise, with his usual attitude, which practically says, "Oh my chin and whiskers! What wonderful things have I been missing!" Instead, he comes in with measured dignity. He casts a sedate glance at Mrs. Garble.

"He seems to be getting much better manners," she says grudgingly. "You certainly are training him to behave like a gentleman!"

I decide that Mrs. Garble, too, seems to be getting better manners. I warm toward her, as I do to all types of characters who have a kind word to say for Gilbert. I even toy with the idea of giving her a drink.

I watch with paternal pride as Gilbert walks slowly over to her. He sniffs at her leg in a genteel way. I beam reassuringly. Mrs. Garble smiles back uncertainly. Gilbert seems about to walk past her. He doesn't. He stops. Trained to observe such matters, I suddenly notice an uncertain attitude, a slight quivering of the muscles of Gilbert's left hind leg.

"GILBERT!" I cry, in the nick of time.

There is no need to go into the next five minutes. It will serve no purpose for me to repeat my weak explanation to the outraged Mrs. Garble that Gilbert, being still in the experimental stage, was merely about to test out a comparatively new idea. And that there was no personal malice or intended criticism involved.

Gilbert and I are alone again—and it is definitely time for me to Take Him Out.

Gilbert *loves* to go out. Five, seven times a day he responds with mad joy to the rattle of his chain, dances with impatience as I attach his collar, and, in a series of chamoislike bounds, precipitates me to our apartment elevator, permitting me to touch the corridor with my feet only intermittently on the way.

If Gilbert is in luck, there will be another passenger in the elevator. This is a stout, very short gentleman with a red face who lives on the floor above us. He is generally on his way to some formal affair. There is something about his frock coats and silk hats which brings out Gilbert's warmest feelings of affection.

It takes Gilbert no time at all to place both his paws on the little man's carefully groomed shoulders. Gilbert's tongue then quickly and deftly leaves a long moist streak from chin to forehead, as Gilbert's body deposits large amounts of hair on the faultless apparel.

The little man's face now becomes even redder, because he does not Understand Dogs. I know he doesn't, because the very first time this occurred, I said to him reassuringly, "It's all right, he is friendly."

To which he replied: "I'm not."

Since then all we say to each other is "Look out!"

Once we have left the elevator and passed through the lobby—a passage too swift for the average vision—Gilbert and I find ourselves outside. It is now that my problems begin and Gilbert's end. This is because we spend a lot of time standing by trees, lampposts, and pillars. It is not the fact that Gilbert is generally standing on one more leg than I am which makes my position more difficult than his. It is rather that I am far more conscious than he of the famous girls' finishing school on our block. Since its dismissal times seem to coincide with our airings, it bothers me to feel that there are hundreds of pretty young girls in the world who believe I spend my entire time standing by upright columns.

It is therefore frequently necessary for me to pretend that I do not know Gilbert. This is difficult, because of the stout chain which connects us. There are various attitudes, however, which I assume:

1. That I happen to be out with a chain and a careless dog got caught in it.

2. That a dog happened to be out with a chain and *I* got caught in it.

3. That a chain happened to be out and the dog and I both got caught in it.

Between lampposts, Gilbert and I walk along with dignity. With as much dignity as possible, that is, considering that we are walking in the gutter.

Sometimes we pause in the gutter and turn around rapidly many times. Then one of us reads a newspaper, while the finishing school, which we are directly in front of, conducts a fire drill.

I could go on interminably. Maybe you think I have already. But anyway, we are agreed that my dog-handling methods are not ideal. Now let me give you some information which is really practical in case you plan to have a dog. Let us examine Gilbert's habits, his point of view, his psychology. I know all about them and it does me no good, but it may forewarn you about your own dog.

I have observed many of Gilbert's moods. They are, I believe, fairly common to his race. Here are a few of them:

1. *The Hooray-Hooray-a-New-Day's-Dawning! Mood.* This manifests itself twice a day. Once at six in the morning,

at which time Gilbert lands heavily on my stomach, knocking both breath and sleep out of me. And a second time at a few moments past midnight, just after he has been bedded down, at which time he insists that I throw his rubber bone for him, or take him out with my coat over my pajamas. There must be some way to stop this.

2. *The Aren't-I-Supposed-to-Have-Any-Normal-Instincts-at-All? Mood.* This is caused simply by the fact that Gilbert is devoid of a sense of shame and I am not. It often results in our not speaking to each other and also in other people not speaking to me. There is no way to avoid this.

3. *The I-Was-Asleep-and-Some-Bad-Man-Must-Have-Come-in-and-Torn-that-Blue-Bedspread-to-Bits Attitude.* This is accompanied by a brazen, hypocritical simulation of overweening joy at my entrance and is unconvincing because of the large piece of blue cloth which Gilbert is unconsciously carrying on his dewlap. One method of avoiding this is always to leave your bed bare to the springs until retiring.

All right. Now that I have revealed my relationship to my dog in all its squalor, the curious may inquire why I have a dog at all. The curious may, but not the wise.

The answer, of course, is simple. In Gilbert I have found a being to whom I am superior in many ways, in spite of the fact that Phyllis insists that a lot more people stop to admire him than me on the street. Gilbert cannot drive a car. I can. Gilbert cannot wash dishes, pour drinks for people, run errands, or do dozens of other things around the house Phyllis considers necessary. Above all, Gilbert is a living, breathing answer to her contention that I am the most inefficient form of life yet devised.

He is also the finest dog in town, even if he did tear up the very best parts of this piece.

Dogfights

J. J. McCoy

IT'S THE RARE DOG that doesn't get into a dogfight sooner or later. The canine gladiators usually come out of the fight with various bites. Before you can render first aid, you'll have to break up the fight. Proceed with caution; too many people have been seriously injured trying to break up a dogfight without knowing how.

Remember that in the fury of the fight, both dogs will be snapping and slashing at each other. Neither of them will pay much attention to your shouts or commands. They're concentrating too hard on the battle and in not getting knocked down. You'll have to provide some strong distraction.

Don't ever try to pull your dog out of the fight by reaching for his collar. That's a good way to lose a hand or some fingers. If you have help, try this technique: Each of you wait for an opening and grab a dog's tail. When you get hold of the tail, pull the dog toward you, quickly swinging him away from the other dog, and heave him as far as you can. If the dogs try to rush back into battle, block *your* dog and give him the command to sit. Have the other person try to chase off the other dog.

If one or both dogs happen to be tailless, you'll have to use another technique. Try banging on a bucket or flinging a chain at the dogs. If near your home, or someone will help you, get out a hose and squirt a stream of water on the fighters.

Dogs usually start a fight very quickly. It can be ended just as quickly, if you can divert the dogs from the battle. Remember, just don't reach for your dog's collar. Use as much distraction as possible, the louder the better. After the fight, you can attend to the dog's wounds.

*"I dare you to come out from under there
and repeat what you just said!"*

The Judges

Maxwell Riddle

THE JUDGES MAY be professionals or amateurs. They may
be licensed to judge one breed or ten, or all breeds. Probably
all the judges who are licensed for one breed only, are amateurs. They may judge solely for the honor of being invited,
or for the additional experience which they will need before
being licensed to judge other breeds. Many amateur judges,
and particularly those who can judge a half dozen breeds,
or who must travel a long distance, will require payment for
some, or all, of their expenses.

But the time comes when the glory of judging wears off.
The judge realizes that he is having to work very hard. If he
is a multiple-breeds judge, particularly one who judges one
or more groups—all sporting dogs, all hounds, etc.—the time
will come when he will demand a fee in addition to expenses.
At this point, the judge has become a professional. And at
this point, also, his work load will increase. Judges with three
or four group licenses, and all-breeds judges, discover that
they could judge at at least fifty weekend shows a year. And
they will find themselves judging as many as two hundred
dogs, and two or three variety groups, on a single day.

This is work, not glory. The judge will be on his feet,
perhaps on a marble or cement floor, for eight to ten hours.
Or he'll be out in the hot sun all that time. He may have no
time out at lunch. And he may have to do as many as three
hundred full knee bends during that show.

So he charges a fee of from $100 to $150 per day, plus his expenses. It seems to be a lot of money, but it is actually a very reasonable amount. Aside from the work involved, he probably has to allow a day to reach the show and a day to get home. If he doesn't, he'll have to sit up all night on planes each way. It is ironic that, whatever his fee, the professional handlers who are exhibiting under him are probably making three or four times as much money as is the judge.

A Sheaf of Cartoons

DOGS ARE just as funny as people. If you don't think so, here are cartoons to help persuade you.

"*He's a good watchdog—but he won't let me into my own home!*"

"No more for him—he's driving . . ."

450

"*I like mailmen.*"

"*You'll just have to choose between us, Edward . . .*"

451

"It probably means he wants to go."

"If you ask me, I think he's terribly spoiled."

453

Fit for a Dog

James Meyers

BELOW YOU will find 36 words, phrases, and expressions. Each one of these should suggest to you another expression which contains the word DOG. For example, a *fairway angle* would be a DOGleg. Fill in the correct expression on the line at the right.

A score of 15 is good; 20 is excellent; 25 is extraordinary; and 30 or more earns you a blue ribbon.

Answers on page 463

1. Worn and shabby _____
2. Deteriorated _____
3. In disfavor _____
4. Trivial or bad verse _____
5. Miserable, drab existence _____
6. Hardwood tree _____
7. Aerial skirmish _____
8. Quick, easy gait _____
9. Loaf on the job _____
10. Established opinion _____
11. Arctic vehicle _____
12. Obstinately determined _____
13. Teeming _____
14. Elementary swim stroke _____
15. Daisy _____
16. Architectural ornament _____

17. Marked by ruthless
    self-interest _____
18. Humorous tale involving
    a talking animal _____
19. Tuckered out _____
20. Small shark _____
21. Darned _____
22. Miserable, shameful end _____
23. One horse carriage _____
24. G. I. identification _____
25. Selfish hoarder of
    unneeded goods _____
26. For a very low price _____
27. Hot sultry period of summer _____
28. Infantryman _____
29. Leave well enough alone _____
30. Ball park refreshment _____
31. Night shift _____
32. Brief sleep _____
33. Pound employee _____
34. They come out in the
    midday sun _____
35. Dress up _____
36. Woebegone, forlorn _____

A Dog's Nervous System

E. B. White

I WOULD LIKE to hand down a dissenting opinion in the case of the Camel ad which shows a Boston terrier relaxing. I can string along with cigarette manufacturers to a certain degree, but when it comes to the temperament and habits of terriers, I shall stand my ground.

The ad says: "A dog's nervous system resembles our own." I don't think a dog's nervous system resembles my own in the least. A dog's nervous system is in a class by itself. If it resembles anything at all, it resembles the New York Edison Company's power plant. This is particularly true of Boston terriers, and if the Camel people don't know that, they have never been around dogs.

The ad says: "But when a dog's nerves tire, he obeys his instincts—he relaxes." This, I admit, is true. But I should like to call attention to the fact that it sometimes takes days, even weeks, before a dog's nerves tire. In the case of terriers it can run into months.

I knew a Boston terrier once (he is now dead and, so far as I know, relaxed) whose nerves stayed keyed up from the twenty-fifth of one June to the sixth of the following July, without one minute's peace for anybody in the family. He was an old dog and he was blind in one eye, but his infirmities caused no diminution in his nervous power. During the period of which I speak, the famous period of his greatest excitation, he not only raised a type of general hell which startled even his closest friends and observers, but he gave a mighty clever excuse. He said it was love.

"I'm in love," he would scream. (He could scream just like a hurt child.) "I'm in love and I'm going *crazy*."

Day and night it was all the same. I tried everything to soothe him. I tried darkness, cold water dashed in the face, the lash, long quiet talks, warm milk administered internally, threats, promises, and close confinement in remote locations. At last, after about a week of it, I went down the road and had a chat with the lady who owned the object of our terrier's affection. It was she who finally cleared up the situation.

"Oh," she said, wearily, "if it's that bad, let him out."

I hadn't thought of anything as simple as that myself, but I am a creature of infinite reserve. As a matter of record, it turned out to be not so simple—the terrier got run over by a motor car one night while returning from his amorous adventures, suffering a complete paralysis of the hip but no assuagement of the nervous system; and the little Scotty bitch returned to Washington, D.C., and a Caesarian.

I am not through with the Camel people yet. Love is not the only thing that can keep a dog's nerves in a state of perpetual jangle. A dog, more than any other creature, it seems to me, gets interested in one subject, theme, or object, in life, and pursues it with a fixity of purpose which would be inspiring to Man if it weren't so troublesome. One dog gets absorbed in one thing, another dog in another. When I was a boy there was a smooth-haired fox terrier (in those days nobody ever heard of a fox terrier that *wasn't* smooth-haired) who became interested, rather late in life, in a certain stone. The stone was about the size of an egg. As far as I could see, it was like a million other stones—but to him it was the Stone Supreme.

He kept it with him day and night, slept with it, ate

with it, played with it, analyzed it, took it on little trips (you would often see him three blocks from home, trotting along on some shady errand, his stone safe in his jaws). He used to lie by the hour on the porch of his house, chewing the stone with an expression half tender, half petulant. When he slept he merely enjoyed a muscular suspension: his nerves were still up and around, adjusting the bed clothes, tossing and turning.

He permitted people to throw the stone for him and people would. But if the stone lodged somewhere he couldn't get to he raised such an uproar that it was absolutely necessary that the stone be returned, for the public peace. His absorption was so great it brought wrinkles to his face, and he grew old before his time. I think he used to worry that somebody was going to pitch the stone into a lake or a bog, where it would be irretrievable. He wore off every tooth in his jaw, wore them right down to the gums, and they became mere brown vestigial bumps. His breath was awful (he panted night and day) and his eyes were alight with an unearthly zeal. He died in a fight with another dog. I have always suspected it was because he tried to hold the stone in his mouth all through the battle. The Camel people will just have to take my word for it: that dog was a living denial of the whole theory of relaxation. He was a paragon of nervous tension, from the moment he first laid eyes on his slimy little stone till the hour of his death.

The advertisement speaks of the way humans "prod" themselves to endeavor—so that they keep on and on working, long after they should quit. The inference is that a dog never does that. But I have a dog right now that can prod himself harder and drive himself longer than any human I ever saw. This animal is a dachshund, and I shall spare you the long dull inanities of his innumerable obsessions. His particular study (or mania) at the moment is a black-and-white kitten that my wife gave me for Christmas, thinking that what my life needed was something else that could move quickly from one place in the room to another. The dachshund began his research on Christmas eve when the kitten arrived "secretly" in the cellar, and now, five months later, is taking his Ph.D., still working late at night on it, every night. If he could write a book about that cat, it would make *Middletown* look like the work of a backward child.

I'll be glad to have the Camel people study this animal in one of his relaxed mods, but they will have to bring their own seismograph. Even curled up cozily in a chair, dreaming of his cat, he quivers like an aspen.

Bull Terriers

The Answers

WHAT DO YOU KNOW ABOUT DOGS?...Page 206

There are freaks and exceptions among dogs just as there are among human beings. The following answers are based on what has been observed to be the reaction and behavior of the overwhelming majority of dogs. The answers to this questionnaire have been approved by some of the leading veterinarians in the United States.

1. *False.* Dogs with cold noses sometimes run high temperatures. Dogs with hot noses are perfectly normal.
2. *True.* Freedom and exercise must not be confused. A dog turned loose will roam about for a time, sniff, investigate, become bored and lie down. If the surroundings are familiar, he will indulge in comparatively less activity. The average dog must be actively exercised to be kept in good health.
3. *False.* A dog doesn't necessarily become strongly attached to the person who feeds him. Many city dogs are fed by the family cook while their masters are away at business. Nevertheless, these dogs prefer their masters, recognize them as such, and pay attention to the cook only at meal times.
4. *False.* Sulphur does not dissolve in water to any extent.
5. *True.* Dogs are naturally carnivorous. They do not relish vegetables, and eat them only when they are very hungry or when vegetables are mixed with other, more appetizing foods. Given both meat and vegetables, a

dog will always eat the meat and leave the vegetables alone.

6. *True.* Puppies are normally born with their eyelids sealed tightly together. This is Nature's way of protecting these delicate organs from injury during the early part of their existence. A puppy's eyelids should never be pried apart. They will open of their own accord in due time, probably when the pup is nine or ten days old.

7. *True.* All authorities are agreed that a good stiff daily brushing and combing is the best and most healthful way of keeping a dog clean. This process will remove surface dirt. If this proves ineffective at times, a dry-cleaning with fuller's earth or plain corn meal is much to be preferred to bathing, which has a deleterious effect upon the dog's coat. Generally, the only dogs that need be bathed now and then are white-haired dogs, and for the sake of appearance rather than health.

8. *True.*

9. *False.* In practically every case docking is performed to add to smartness of appearance; health is no consideration.

10. *True.* The standard solution is a tablespoon of kerosene to a quart of milk. This should be rubbed into the coat. After half an hour, the dog should be bathed in soap and water.

11. *False.* Since it is more difficult to keep a dog in the city than in the country, city-dog-owners are honest-to-goodness dog lovers, and take exceptional care of their pets. The average life span of the city dog exceeds 11 years. The country dog, on the average not as well cared for, exposed to natural hazards and dietary maladjustments, lives on the average two or three years less.

12. *True.* Therefore, most puppies need worming at one time or another.

13. *False.* No such hard-and-fast rule can be laid down. Individual dogs differ in capacities and dispositions much the same as individual human beings differ. There are docile and sullen dogs among both mongrels and pure-breds, and very intelligent as well as stupid dogs in both classes.

14. *True.* Most dogs rely mainly on their senses of smell and hearing. The only class of dogs whose sight is definitely keener than its smell are the dogs of the sight-hound group: the saluki, greyhound, whippet, Afghan, et al.

15. *True.* Although distemper inoculation is more or less effective, and although veterinarians know how to prescribe for and treat distemper, there is no known specific cure.

16. *True.*

17. *False.* Generally, clipping instead of conferring comfort increases discomfort. A dog naturally sheds his coat when seasonal changes render a heavy coat unnecessary. Removal of a dog's coat by clipping leaves his skin without protection from gnats, flies, and the hot sun and, moreover, exposes him to colds.

18. *False.* Dogs gulp their food. That is natural. The dog's habit of bolting food probably derives from the time when dogs traveled in packs and each dog had to eat fast to get his share of the kill.

19. *True.* All authorities subscribe to this statement. Experience proves that a vicious dog will chase—and usually catch and bite—the person who runs away from him; but the dog will generally be held at bay by the person who stands still, confronts him calmly, without show of fear or of intention to attack. It is held to be wise to place one's hand flat on one's chest and to talk to the dangerous dog in soft, quieting and disarming tones.

20. *True.* Dogs are basically carnivorous. Vegetables and prepared foods can only supplement and not substitute

for lean meat, which is absolutely necessary to keep a dog in good health.

21. *False*. Mongrels frequently have mouths whose roofs are much blacker than prize-winning thoroughbreds.
22. *True*.
23. *True*. Dogs are easily frightened by sudden loud noises. Firecrackers, blowouts, and thunderclaps have thrown many a dog into hysteria. If a dog crawls under a bed or shakes all over with fright at the approach of a thunderstorm, a small dose of Luminal will quiet him down.
24. *True*.
25. *True*. Many a puppy is brought to the dog hospital with a bellyful of extraneous objects.

FIT FOR A DOG.........................Page 454

1. Dog-eared
2. Gone to the dogs
3. In the doghouse
4. Doggerel
5. Dog's life
6. Dogwood
7. Dogfight
8. Dogtrot
9. Dog it
10. Dogma
11. Dogsled
12. Dogged
13. Raining cats and dogs
14. Dog paddle
15. Dog flower
16. Dogtooth
17. Dog-eat-dog
18. Shaggy-dog story
19. Dog-tired
20. Dogfish
21. Doggone
22. Dog's death
23. Dogcart
24. Dog tag
25. Dog in the manger
26. Dog-cheap
27. Dog days
28. Dogface
29. Let sleeping dogs lie
30. Hot dog
31. Dogwatch
32. Dog nap
33. Dogcatcher
34. Mad dogs and Englishmen
35. Put on the dog
36. Hangdog